The Seattle *Street-Smart* Naturalist

The Seattle Street-Smart Naturalist

FIELD NOTES FROM THE CITY

David B. Williams

WESTWINDS PRESS®

To Marjorie

This book was previously published under the title *The Street-Smart Naturalist: Field Notes from Seattle.*

Library of Congress Cataloging-in-Publication Data

Williams, David B., 1965-
 The Seattle street-smart naturalist / David B. Williams.
   p. cm.
 Includes bibliographical references.
 ISBN 978-1-55868-859-9 (softbound)
 1. Natural history—Washington (State)—Seattle Region—Anecdotes.
 2. Williams, David B., 1965- I. Title.
 QH105.W2W55 2005
 508.797'772—dc22

                                                              2004012542

WestWinds Press®
An imprint of Graphic Arts Center Publishing Company
P.O. Box 10306, Portland, Oregon 97296-0306
503-226-2402 / www.gacpc.com

President: Charles M. Hopkins
Associate Publisher: Douglas A. Pfeiffer
Editorial Staff: Timothy W. Frew, Tricia Brown, Jean Andrews, Kathy Howard,
         Jean Bond-Slaughter
Production Staff: Richard L. Owsiany, Susan Dupèré
Editor: Colin Chisholm
Design: Andrea Boven Nelson, Boven Design Studio

Printed and bound by Lightning Source, Inc. in the United States of America

CONTENTS

ACKNOWLEDGMENTS

I could not have written this book without the generous support and encouragement of the following people: Sally Abella, Bud Angerman, Clay Antieau, Esa Ärmänen, Jeremy Bell, Becky Benton, Nick Bond, Derek Booth, Sharon J. Collman, Brad Colman, Rod Crawford, Frank Danes, Bernadette Donald, Jean-Pierre Garcia, Curt Hedstrom, Arthur Lee Jacobson, Roger Kiers, Cheryl Klinker, Dave Knoblach, Louise Kulzer, Ray Larson, Estella Leopold, Meredith Lohr, Nate Mantua, John Marzluff, Kathy Mendelson, Martin Muller, Ralph Naess, Dennis Paulson, Keel Price, Sarah Reichard, Diane Sepanski, Brian Sherrod, Evan Sugden, Paul Talbert, Coll Thrush, Kathy Troost, Bob Vreeland, Dave Waters, Jim Watson, and John Withey. They answered my persistent questions, tracked down obscure facts, took me out in the field, and fact checked chapters. Any errors or misinterpretations of their data, of course, are mine.

I wish to thank the librarians in Special Collections at the University of Washington, who helped me track down many obscure documents. In the Internet Age, librarians' skills and knowledge are more important than ever.

The Cultural Development Authority of King County, through their Heritage Special Projects and Arts Special Projects programs in 2002 and 2003, and the Office of Arts & Cultural Affairs Seattle Artists Program for Literary Arts provided funds that allowed me to work on this project.

A big thanks to Tricia Brown at Graphic Arts for her support throughout this project.

I am grateful to Lisa Wogan and Bob Benton for reading the entire manuscript and making helpful suggestions, to Megan Ernst for her exquisite drawings, and to Colin Chisholm for his astute copyediting and editing.

To my parents for their inspiration and support.

And finally to my wife, Marjorie Kittle, for reading and rereading each chapter and for listening to me ramble during this four-year-long project on seemingly endless walks. I couldn't have done it without you.

I have been fortunate to spend an important part of my life outdoors. After I graduated from college with a degree in geology I moved to Moab, Utah, where I had lined up an internship with a nonprofit education organization. I planned on staying for three months but ended up leaving nine years later. As a program coordinator at the field school and later as a park ranger at Arches National Park, I explored some of the most beautiful and desolate landscapes on the planet with a vibrant and enthusiastic group of folks who loved the desert and who had a passion for sharing their knowledge of the flora and fauna. It was an amazing lifestyle that I was lucky to experience.

My years in the desert ended when my wife, Marjorie, and I moved to Boston so she could go to graduate school. The change was a shock, to say the least. I can best sum it up with a simple set of numbers. Population density in Grand County, where we lived in Utah, was a little under two people per square mile. In Somerville, Massachusetts, there were roughly 19,713 more people in that same space. We remained in Boston for as little time as necessary, arriving one day before Marjorie's graduate program started and leaving three weeks before graduation ceremonies.

What saved my sanity in Boston was the natural world. I discovered five-inch-wide fossils in limestone building blocks of the city's second-tallest skyscraper. I watched red-tailed hawks hunt in the gardens across the street from our apartment. I joined a pilgrimage of birders to one of the city's toniest sections, when a boreal owl made a rare visit. I found solace in a 3.5-mile-long river. Unlike the previous decade of my life, when I had to travel only a few minutes to find spectacular natural features, these expeditions required planning and determination. To succeed in finding wildness in the city, I had to hone my observational skills and learn the importance of patience. I became an aficionado of small wonders.

Moving to Boston also forced me to be a hunter and gatherer, not only of nature, but also of stories, one of the most sustaining parts of my life. For me, a good natural history story is as much about history as it is about nature. I am someone who wants to know why a plant or place has a certain name, why a scientist decided to study his or her subject, or when and how a particular species was introduced. I want to examine the inter-section between people and nature, and the urban landscape is as good a place as any to do this.

Since Marjorie and I moved back to Seattle 7 years ago, after an absence for me of 15 years, I have tried to use my new skills to hunt, explore, and ask questions in the city where I grew up. Although Seattle is young, our stories are as complex as our topography. They have given me a deeper appreciation of and connection with my hometown. Maybe it is hyperbole to say that I have found myself or that without my forays into urban nature I could not survive, but I do know that I like Seattle better after spending so much time exploring and discovering new and old places. I take greater pleasure in the city. I am comfortable here.

What these stories and my adventures in Seattle confirm for me is that you don't have to go to exotic places to find interesting natural history stories, despite what you might see on the Discovery Channel or in the pages of *National Geographic*. These fine purveyors of nature leave you with the distinct feeling that nature is out there, away from most people's ordinary lives. They fail to show that stories are in our yards, under our feet, and on the walls of our buildings. Stories and nature are all around us, if we take the time to look and wonder.

I am not saying that we should substitute urban experiences for wild ones, but I recognize that most urban dwellers stand a better chance of developing a relationship with a goose than with a gorilla. We will develop connections with nature more often in our neighborhood parks than in national parks. We will have our first childhood encounter with a wild, undomesticated animal while exploring our backyards or nearby green spaces. These encounters and experiences will become more important as we continue to become a more urban planet.

Getting to know the urban wild will also influence how we react in wilder places. What lessons will people learn when they see public officials killing Canada geese in Seattle? What if instead citizens heard public officials challenging us to make changes in order to coexist with thousands of geese? I cannot help thinking that positive experiences with wildness in urban settings will lead to a positive land ethic in wilder places.

Another fine attribute of life as an urban naturalist is that it does not require specialized equipment. My field bag consists of notebook and pencil, binoculars, flashlight, magnifying lens, and an insulated coffee mug (one benefit of urban natural history is the proximity to good food and drink). I also wear metaphorical blinders. I have found them to be quite helpful in ignoring trash and ivy on a search for skunk cabbage. They have allowed me to bypass the mall while hunting for a bog, or to block out freeway sounds when listening to chorus frogs.

It also doesn't hurt if you don't mind doing odd things, like crawling around the floor of a mall to look at 150-million-year-old sponge fossils, posting up in a car at 7:00 A.M. waiting for crows to come and find a bag of old french fries, traipsing around under an interstate highway in search of evidence for plate tectonics, or touring a wastewater treatment plant. These experiences may not fit the picture of "classic" nature, but they certainly have made my days more fun and interesting.

To be an urban naturalist one must also be an optimist. You have to be open to possibilities. You have to trust that urbanization will not drive away every living species except starlings, rats, blackberries, and English ivy. You have to believe that humans can learn from the past. You have to believe what Henry David Thoreau once wrote, that "In wildness is the preservation of the world," whether you find that wildness in your backyard or in the back of beyond.

For my own part, I wish the bald eagle had not been chosen as the representative of our country; he is a bird of bad moral character; he does not get his living honestly; you may have seen him perched on some dead tree, where, too lazy to fish for himself, he watches the labor of the fishing-hawk; and, when that diligent bird has at length taken a fish, and is bearing it to his nest for the support of his mate and young ones, the bald eagle pursues him, and takes it from him.

LETTER FROM BENJAMIN FRANKLIN
TO HIS DAUGHTER, SARAH BACHE,
JANUARY 26, 1784

I first saw the bald eagle while visiting Seattle's most popular park on Thanksgiving Day, 1998. Marjorie and I were taking advantage of the cool, overcast morning to walk around the three-mile-long trail that skirts the park's central feature, Green Lake. We had just started around the water when we saw the bird's brilliant white head, which stood out from the barren limbs like a lighthouse on a foggy coast.

The two-foot-tall bird sat atop one of the many black cottonwoods on Duck Island, a small, man-made dab of land at the north end of the lake. With my binoculars I could discern the chocolate brown body, the 12-inch-long white tail, and the yellow beak. After admiring the eagle for several minutes, we resumed our walk. It seemed appropriate to see our national symbol on this particular holiday, for we could be thankful for the return of bald eagles from the edge of extinction.

Just seven months after my first encounter with an urban eagle, on our nation's other great patriotic day, President Clinton proposed removing the bald eagle from the federal List of Endangered and Threatened Wildlife. "The American bald eagle is now back from the brink of extinction," he said. "I can think of no better way to honor the birth of our nation than by celebrating the rebirth of our proudest living symbol."

Concern over the bald eagle decline first became a national priority when a 1963 National Audubon Society study found only 417 active nests in the lower 48 states. This compares with an estimated 250,000 to 500,000 eagles on the North American continent before the first Europeans landed.

Despite the publicity caused by the report, another 15 years would pass before bald eagles got official designation under the aegis of the Endangered Species Act (ESA) of 1973. In addition to prohibiting harming, pursuing, and killing eagles, the listing also required that habitat be protected, with an ultimate goal of recovery of the species. In 2003 the number of nesting bald eagles exceeded 7,678 pairs.

My sighting of the eagle occurred a little over five months after Marjorie and I had moved to Seattle and two months after we had purchased a home just north of the lake. The move back to my boyhood home had been a major change in our lives. Marjorie and I had met in September 1991, in Moab, Utah, and spent five years working outdoor-oriented jobs. The red-rock desert of southern Utah was the landscape that I knew and loved more than any other. It was where I had become a naturalist and developed my passion for hiking, backpacking, and exploring. It was the place I felt most centered and at home.

When we moved to Boston for Marjorie's MBA program in 1996, we knew it was only temporary and that we would probably end up back in Moab after two years in the East. The sojourn in Boston and a scare I had with skin cancer, however, made us realize that a small town that gets 300 days of sun a year was not the best place for us. Although we knew we would dearly miss the desert and our friends, we decided to return to Seattle, which we hoped would offer us a good mix of urban life and access to the outdoors.

We were nervous about making Seattle our permanent home. I had enjoyed growing up in the city and we had liked our visits to see my family, but living here as an adult would not be the same. I wondered how it would be to live without the wildness of the desert; I had learned how to do it in Boston but I had also returned to the desert six times in 18 months. In Seattle, we would not have the luxury of going back so often. Nor did we have the mind-set that we would be in Seattle for only a short time with the desert waiting for us at the end of our time here. I took our sighting of the Thanksgiving Day bald eagle as a fortuitous omen.

I continued to see an eagle soaring elegantly above Green Lake through the holidays and into the new year. I was pleasantly surprised each time I saw the handsome bird and wondered when it would leave. Although this urban oasis provides eagles with many tall Douglas-firs for perching and an abundant food base of fish and fowl, why would this symbol of wildness nest in a park teeming with people and traffic, especially when much quieter and more secluded habitat exists just an hour north along the Skagit River?

The Green Lake eagle inspired Marjorie and me to drive to the Skagit in early February. We saw 48 balds in a little over two hours, including a single tree with 13 white-headed apparitions perched silently like avian gurus waiting to bestow knowledge. Or maybe they were just sated from feeding on the abundant three-foot-long chum salmon, which littered the river banks by the thousands after spawning and dying.

The upper Skagit contains one of the densest concentrations of wintering balds in the lower 48 states, with as many as 400 birds consuming the spawned-out fish. After I saw these abundant eagles, I wondered if the Emerald City eagle was a loner who left the Skagit and found that it could exploit Green Lake's migrant waterfowl by itself.

About a week after our Skagit trip, I saw an eagle flying across Green Lake with a stick in its talons. I didn't think anything of this potential domestic display until local birder Martin Muller told me that he thought the eagle and a possible mate were constructing a nest in a large conifer in lower Woodland Park at the southwest corner of the lake. According to Martin, this was the first recorded bald eagle nest at Green Lake, which sits just five miles from downtown Seattle.

Unlike most of the country, Washington state has historically had a relatively high bald eagle population. When the species was listed as "endangered" in the lower 48 states, they were listed as only "threatened" in Washington. Bald eagles, though, were not common in the urban landscape.

Seward Park was the first Seattle park to have a nest. The birds exploited the city's best habitat, abundant Douglas-fir, the wild shoreline of Lake Washington, and few close houses. Birders found the first nest in 1981; a second pair of eagles built another nest at the park in 1998. As of 2003, there were 16 eagle territories with 37 nests in and around Seattle. Nest sites include West Seattle, Discovery Park, Mercer Island, and Bellevue.

With Martin's help I eventually found the Green Lake nest. It appeared that the bird constructing its new nest had done its aeriework because the nest's location fit perfectly into the ornithologist's descriptions of bald eagle nests. Studies of Pacific Northwest bald eagles show that a pair generally builds a nest in a conifer, most often a Douglas-fir that is taller than the surrounding forest canopy. The nest tree grows on the upper portion of a slope within 750 yards of open water. About half the nest is obscured from the ground and an overhead canopy protects it from above. A damaged tree top or a structural peculiarity that eases nest construction is also common. The nest tree grows near other potential nest sites and good perching spots, which provide the birds with prime views of their hunting grounds. I cannot describe the Green Lake nest better than this.

Unfortunately, the Green Lake eagles had chosen a difficult housing site—the nest had to span two limbs that forked off the tree at a 120-degree angle. Despite the challenge, they had succeeded in constructing a three-foot-wide base of tangled and interwoven branches. The big question would be whether the nest would survive the winter storms.

Whitecaps covered the lake two days after my first nest observation, as yet another front oozed across Seattle. This winter was rapidly becoming well known for its precipitation. A radio story on February 24 reported that over 32 inches of rain had dropped in the city since November, a new record. Mount Baker, only 90 miles north of Seattle, eventually received a world record of 95 feet of snow from November 1, 1998, through August 4, 1999.

When I saw no eagles on the nest during the storm, I hurried over to their tree and discovered that I could just barely wrap my arms around the trunk. Numerous cones with three-pointed bracts littered the ground and confirmed that the tree was a Douglas-fir, generally the tallest and definitely the most common conifer in the second-growth wooded lands that cover Seattle.

I returned the next day to find both the male and a female eagle in the vicinity of the nest, which had weathered the storm without ill effect. She sat on a nearby western red cedar, one of their favorite perching spots for hunting and eating. With my binoculars I could see the dark patches that wrapped around her eyes like a bandit's mask and provided the easiest means of distinguishing the sexes. While watching her, I heard the male land on the jumble of sticks that made up the ever-expanding aerie. He was wrestling with a wishbone-shaped branch nearly twice his height. He held the unruly stick with his beak and tried to place it along the southeast corner of the nest, but it bounced back at him as he let it go. Picking it up again he tried another spot with the same result. After several more tries he seemed to jam the branch down in disgust. It remained in place and he disappeared to the south. I wondered if males of all species are the same.

The sound of a slowly turning, poorly greased wheel pulled me from my note taking. The noise traveled over my head but I could not locate its origin. In the general direction of the squeal, though, I saw the male eagle swooping down on the female, who was eating in the nearby cedar. I could not tell if he was trying to steal part of her meal, but he settled down, began to preen himself, and emitted a distinctly squeaky call. I was disappointed; other eagles I had heard before sounded haunting and wild. I had hoped that the local representative of our national symbol would not be such a whiner.

With the two birds perched side by side, I could compare them and see what ornithologists call "reverse sexual dimorphism." She stood two or three inches taller than he did and although I could not see the weight difference, I knew she probably outweighed him by a couple of pounds. A normal female averages 11 to 13 pounds with a wingspan of 88 inches, while a male may weigh 9 to 10 pounds and have a wingspan of 83 inches. One way to visualize an eagle's wingspan is to stretch your arms out; a typical adult has a 72-inch-wide arm span.

Ornithologists debate why raptors, a group that includes hawks, falcons, and eagles, reverse the usual bird archetype of males being larger than females. One camp has proposed that this may allow larger females to protect themselves against males, who might aggressively use their talons and beaks against females. Another group believes that different-sized mates can hunt different-sized prey, allowing a pair to share a territory and not compete for food. For the present time, the conundrum remains unresolved.

The next day I saw the pair on the nest together for the first time. Both were gathering material. When collecting they invariably flew into Woodland Park, which contains more Douglas-firs, red alders, and bigleaf maples than the lakeshore. They usually returned within 10 minutes, an event heralded by a loud squawk-and-caw session from the omnipresent crows. Each time one of the eagles returned, he or she added another layer to the exterior walls.

The center of the nest, which had been constructed first, is reserved for the eggs, which rest on a soft bed of grasses, conifer needles, and feathers. Eagles may also adorn the rim of the nest with fresh foliage, often replacing it throughout the nesting season.

Once they establish a nest, a bald eagle pair will continue to reuse and add to it year after year. The most famous and possibly the longest surviving nest was first noted on June 14, 1805, by Meriwether Lewis and William Clark. They reported seeing an eagle nest in a cottonwood tree on an island at the Great Falls of the Missouri River in Montana. Fifty-five years later, Captain William F. Raynolds, leader of an exploration up the Yellowstone River, believed that he saw the exact same nest with an eagle perched near it. Which generation of the family was living in that nest is unknown, but eagles generally live less than 30 years.

Balds also require large nests, the grandest of any bird in North America. A nest in Florida measured over 9 feet across by 20 feet deep and weighed two tons. Northwest nests do not reach such proportions. Our typical disk-shaped aerie measures 5 feet across by 2.5 feet deep. Nor do ours survive as long as the Great Falls nest. In Saskatchewan the average nest life expectancy is only 5 years. In Alaska, nests are often 20 years old, although severe storms have been known to destroy 20 percent of all nests in a single year.

During January and February, when most of the nest building took place at Green Lake, Marjorie and I had our first inklings that we would be comfortable making our home in Seattle. I had my first articles published in the Seattle market. A third story would come out in late February, and I had another piece due soon at the *Seattle Times* Sunday magazine. My decision to pursue writing full time, which I had wrestled with since moving to Seattle, was now paying off. Marjorie had recently started a new job using the skills she had learned at graduate school. We both felt that we were finding our places in Seattle.

After a brief respite of clear days (what some might call partly cloudy days in other parts of the country), normal weather returned. Back at Green Lake one day, I stood on the shoreline observing a sord of mallards paddling around. They seemed focused on finding food under the water's surface, when suddenly most of the raft looked straight up and immediately flew away. I saw a black silhouette pass overhead. Through my binoculars I watched spellbound as the specter soared toward the middle of the lake where it swept down, scooped up a fish, rose, and turned back to the nest.

I must have looked peculiar standing at the shoreline with my mouth agape, eyes stretched wide, and binoculars dangling down. I have spent a fair amount of time in the outdoors, backpacking, canoeing, and biking, but I had never seen an eagle catch a fish. And it occurred only a mile and a half from our house in the city.

Two aspects of the kill stood out for me. The first was that I was witnessing a natural act as I think it should happen. No humans interfered. An animal wanted food and went to get it. With its keen eyesight, the eagle had found a fish close to the surface and had simply flown across the lake and used its powerful talons to get its meal. An elegant display of evolution at its most basic level of predator and prey. Allied with this notion was the bird's air supremacy. I could detect no apparent deviation in the eagle's deadly flight from nest to fish to nest, even with several ring-billed gulls harassing it.

A few days later, though, I saw a slight variation on the predator-prey theme when I wandered over to the nest to see how it had withstood the season's most severe windstorm. The nest was fine but a western hemlock limb thicker than my thigh lay shattered on the ground next to my favorite viewing spot, near a red alder that offered a direct view of the nest. As I sat resting against the alder, I saw the male eagle leap off the nest and glide toward the lake. Curious, I looked at my watch to time how long he was away. He landed on the nest precisely two minutes later with a wriggling fish clutched in his talons. I was silently applauding the eagle's hunting prowess when the fish became airborne again; it had flopped out of the nest and was dropping to the ground. Although I know that birds do not express themselves in profane English, the bald eagle standing on the edge of his nest looked like he was thinking, "Shit. I hate it when that happens."

He continued standing on the nest's edge for several minutes before flying away. As his squeaky voice trailed off, I approached the fish. It was about 13 inches long with a reddish tail, bluish top, and silvery mouth—a native rainbow trout, which are stocked by the thousands at Green Lake. A streak of blood was visible near the gills, but I could find no distinct markings from the eagle. Within a half minute of my departure, the first crow had landed. A true lagniappe from their enemies. No trace of the trout remained the next day.

On another day I saw the female eagle return from a jaunt over the lake with something larger than a fish in her talons. She landed on her customary perch in the western red cedar, bent over, ripped a chunk out of her catch, shook her head, and produced a spray of white and black feathers. After several minutes of shredding and shaking she reached the meat. Sunlight glistened off the blood covering her beak and chest. In a simple process of alchemy, a bufflehead was being converted to an eagle.

Crows dove and cawed at the eagle, blackening the surrounding branches. One crow practically sat on the eagle's shoulder cawing advice on how and what to eat. This situation was typical; I rarely visited the nest without seeing one, two, or generally more crows nearby. They even landed on the nest when the eagles were out hunting.

Crows can do little harm to an eagle. Their harassment is more proactive, alerting other crows to the predator and showing juveniles which predator might eat them. Mobbing might also discourage the predator from hanging around or from attacking. Some ornithologists also think mobbing results from boredom. The Corvid family (crows, ravens, magpies, jays) is an intelligent, impish bunch who like to play and create mischief. What could be more enjoyable than harassing a bird who is minding its own business, especially when that bird is much larger and lethal?

When I approached the nest on March 16, I could see only the female's head above the nest's rim. When the male showed up with a branch, though, she stood and immediately flew to a snag on a Douglas-fir. He placed the branch and then poked around the nest with his beak, stamped his feet, and finally hunkered down into the nest with his beak visible just above the rim. The reverse occurred the next day with the female landing and the male flying to the snag.

I continued to visit the nest over the next several weeks, always seeing one of the bald eagle pair, usually the female, sitting in the nest. Once again, it appeared that the eagles had read the biologist's reports. Middle March is the typical time for a Pacific Northwest bald eagle to lay eggs. One or two eggs is the norm, with an incubation period of 34 to 36 days. During this time the eggs are rarely unattended.

The eagles' nearly constant vigil on the eggs is essential since incubation time is the most critical factor for nest success. A 1998 Washington state Department of Fish and Wildlife (DFW) report examining bald eagles and human activity stated that "During incubation unsuccessful nests were exposed an average of 20 minutes per hour and were incubated 14 minutes per hour less than successful nests." The report also listed temperature, precipitation, wind, nest tree characteristics, and conspecific aggression as factors affecting incubation in wild populations.

Beginning in the 1940s, however, another factor had played a more significant role than any of those mentioned by the DFW report: the development of DDT (dicloro-dephenyl-trichloroethane). As the well-known story goes, DDT was first used on mosquitoes and then as a general crop insecticide. Bald eagles did not directly ingest DDT; instead DDT entered their bodies through the animals they ate, which concentrated the pesticide in ever increasing amounts up the food chain.

DDE (dichlorophenyl-dicloroethylene), a breakdown product of DDT, was actually the main agent of destruction because it caused eggshell thinning and led to eggs breaking during incubation. Low moisture content in the shells, one more result of DDE, caused eggs to dry out too quickly, killing the chicks. Another dangerous class of pollutants, PCBs (polychlorinated biphenyls), bears additional responsibility because they delayed the onset of breeding, lowered sexual drives, and led to feeble parental care.

DDT and PCBs almost finished off the dwindling population of bald eagles, which had begun to drop in the mid- to late 1800s with the widespread shooting of the birds for trophies and feathers. The eagles' consumption of carrion, which ranchers had baited with strychnine, thallium sulfate, and other poisons in a misguided effort to eliminate livestock predators, also drove down population numbers. Add to this the loss of habitat through development and deforestation and the recipe was nearly perfect for extirpating bald eagles, as well as many other birds of prey.

A 1972 ban on DDT, however, prevented the completion of the recipe. Within six years of the ban, concentrations of DDT in fish, its primary breakdown products, and total PCBs had dropped in half and nesting eagle pair numbers had doubled. In addition, the 1978 listing of bald eagles provided the habitat protection that the growing population needed. Seventeen years later, the bald eagle was downlisted from "endangered" to "threatened" across the country. Clinton's proposed delisting would have removed the bird from the list entirely. However, as of 2004, the bald eagle remained on the federal List of Endangered and Threatened Wildlife.

Even though DDT no longer affects incubating urban eagles, they face a problem that birds in the past did not have to contend with: human disturbances. The DFW report describes many obvious human-related activities such as construction noise, aircraft and boat disturbances, and automobile traffic, but notes that "non-audible pedestrian activity (e.g. walkers)" leads the pack of disturbances. This does not mean that the other activities do not bother the birds, but that they seem to adapt to regular, repetitive sounds. Although walkers and bird-watchers may think their quiet interactions with the eagles are benign, approaching nests for a better view, especially during breeding season, can drive the parents away and result in unsuccessful nesting.

According to Jim Watson, coauthor of the DFW report, we cannot let the bird's adaptive ability make us complacent around eagles. "An increasing proportion of eagles recruited into the nesting population will have been raised in environments with greater human activity, perhaps resulting in a greater population-wide tolerance of humans and human activities," he said. "The caution, however, is that with any wild species there are limits to what animals can and will tolerate." I understand the desire to get close, to feel a connection with an animal's wildness, but maybe we should consider that the interaction can travel both ways and that our touch imparts our domesticity.

April 23 was the next big day for the eagle family, which now numbered three or four. On that day, the adults started flying into the nest with food and then ripping it into smaller pieces. I could not see into the nest but knew that the parents would dangle the morsels from their beaks. Feeding of fish, mallard, or crow took place several times a day, mostly by the male, since he had more time to hunt. The female spent most of her time at the nest keeping the nestling warm.

After watching for nearly a month, I was startled on May 20 by a gray mass rising over the nest's rim. The nestling was copying its father. Each bird was opening its beak, yellow for dad and blue-black for junior, tracking the omnipresent crows above the nest. The youngster's dark eyes shimmered like bits of muscovite catching sunlight in a matrix of gray granite. At one month of age, the nestling was already larger than its harassers.

Over the next month the eaglet began to replace its youthful coat of sooty down with feathers. It also continued to gain weight, eventually growing from 3.5 ounces at birth to between 9 or 11 pounds in about three months, the fastest rate of change of any North American bird.

With each passing day, the thousands of generations of flight that coursed through the young bird's veins expressed themselves. The nestling started by stretching, sometimes one wing and sometimes both. In late June it hopped about the nest, catching wind currents with its wings wide open. At times it appeared to be attached to a bungee cord as it leapt high, flapping into the wind, only to make a quick descent back to the nest.

By early July the nestling looked ready to become a fledgling. Dark brown feathers had replaced the ashen down. The soon-to-fledge bird was larger than the adult. Eagles reach their greatest size in their youth, when their tail and wing feathers are longest. The nestling, however, was most likely lighter than the adult. Ornithologists do not know the reason for this size change, but a larger bird can soar more easily and the large fledgling might be better equipped to successfully steal food from other birds or smaller eagles.

On July 12 I finally saw the female and a juvenile on one of the eagle's preferred perches in a nearby Douglas-fir. Splotches of white on the chest of the younger bird gave the impression that a small can of white paint had spilled down its front. The family was punctual as ever, the average time between hatching and fledging fitting precisely into the lifestyle described by the ornithologists. As I sat looking at these two, I noticed movement at the nest and realized that my eaglet had not fledged; the juvenile I was watching was an alien, being watched by the resident female. I was disappointed because Marjorie and I were leaving town on the twelfth, and this was my last opportunity to see the eaglet fledge.

We left soon for Rocky Mountain National Park for five days, and then I went to Moab for a week, my first trip back in over a year and the longest I had been away in 14 years. The two-week trip went well. I saw old friends, went on great hikes, exploring new territory and revisiting my favorites haunts. My visit reminded me once again what I missed about the desert.

I never saw the baby eagle at Green Lake again and I did not get to see the young bird fly. According to notes taken by Martin, the eagle fledged while I was on vacation, flying to a nearby treetop. It was a strong flier and spent its first week practicing takeoffs and landings. During its second week of flight, the dark brown youngster ventured out over Green Lake and landed at Duck Island, where I had first seen one of its parents.

The adults continued to feed the eaglet. I asked around but no one saw it catch anything. I can only assume that it had learned to hunt because the last sighting of the young eagle occurred in early August, when it began its probable migration north above the 49th parallel. If it didn't know how to hunt, the migration would not last long.

The entire family was soon gone from Green Lake. Right on schedule for a final time. Most Washington state bald eagles leave the country in summer and autumn. They spend an average of 112 days along coastal and interior British Columbia, and as far away as southeast Alaska. They head north for what one report calls the "superabundance of salmon carrion" found in the rivers that empty into the Pacific Ocean. When spawning season ends eagles start to migrate back. Territorial adults, like the pair at Green Lake, will often return to their previous season's nest, while the juveniles and non-breeding adults might come back to Puget Sound, but may end up elsewhere in the area.

Despite missing the young eagle's flight debut, I was quite fortunate in being able to amble out my front door and walk or bike a mile to Green Lake to see this magnificent family. To watch them soar effortlessly across our cerulean skies. To marvel at their snaring an unsuspecting fish. And to see them raise the next generation of our nation's symbol.

This good fortune is due in part to the geography of the city with its vast fresh- and saltwater shorelines, good perching and nesting trees, and abundant fish and fowl food sources. A simple question remains, however, about the increasing number of eagles in our urban landscape. Can we pat ourselves on the back because we have done something right in our stewardship of the Seattle landscape? After all, during breeding season as many as 150 eagles may be living in the state's most populated county.[4]

We should refrain from excessive congratulations. Most biologists with whom I corresponded thought that the DDT ban was the most important reason for the eagles' return. DFW biologist Watson said, "I don't think the eagle increase has much of anything to do with how we have treated the urban environment. In residential areas, the fact that all the trees are not cut down and some people prefer to leave large trees has had the secondary benefit of providing eagle perches along the shore and occasionally a nest tree." We are fortunate that eagles adapt well and are resilient.

We should probably give the early city residents more applause because of their creation of a decent park system, which protected the large trees that our newly returned eagles use for nesting and perching. The onus is now upon us to ensure that this legacy is not lost. The future will be the true measure of whether we deserve that back patting. What will happen when the bald eagle is delisted and the requirement for long-term habitat protection is removed? Even though the eagles will still be protected by several federal and state laws, nest and roost habitats will not. Landowners will be able to cut down any tree they want, no matter what the impact is on wildlife, a process that is already occurring as more people build and remodel houses along Lake Washington and Puget Sound.

Nor will state or federal agencies have a long-term mandate to survey the birds and monitor population trends. The Endangered Species Act requires a five-year monitoring program after a species is removed from the list, but this hardly suffices. Why else would the bird be delisted if its population is not on the upswing? One reason why biologists did not clearly recognize the DDT-caused drop in eagle numbers was the lack of long-term population analysis.

Despite the presently abundant eagle population, most biologists I talked with expressed a concern about a potential decline in eagle populations. They worry that without the federal mandates we will remove perching and buffering trees, and most importantly, will cut down future nest trees.

We may have the nest sites now, but we need to ensure there will be many for the future, too. To meet this exigency, we must cultivate and maintain Douglas-fir trees within a quarter mile of the shoreline so they attain mature size and are capable of supporting eagle nests. I hope that we do not bow to our all-too-common habit of moving to places that offer wildness and then taming them to meet our immediate desires.

Another key factor in ensuring that eagles remain here is for us to get to know them. The best way, of course, is to take advantage of the eagles' urban abundance and to watch and enjoy them, but at a distance with binoculars and spotting scopes.

We may be living in the halcyon days of urban eagles. The DDT ban and the ESA have given bald eagles the opportunity to increase their population and to refill previously occupied habitats, as well as to move into marginal (urban) habitats. Our local environment serves the eagles well and has been protected by the ESA. Our attitudes toward bald eagles have changed for the positive, and we want the birds to thrive. We need to live like we believe this.

Part of me worries that these days will not last long. I am hopeful, though, that we will start to act as if we are thankful for this second opportunity to see healthy eagles. On Thanksgiving Day 1999, I walked down to Green Lake to express my thanks to the resident bald eagles, who had recently returned from the north to their home and to the place Marjorie and I were now considering our home, too.

In Yosemite Valley, one morning about two o'clock I was aroused by an earthquake; and though I had never before enjoyed a storm of this sort, the strange, wild thrilling motion and rumbling could not be mistaken, and I ran out of my cabin, near the Sentinel Rock, both glad and frightened, shouting, "A noble earthquake!" feeling sure I was going to learn something.

JOHN MUIR, *OUR NATIONAL PARKS*, 1901

In an exhaustive report published at the time, he (Dr. Collier Cobb) emphasized the opinion that when the great glaciers swept down over this portion of the country (Seattle) they rendered it immune from severe earthquakes for all time... Dr. Cobb's findings created considerable discussion at the time but as nothing has happened in fifteen years to disprove them, those who scoffingly disagreed with him should be willing to admit that he may possibly have been correct in his findings.

THE ARGUS, JANUARY 11, 1936

In most parts of the country, people would call a magnitude 6.8 earthquake the BIG ONE, but not in Seattle. Although the February 28, 2001, Nisqually tremor caused over a billion dollars in damages, it occurred in what geologists consider the wimpiest of the three active fault zones under western Washington. They were glad that the other two centers—the Cascadia subduction zone, which has the potential for the most powerful quake, and the Seattle fault zone, the one they fear the most—had not moved, because damages from one of these quakes could total in the tens of billions of dollars with numerous deaths more than likely.

Although the *Big One* didn't hit that day, I doubt I will forget the seconds following 10:54 A.M. on that not-so-tranquil Wednesday. I had just picked up the February issue of *Audubon* magazine at the University Bookstore when the shaking began. It started slowly and gently, as if a large truck was passing on University Way. As the seconds seemed to stretch longer and longer, however, the shaking became a rumbling, and concrete walls, bookshelves, and windows swayed and rattled.

Despite the years of training I had as a child in Seattle, when we were all taught to crawl under our desks during an earthquake, I didn't scurry under a doorway or heavy desk. Instead, I stood still, mesmerized by the undulating, out-of-focus structure. I don't know why I didn't move, but I had no fear that anything would collapse. Maybe I was just naïve. I had been through a few small tremors, and this was by far the biggest one, but it just seemed that all would be okay.

An employee at the cash register closest to me yelled and leapt into a coworker's arms. Other people ran toward the doors. I followed slowly, caught up in the realization that I was watching one of the greatest ideas in science, the theory of plate tectonics, come to life. When I finally made it outside, standing still was not an option; either my legs were wobbling or the ground was continuing to shake. Stillness eventually returned and I began to turn my mind back to geology and to wonder where the quake had hit and how big it had been.

From what I had learned over the previous few months while spending time with geologists studying the Seattle area, I suspected that I had felt a Benioff zone quake, one of the more common manifestations of plate tectonics, at least in the Pacific Northwest. (The theory holds that the surface of the planet is made of a thin crust of rock separated into ten large and several smaller constantly moving pieces, or plates. Where the plates interact, whether by a head-on collision, sliding past each other, pulling apart, or by one diving under another, earthquakes happen.)

In the case of the Nisqually, two plates play central roles, the small Juan de Fuca and the massive continent of North America. During the past 20 to 30 million years, the leading edge of the denser Juan de Fuca has slid under, or subducted, the lighter North America, and its diving top now rests between 20 and 50 miles underground, directly beneath Puget Sound. As the tongue has descended deeper it has slowly bent and become much hotter, which creates two problems for us at the surface. The first is that bending stretches the plate. The second problem occurs because heat drives water out of minerals and shrinks the plate. This bending and contraction of Juan de Fuca deep under Puget Sound is one cause of the earthquakes we feel in Seattle.

Along with producing the Nisqually quake, the Benioff zone generated the two other memorable quakes that hit Puget Sound in the 1900s, a 7.1 magnitude event on April 13, 1949, and a 6.5 magnitude tremor on April 29, 1965. All three quakes had epicenters at least 30 miles underground. Pacific Northwest geologists estimate that major earthquakes at these depths occur about once every 30 years, with a potential magnitude range of 6.0 to 7.5, certainly big and frequent and much cause for excitement, but not the *Big One*.

Interaction between Juan de Fuca and North America, however, does have the potential for producing a quake that dwarfs these recent ones. Such a massive disturbance would occur closer to the surface off the Washington coast in an area called the Cascadia subduction zone, where Juan de Fuca and North America are moving toward each other. At present they cannot move because the plates are locked together like two pieces of Velcro, but this bond is not permanent; it will break someday and the plates will snap forward, sending a titanic wave of energy to the surface.

Geologists predict that this lock should break once every 300 to 600 years. Cascadia last moved at around 9:00 P.M. on January 26, 1700, dropping coastal Washington several feet and flooding and killing coastal forests. This created miles of marshes, punctuated by thousands of western red cedar and Sitka spruce snags. These "ghost forests" confused naturalists for over 100 years until United States Geological Survey (USGS) geologist Brian Atwater saw the forests in 1980.

Atwater knew that subduction quakes in Alaska and Chile had created similar areas of dead trees with a distinctive layering of sediments. When he examined the Washington marshes he found the same pattern. Carbon dating showed that the spruce and cedars had died between 1680 and 1720. Atwater narrowed the date by consulting Japanese researchers, who discovered that a six-to-nine-foot-high tsunami damaged houses and flooded rice paddies across 600 miles of Japanese coastline on January 27. No earthquakes occurred in Japan on that day and an earthquake-generated wave would have taken about 10 hours to cross the Pacific.

Geologists estimate that the 1700 Cascadia earthquake had a magnitude of 9.0 and that a future quake could be worse. We will have little doubt that it is the *Big One*. A one-unit increase of magnitude (for example, from 5.1 to 6.1) represents an approximately 32-fold increase in the energy released. In other words, a Cascadia zone 8.8 earthquake would release over 1,000 times (32 times 32) the energy of February's 6.8 quake. It would take more than 1,000 Nisqually earthquakes to equal the energy released in the 1700 Cascadia event.

The third local earthquake area sits directly under Seattle. Known as the Seattle fault zone, it is a 45-mile-long, 2.5- to 4-mile-wide, east-west trending series of fractures. Of the three earthquake zones, this one fascinates me the most, in part because of the way geologists pieced together the clues for its location and most recent movement; and in part, because it shows how good science can and does occur in urban settings. Furthermore, this fault zone has the most capacity for damage to my hometown. Geologists discovered this zone last, which is surprising, considering it is the only one where the evidence can be seen while you are stuck in traffic on I-5.

I first saw this evidence not while waiting in traffic, but on a field trip with Kathy Troost, a geologist at the University of Washington (UW). Kathy coleads the Pacific Northwest Center for Geologic Mapping Studies (GeoMapNW), a collaborative effort between the city of Seattle, the UW, and the USGS to put together, in unprecedented detail, a map of Seattle's surface and subsurface geology. The project will be incorporated into the Federal Emergency Management Agency's (FEMA) "Project Impact," a program to help make cities proactive instead of reactive to natural disasters. (Coincidentally, less than a day before the February quake President Bush had proposed a 17 percent cut in the FEMA budget, including terminating the $25 million Project Impact.) Seattle is one of only three localities, along with Memphis and Oakland, where such detailed maps are being developed.

Kathy was a geology consultant for 19 years before returning in 1998 to the UW for her master's and Ph.D. Her obsession with understanding this region better led to her assembling information for a map of Seattle's geology in the 1980s. "I got involved with this project because I love puzzles. We have been given a unique opportunity to put together a map that will make a positive influence on people's lives," said Kathy.

In late August 2000, she and I spent the day exploring the Seattle fault and other features of Seattle geology. We had parked her dark blue Miata just south of the intersection of I-5 and I-90, closed the convertible soft-top, put on yellow hard hats and hunter's orange reflective vests, passed through a gap in a fence, and climbed under the southbound traffic roadway. Normally, this area is off-limits but Kathy has a special permit from the Department of Transportation (DOT).

As we walked north, we followed a slender road cut, which DOT made in 1998 when it was retrofitting the northbound I-5 lanes to meet new seismic standards. About 50 feet from where we started, Kathy got out her shovel, macheteed off a few blackberry vines and revealed a set of one-eighth- to one-quarter-inch-thick, gray beds of alternating silt and clay. "These were deposited roughly 70,000 years ago in a glacial lake. The rhythmic banding probably represents seasonal changes, with finer sediments in winter. We don't find any pollen or other microfossils, which indicates a cold climate," she explained.

To my left I could see small folds in layers that dipped slightly back into the hill. I knew we had come to see evidence of deformation and expressed my excitement. "Oh that's nothing," said Kathy. Near the base of the next concrete support column I realized the error of my initial twittering. The once-horizontal beds now resembled an EKG-readout with complex zigzags connecting to less folded beds. They appeared to have been compressed from either end by two colossal bulldozers. Looking closer I could see that whatever force squeezed this area had sanded the clay beds into a smooth surface. Geologists calls these surfaces "slickensides." They form where two layers of rock have slid by each other in a fault. The fine-grained, more cohesive clay layers under the freeway slid along the gritty, silt layers, which created a polished, faintly striated surface.

Neither Kathy nor I was the first to get excited by these folds and faults. USGS geologist Brian Sherrod discovered these deformed beds in December 1998. "I was stuck in traffic listening to music on my way home to Federal Way, when I happened to look over and see the nearly vertical beds next to the pillar. I said 'Holy shit,' but of course couldn't do anything then," exclaimed Brian, when we met together to explore some of his recent work around Bellevue.

Like Kathy, Brian's eyes light up when he describes geology in Seattle. "We've got a world-class problem right here in our backyard," he said, as we drove from spot to spot examining the trace of a fault on the east side. "The older generation trained to go out to pristine landscape and study geology. That is not as easy to do now, plus we have problems here relevant to society, which makes it that much more fascinating."

Brian eventually returned to the road cut under I-5 with Kathy and Derek Booth, the other coleader of the GeoMapNW. "When we finally got up close to these beds, I was amazed to see that much deformation in one small outcrop. What I once thought was just a very small patch of dipping beds turned out to be several sets of folds with overturned limbs and several faults," Brian told me on our field trip. This amount of deformation clearly indicated that whatever disturbance created this deviation was a significant geologic event and not merely the product of the construction of I-5, which did produce a landslide, forcing workers to build the large wall that rose above the highway near where we stood.

One of three events could have folded and faulted these layers: landslides, glacial compression, or tectonic forces. Although you will find those who disagree, Brian, Kathy, and Derek lean toward a tectonic origin.

"We can blame California for our geologic problems," Brian explained. North-northwest movement of the Sierra Nevada and Klamath Mountains over the last 10 to 15 million years has created a zone of compression in the Puget Sound area. Interaction between the North America and Pacific plates moves California's block of hard granitic mountains north at almost a half inch per year (twice as fast as a toenail grows) and butts it into another block of hard rock, the Coast Range of Oregon, which in turn slides north into Washington state. "It's like a train with one car pushing against the next. The cars continue to move until they hit an immobile object, which in this situation is Canada," added Brian.

Seattle is literally being compressed between a rock and a hard place, at about a quarter to a third of an inch per year, which has created the Seattle fault zone. Geologists call it a zone because it consists of at least three or four separate faults, or splays, cutting east-west across the Seattle area. Only the northern splay, the one geologists call the Seattle fault, shows signs of recent movement. It basically follows the route of I-90 from Issaquah to Safeco Field, south of downtown, and continues west through Alki Point, Restoration Point on Bainbridge, and Bremerton before terminating at Hood Canal.

Geologists estimate that in the past 10 to 15 million years, the Puget Sound lowlands have been horizontally compressed between five and nine miles on a north-south axis between the southern Scylla of Oregon and northern Canadian Charybidis. Vertical movement totals about five miles between the uplifted and downdropped walls of the Seattle fault zone. If we could see this process occur over the next 10 million years in time-lapse photography, we would see Boeing Field pushed north to about the location of the Seattle Center and up to the elevation of the summit of Mount Rainier.

This process of compression generally occurs in small increments, as exemplified by the deformed I-5 beds, but it can also thrust an entire river bank out of the water in a single event, which it did most recently a little over 1,100 years ago. One good spot to see this once-submerged river shoreline is along the Duwamish River.

To reach this location, Kathy and I went to the Duwamish Public Access on West Marginal Way and Southwest Edmund Street and took a short path down to the river. Upright pipes, old pier supports, broken bricks, a retaining wall—the detritus of bygone industry—dotted the shoreline. On the other side of the Duwamish, blue, red, white, and rust-colored container cars rose five stories high, while great blue herons and Canada geese stalked the mudflats between us and Kellogg Island, a 15-acre crescent of battered land dotted by industrial fill and few trees.

We had come to examine the eight-foot-high riverbank, accessible only at low tide. Thousands of white, tan, opalescent, and bluish shells littered the gray wall of silt and sand. Most of the shells were fractured beyond recognition but I could distinguish bits and complete shells of clams and mussels, ranging up to about three inches wide. After examining the wall of shells for a few minutes, I used a piece of rusted pipe to pry two intact clam shells out of the riverbank. The thinner of the two, called a bent-nose clam (*Macoma nasuta*), measured about 1.5 inches wide. Fairly smooth and white, it looked as if the left side of the shells had been stretched and then turned up slightly. The thicker clam was the common Pacific littleneck (*Venerupis staminea*). Locals might know these latter bivalves because they are a popular clam, relished for their fine taste.

This shell-rich locality, which covers three acres, first attracted attention in November 1975, when David Munsell, staff archaeologist for the Seattle District of the Army Corps of Engineers, found abundant beds of shells on the upper bank of the Duwamish River, just north of where Kathy and I stood. A 1981 archaeological report concluded that this refuse, or midden site, as archaeologists call it, had been a major domestic habitation site from late fall to early spring, between 670 and 1700.

The report did note the clam layer that brought us to this spot but did not state that the beds predated the earliest midden date by about 500 years.

The two clams in my hands died roughly 1,850 years ago. "What makes these shells interesting is that they were intertidal organisms and they are not below the tidal line at present," Kathy said. "This means one of two things: either sea level was once higher or they were uplifted sometime between 1,850 years ago and the present. We know that sea level is now as high as it has been for thousands of years."

"We believe that these beds of clams were uplifted at least 15 feet, 1,100 years ago during the last major movement of the Seattle fault. Twenty years ago we wouldn't have thought much about this cross section of shells, because we didn't know anything about this structure. Now, the more we look, the more evidence we find for the fault."

Realization that the Seattle fault moved relatively recently first began to gel in the late 1980s when geologist Robert Bucknam discovered that Restoration Point on Bainbridge Island had been shoved out of Puget Sound less than 1,700 years ago. In 1986, he had been working on earthquake hazards along the Wasatch Front, in Utah, when the program focus changed to other, less understood seismically active areas, including the Puget Sound region. Bucknam examined aerial photographs to locate faults on the surface, but this approach did not work in the Pacific Northwest, which has slightly denser vegetation hiding most of the evidence. He was in luck, however, because recent research showed that in coastal areas the deformation near faults from large earthquakes could change the elevation of shorelines adjacent to the fault. Now all he would have to do was find an uplifted marine terrace near a suspected fault zone.

Serendipitously for Bucknam, only a year earlier three geologists had published a report that indicated a recently uplifted marine terrace at Restoration Point. The authors noted that the terrace was near a geologic anomaly that previous researchers had interpreted as evidence for a possible fault. Bucknam spent the next few years examining Restoration Point, before reporting his findings in the December 4, 1992, issue of *Science*.

Along with four other articles in the same issue, Bucknam's paper made a startling report: one day about 1,100 years ago the land south of the Seattle fault line shot up 20 feet and the area north of it dropped at least three feet during a massive earthquake. Comparing the offset on this quake to a 1980 one near El Asnam, Algeria, geologists estimate that the last movement on the Seattle fault measured at least magnitude 7.5.

On a cool, clear Sunday in October 2000, Marjorie and I took the Bainbridge Island ferry to see the rocks that had fascinated Bucknam. After deferrying in Winslow, we drove south and west until we reached a narrow road that led to the island's westernmost point. We parked in a small turnout a quarter mile before a sign reading *Private Property—Restoration Point Golf and Country Club*, left the car, and walked to the edge of a flat rocky platform that dropped straight down 20 feet to the Sound. Several six-inch-wide, parallel, dark brown fins of rock extended out from the cliff. These hard, well-cemented layers had originally been deposited as horizontal sands, like the beds under I-5, but the slow squeeze of the Seattle fault zone had tilted them nearly vertical. Bucknam interpreted the vertical fins as proof of sudden uplift; waves would have eroded them if Restoration Point had risen slowly from the Sound.

About 100 yards from our parking spot, we found a route down a slope of tan sandstone. Sand, shells, and broken jewels of glass covered the beach, while waves washed against another layer of tan sandstone barely emerging from the water. The nearly smooth, raised ledge we had descended from indicated rapid emergence from the sea. Slow uplift would have produced intermediate shoreline features on the middle slope, such as bars of beach gravel or small erosional steps. We found only empty beer bottles, cigarette wrappers, and a couple of tattered blankets.

After collecting a few shells, we climbed back to the upper platform. I wondered what it would have been like to have been fishing on this spot when the Seattle fault last moved. One second you're standing at the shoreline, waves lapping against your feet, and the next you're 20 feet out of the water, your fishing line dangling in the air. Despite my passion for natural disasters, I am not sure I would want to take such an unexpected ride.

In addition to Bucknam's paper, four other articles in the same issue of *Science* describe how geologists had turned to an array of seemingly disconnected evidence to show when the Seattle fault last moved. The most distant data came from the Olympic Mountains. Five large rock avalanches had dammed streams, which created lakes that had submerged trees. Snags collected from three of the lakes, Jefferson, Lower Dry Bed, and Spider, indicated that an earthquake occurred between 1,000 and 1,300 years ago.

Researchers in Seattle also examined a layer of fine sediment in Lake Washington, deposited by multiple, same-age, subsurface landslides that could only be set in motion by some event as ground shaking as an earthquake. The mean age for organic matter in the sediments was 1,117 years before present, plus or minus 142 years.

An analysis of Douglas-fir trees from Seattle also gave a date for the last movement of the Seattle fault at about 1,100 years ago. The initial evidence came from three groves, which a fault-induced landslide had carried from their original habitat on the shores of Lake Washington to their present resting place 90 feet underwater. One stand slid off the southeast corner of Mercer Island. Another settled on the west side of the island, across from the south end of Seward Park, and the third slumped between Holmes Point and North Point near St. Edward Park, north of Kirkland.

When divers explored the trees in 1957, they discovered that many were still upright and appeared to have slid to their present position with little movement relative to the soil where they had grown. The largest had a circumference of over 28 feet and the longest measured 120 feet with a 5.5-foot diameter. They were so waterlogged that they sank readily.

In 1990 three geologists pulled up several trees from the submerged forests, which they used to obtain radiocarbon dates. Once again the dates were between 1,000 and 1,300 years ago, but this was not the only telling piece of information from these Douglas-firs. Researchers also analyzed the trees' annual growth rings. First they determined that the firs all died in the same year and season. Next they compared their tree-ring data with a Douglas-fir found at West Point, the westernmost point of Magnolia Bluff. This tree, discovered in February 1992 by Brian Atwater of Cascadia fame, was one part of an extensive archaeological and geological record removed from a trench dug for an effluent pipe connected with the West Point Treatment Plant.

The earliest material consisted of shell middens, which is what initially caught Atwater's eye, bone and stone artifacts, and fire-burnt material left by people who inhabited the area 4,000 years ago. People continued to live around the sandy beach and adjacent saltgrass and bulrush-rich marsh for the next 3,000 years, although landslides cascading off the adjacent cliffs periodically plowed through their beachfront property. And then came an ominous day about 1,100 years ago, when the Seattle fault dropped West Point three feet into the sea and created a tsunami that surged across Puget Sound.

As the wave of water spread across the now submerged tidal marsh, it deposited a 1.5- to 2.5-inch-thick sheet of sand and at least one Douglas-fir log. Over time another marsh developed atop the older one, which is what happened to Atwater's Cascadia zone coastal ghost forests. The West Point marsh persistedfor another 900 years or so, until the 1940s when the U.S. Army began to practice amphibious landings and beach assaults. Construction of the sewage treatment plant in the early 1960s finally obliterated all surface evidence of the marsh, until Atwater's 1992 observation of the trench-bound shell midden.

When Atwater found the tsunami-deposited log, it rested on a patch of the sand sheet and on toppled, flattened bulrush stems. Radiocarbon dating put the tree's death at between 850 and 1,350 years ago. In order to narrow this window of death and to pinpoint the date of the tsunami, Atwater compared his tree-ring widths with data from the submerged forest trees. He discovered that the trees died within a half year or less of each other, most likely between A.D. 900 and 928.

With this final clue, the geologists had solved the mystery of date and magnitude for the last big movement of the Seattle fault. One significant question that remains to be answered, however, is when it will happen again. At this point in time geologists cannot predict quakes. Nor will they be able to at any point in the foreseeable future. Geologists know that the Seattle fault last moved 1,100 years ago and have evidence indicating two or three additional movements in the last 2,500 years, but that offers no more accurate prediction for a future event than sometime in the next several thousand years.

We have two ways to examine this data. On one hand, a human one, the last big movement of the Seattle fault occurred in the distant past, over 1,100 years ago, implying that this subsurface defect doesn't move often and that it won't move in our lifetimes. On the other hand, a geologic one, the last big movement of the Seattle fault occurred only about 1,100 years ago, the merest blink of geologic time, implying that the fault is still active and ready to move. All geologists know for sure is that the *Big One* will hit Seattle, most likely sooner rather than later. We just have to wait and see which time scale will prevail: human or geologic.

When I think back to February 28, one aspect of the earthquake that stands out was how slowly time seemed to progress. I did not expect the shaking to both increase in scale and to continue for so long. Despite what the reports said, I am sure that I felt vibrations for several minutes and not just 45 seconds, which is how long the geologists say the quake lasted. The intersection between geologic and human time was both exciting and scary.

One important question that geologists can answer is the depth of the Seattle fault. Subsurface data shows that the epicenter for the 1,100-year-ago earthquake occurred fewer than 10 miles beneath Seattle. This is what scares geologists. When a fault moves deep underground, such as in a Nisqually-type event, most of its high-frequency energy dissipates before reaching the surface, which reduces the level of ground shaking. In contrast, a shallow earthquake's high-frequency energy remains strong at the surface. During the shallow 1995 Kobe, Japan, and 1994 Northridge, California, earthquakes, ground shaking ranged between 2.5 and 5 times greater than what has been recorded in subduction-generated faults.

The other problem with the Seattle fault relates to Restoration Point: a shallow fault can push up material that pierces the surface. Considering that the last movement on the fault thrust rock 20 feet out of the Sound, ground ruptures could sever natural gas, liquid fuel, sewer, and water supply pipelines, all of which cross the Seattle fault zone. And this does not even address the numerous bridges and roads that an earthquake could destroy.

We weathered the 2001 quake well, in part because it was so deep and in part because the city of Seattle has taken significant steps to retrofit our infrastructure. Structural damage in Seattle was mostly limited to chimneys and brick facades. We had no loss of life and few major injuries. We are fortunate that millions of dollars have been spent on retrofitting roads and bridges and that our stringent design regulations require that buildings be built to withstand most seismic problems. We are fortunate that small earthquakes periodically hit and remind us that the work of people like Derek, Kathy, and Brian is not just esoteric studying of bygone events. In addition, we have good emergency life-support systems and vast pools of money available when a disaster hits.

This was most evident to me the week following the Nisqually earthquake, when Marjorie and I traveled to El Salvador to see friends. We had been planning the trip for months and El Salvador's January 13, 7.6 magnitude and February 13, 6.6 magnitude earthquakes gave us a firsthand chance to see the destruction. While damage such as cracked walls and rubble piles was evident across the capital of San Salvador, we did not see true devastation until we went out into the countryside.

At San Agostin, a dot of a town in the foothills of one of El Salvador's many volcanoes, I felt like a voyeur, because only the floors remained in most houses. A few had walls standing but even these had wood supports propping them up. Electrical boxes and bare bulbs hung from trees. At what was left of the school, people stood in line, waiting to receive food from aid workers. It appeared that many were living in a tent village, set up on the school grounds.

We also saw Santa Tecla, a middle-class suburb of San Salvador that was leveled by a landslide. During the January quake a ridge above town collapsed, sending a wall of soil and rock down and over several blocks of two-story cinder-block houses. The landslide's path through Santa Tecla was two blocks wide and a half mile long. At least 700 people died. The final number will probably never be known because people are still buried in the rubble. No one is allowed to live in neighborhoods below the landslide, and a tent city outside the cordoned-off zone houses over 2,100 people.

As I stood below the landslide ridge, I thought about how much we take for granted in Seattle and was struck by how little damage was evident. El Salvador was the first place where I had ever witnessed geology overprinted by such a human face. The death and destruction was sobering and I am less eager to revel in the process of natural disasters than previously, though this is still the way I think the world should work.

I like that I live in an area of active geology. I like knowing that the potential exists for a natural cataclysm right under my feet. This does not mean that I advocate movement on the Seattle fault, or that I look forward to the destruction that will follow. The Seattle fault starkly reminds us that nature bats last, even in the environment that we think we have tamed the most, the urban zone.

There is good reading on the land, first-hand reading, involving no symbols.

The records are written in forests, in fence-rows, in bogs, in play-grounds, in pastures, in gardens, in canyons, in tree rings.

The records were made by sun and shade; by wind, rain, and fire, by time; and by animals.

As we read what is written on the land, finding accounts of the past, predictions of the future, and comments on the present, we discover that there are many interwoven strands to each story, offering several possible interpretations.

Interpreting this reading matter, in place, on the land, seeing living things in their total environment, is an adventure into the field that is called ecology.

MAY THEILGAARD WATTS, *READING THE LANDSCAPE: AN ADVENTURE IN ECOLOGY*, 1957

I like to think I am knowledgeable about Seattle's early natural and social history. I generally do well on those local history quizzes that newspapers publish during a slow news week, and one of my earliest memories is of interviewing a descendent of a pioneer family for a story I wrote in third grade. I know when the locks were built, who first uttered the name Lake Union, why the streets are skewed around Pioneer Square, where the Great Fire started, and what the first industry was.

Despite this astounding accumulation of important facts, for many years I had a skewed image of what Seattle looked like when the first settlers arrived. My botanical ignorance centered on big trees; I thought that a nearly unbroken Douglas-fir forest covered the hilly terrain from the shores of Puget Sound up into the purple mountain majesty of the Cascades. I pictured trees so big that it took "two men and a boy to look to the top," as one early writer described them. I pictured a forest "whose dark verdurous hue diffused a solitary gloom—favorable to meditations," as naturalist Archibald Menzies wrote in 1792. It was an image fashioned partially by the women of the Denny party, Seattle's founding families, who wept when they first arrived at Alki Point and discovered a dripping forest of giant trees.

When I began to investigate Seattle's past I discovered my ignorance. As I looked through old scientific journals and early survey reports, read modern ecological studies of the region, and talked to botanists, historians, and ecologists, I found far more complexity than I expected. Just as important I began to realize that there were clues left in the modern landscape that could help me both see and understand the ecological diversity of Seattle on November 13, 1851, the overcast day that the schooner *Exact* dropped off the 22 people of the Denny party. (Unfortunately, the founders were not nature lovers, and little information can be gleaned from their journals and memoirs, except that the first thing they did after building their winter quarters was to cut down Douglas-firs to ship to San Francisco.)

My education began close to home with the name of the neighborhood where we live. Licton Springs is the only neighborhood with a Native name that gives a clue to what the area may have looked like prior to the arrival of pioneers. The name is a corruption of the Lushootseed word *liq̓ted* (LEEK-tuhd), which means "red" or "paint." It refers to the iron oxides that still precipitate from springs bubbling out of the ground.

At present, the springs are preserved in a nine-acre park, which contains a small stream, a pond, a large grassy field, and a kids' play area. The lone reference to the past spills out of a rusty-rimmed, concrete cistern and flows down an ochre-colored rivulet to the stream, which feeds the pond at the park's south end. Alders dominate the tree canopy, complemented by a few red cedars, a smattering of English holly, English laurel, snowberries, and far too much reed canary grass and Himalayan blackberry.

I remember the first time I walked through this small park. I had never heard of it before moving to this neighborhood. I was walking our dog, Taylor, when I saw the green lawn backed by Lombardy poplars and alders. I found the pond, explored what I could, and followed a path north by the playground. This path forked, one route leading across the main stream and the other heading north on a boardwalk. I ventured north and would have passed by the blackberry-shrouded cistern if there had not been a sun-baked sign that related the history of Liq̓ted.

I learned that the Native people of the area considered the springs a spiritual place. They used the red mud for face paint in winter ceremonies, such as the spirit canoe and power spirit dancing, drank the mineral-rich waters medicinally, and camped and built sweat lodges nearby. They also followed trails from liq̓ted to Green Lake, a nearby cranberry marsh, and Haller Lake. Considering how few place-based Native names remain around Seattle, the survival of Liq̓ted, or Licton, testifies to the importance of the site.

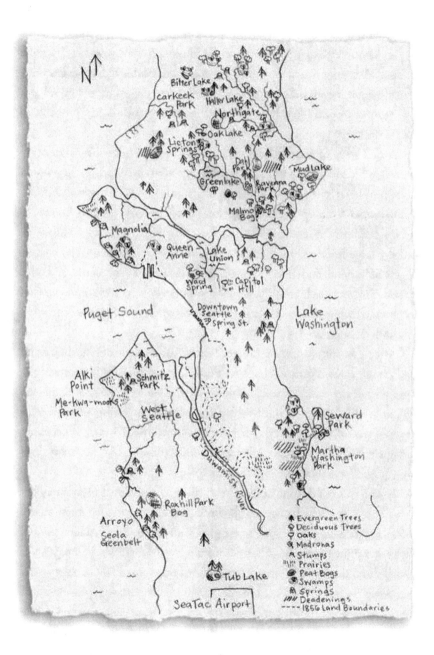

So what did this site look like in 1851? How did springs interrupt my image of unbroken forest? Judging from early photos and descriptions of the area and from my experience with springs in modern-day forests, western red cedar and red alder would have grown near the seeps at Liq'ted, as well as along a small stream, which early maps show flowed from the springs to Green Lake. The ground around Liq'ted would have been marshy or muddy, probably in shades of terra cotta.

A rich array of water-loving undergrowth would have thrived beneath the cedar and alder. When Native people visited in early spring, they would have seen the bright yellow cloak-and-dagger of skunk cabbages (*Lysichiton americanus*). A damp habitat obligate, skunk cabbage is also known as "swamp lantern," a reference to the yellow flowering spike, called a spadix, and the large hooded bract, the spathe. They could also have seen narrow fingers of horsetail and cattail, thorn-covered devil's club and nettle, and odd-shaped blossoms such as brilliant yellow monkeyflowers (*Mimulus guttatus*) and hooded white ladies' tresses (*Spiranthes romanzoffiana*), flowers now less common in Seattle.

After a recent restoration project cleared out a jungle of blackberry and reed canary grass, skunk cabbage reappeared at Licton Springs. One of the highlights of my morning walks with Taylor was seeing these striking plants, which lived up to their light-inspired moniker. As spring progressed, I watched the unfurling of skunk cabbage's 3-foot-long, 15-inch-wide, shiny dark green leaves. I looked for other spring-loving flowers but the canary grass appeared to have outcompeted them.

Liq'ted was not the only well-known spring around Seattle. Ravenna Park once had springs, which owner William Beck charged 25 cents to visit in the 1890s. Other examples of such soggy places are Spring Street, which honors the former principal source of Seattle's drinking water, and Ward Springs Park, a small site at the base of Queen Anne Hill that opened in 2002 and that commemorates the spring that once provided 80,000 gallons a day of drinking water. We will never know the total number but it is safe to assume that tens and maybe hundreds of small seep-created wetlands once dotted the Seattle landscape. Land surveys conducted in the mid-1800s refer to crabapple, skunk cabbage, alder, and hardhack swamps, just in the northwest end of the city.

Concrete and piping have eliminated most of Seattle's springs, but one can still see signs of their persistence. When I see a dense growth of horsetails, nettles, or devil's club, I know I have found one. The persnickety flows appear as wet spots on pavement, damp patches on lawns, or small pools at the bottom slopes. This is especially true in winter when it appears that city streets have sprung leaks. Landslides generally indicate the presence of a spring, too.

Another name close to our neighborhood also offers a clue to Seattle's early-day plant life, but this time to a much rarer plant community than the springs. Oak Tree Village, at N 100th Street and Aurora Avenue, refers to a school that stood on this site from 1886 to 1982 and that bore the name Oak Lake School, in reference to a nearby pond where a grove of large oak trees grew. Neither the oaks nor the lake remain at this location. Despite the fact that I shop here once a week, I only recently noticed that the developers have honored the name by planting oaks around the buildings and parking lots. These oaks, although a nice gesture, are pin oaks, natives of the east coast.

Washington state has only one native oak, the Garry or Oregon white oak. David Douglas bestowed the scientific name, *Quercus garryana*, to honor Nicholas Garry, secretary and later deputy governor of the Hudson's Bay Company. More common south of Tacoma, particularly on the prairies around Nisqually and Fort Lewis, and on islands in Puget Sound, Garry oaks prefer sunny, open, well-drained sites. In describing oak prairies, early naturalists often mentioned the broad, flat terrain, luxuriant grass, and abundant wildflowers, in particular the blue camas, which made some prairies look like a lake reflecting an azure sky. These prairies were and still are important refuges for threatened animals, such as the western gray squirrel and western pocket gopher, and two butterflies, the mardon skipper and valley silverspot, as well as several plants, including Torrey's pea and smallflower wakerobin.

Garry oaks grew only in isolated plots in Seattle and I know of only three spots where one can still see large Garry oak trees: Seward Park, Martha Washington Park, and 730 Belmont Avenue, at Oak Manor, on Capitol Hill. Each of these localities has or recently had oaks that could have been growing on November 13, 1851. The Oak Manor oak, a lone tree, is several hundred years old. It is awe inspiring, its canopy of dark green leaves towering over the nearby apartments and its 12-foot-circumference gnarled trunk split-ting into numerous arms, many larger than typical street trees. No one I talked to knows why this single oak survived the logging of Capitol Hill or whether others grew nearby.

The oaks at Martha Washington and Seward Parks, on the other hand, grow in groves, particularly at Seward. Of the two sites, Seward is easier to explain. First, the site faces south, and the grove grows on relatively thin, well-drained soil that sits directly atop bedrock, instead of the more typical Vashon till, Lawton Clay, or Esperance Sand. Additional dry-site plants at Seward include two other rare natives, poison oak (*Rhus diversiloba*), not actually an oak but a sumac, and snowbrush (*Ceanothus velutinus*), as well as snow-berry (*Symphoricarpos albus*), tall Oregon grape (*Mahonia aquifolium*), and serviceberry (*Amelenchier alnifolia*). Although never very prevalent in Seattle, this is ideal habitat for oaks and these cohorts but marginal habi-tat for Douglas-firs.

Martha's oaks, although fewer and smaller, require more explanation, and ultimately add more detail to my picture of Seattle's presettlement forest. Until the winter of 1987–88, a 14-foot circumference, 75-foot-tall (and this with the top broken off) Garry oak dominated the small park, which encompasses 10 acres on Lake Washington where the Martha Washington School for Girls once stood. Like the Oak Manor tree, this one started to grow long before the Dennys and their clan arrived. Two nearby streets, Oaklawn Place and Oakhurst Street (*hurst* is an ancient word meaning "grove of trees"), also indicate that oaks were abundant or noticeable enough to merit street name recog-nition. Add to these clues an early name for land around the Seward Park penin-sula, Clark's Prairie, and it is clear that an unusual plant community grew in this area. It is less clear why.

I hoped that a visit to the former school site would help answer this ques-tion. All that one can now see of the giant oak is a stump, but I found 15 to 20 smaller, but still 30- to 40-foot-tall, oaks growing near the water. I spent about an hour wandering around, but I did not locate the one clue I sought, acorns, which could have offered an insight into why oaks grew there. Acorns were a prominent food source for Native peoples. Edward Curtis, in his multivolume *The North American Indians*, wrote that tribes from around

Puget Sound would canoe down to the Nisqually plains and collect hundreds of bushels of acorns, which they roasted, ate raw, and used for bread making. In addition to collecting acorns, Native tribes, such as Skagit, Duwamish, Snohomish, Cowlitz, and Clallam, harvested bracken and camas from the prairies of Nisqually and further south, and from Whidbey and Camano Islands.

Harvesting these delicacies, however, was not simply a matter of going to the local prairie year after year and collecting the early day equivalent of fast food. It involved active management of the land: in particular, setting fires. Fire destroyed the Douglas-fir seedlings, which grow faster, eventually shade out oaks, and can take over an oak prairie if not prevented from doing so by fire, a process now occurring around Fort Lewis and on the Mima Mounds, south of Olympia. Annual blazes would also help check undesirable grasses and shrubs, and facilitate the growth of camas and the spread of bracken, which quickly invades disturbed land. Tribes supplemented fire by transferring camas bulbs to recently burned areas and by gathering them with digging sticks, tilling the soil as they did so. Some botanists have also surmised that Native people transported acorns to prairies, which may account for the spotty distribution of oaks in Washington state. For some unknown reason, possibly aggressive nonnative squirrels or lack of fire, Seattle's native oaks are not reproducing and I have found neither sapling nor seedling in the city.

But did the Native people set fire to this area? Two lines of evidence may help answer this question. The first comes from the 1850–60s surveys I mentioned earlier. Known as Government Land Office (GLO) or cadastral surveys, they were done to establish township and range boundaries around the country. At each section and quarter section, surveyors designated bearing trees, as well as noting four large trees around the bearing tree. For the survey of Township 24 North, Range 4 East, Sections 23 and 26, which encompasses the oak communities in question, the surveyors recorded two "deadenings," shorthand for burned-out areas.

I found the second set of clues for this story atop Seward Park, in one of the last old-growth forest areas in Seattle. I had gone to the park to show a friend from Moab, where the dominant ecosystem is known as a pygmy forest, what big trees looked like. We began by walking on the road around the north end of the peninsula, passing by poison oak, a few madronas, and many conifers. This array impressed my tree-challenged visitor but it was not until we followed a path up and over the center of Seward that she got to see what even we in the Pacific Northwest consider big trees.

The one that caused the most excitement for us grew next to the trail. A sign on the path indicated it was Seattle's largest Douglas-fir. With a circumference of 23 feet, it probably started growing at least 500 years ago. Of particular interest to me were the fire scars that blackened the base of the deeply furrowed trunk. As we continued to walk around Seward, we found at least a dozen more large Douglas-firs with blackened bases. Burn marks reached no more than 25 feet or so up the trunks and had no consistent orientation. None of the smaller Dougs showed any indications of fire. Most were about the same size, indicating that a disturbance cleared the way for them to start growing and that they post-date whatever fire burned through the peninsula, scarring the big trees.

It is not possible to say if the fire that blackened the big trees was started by the people who were burning the nearby oak prairie. Lightning could have created the blaze. Fire ecologists hypothesize that fires around Puget Sound may have had a recurrence interval of once every 100 years, as opposed to a 500 year interval on the Olympic Peninsula. We had more fire because of our relatively dry climate and because people set blazes. Native people relied on fire to clear prairies but they also burned wooded areas, which attracted game and improved habitat for various food plants such as berries. These openings were probably not large and most likely occurred where trees had blown down, opened the canopy, and allowed smaller plants to flourish. The cadastral surveys record several such burned areas of forest across Seattle.

Whether natural or anthropogenic, fire did play a key role in the composition of Puget Sound forests. Without fire, western hemlock, in particular, and western red cedar to a lesser extent, should become the climax conifers of this region. This means that, if left undisturbed, hemlocks would eventually replace Douglas-fir and take over as the dominant tree in our forests. Fires have changed this situation by favoring firs, which thrive in full sunlight, outcompete hemlocks in their youth, and resist fire better in old age. Dry site conditions have enhanced the fire effect and made much of Seattle a nearly perfect locale for Douglas-firs.

Some of the largest known Douglas-firs of Seattle's past, nationally recognized "vegetable skyscrapers," as a promotional brochure called them, grew in Ravenna Park. One known as the Robert E. Lee supposedly topped out at nearly 400 feet, and another, the Roosevelt, in honor of Teddy, measured 44 feet around and was called "the single most famous thing in Seattle" by a Chamber of Commerce publication. The Ravenna trees survived until at least the 1909 Alaska–Yukon–Pacific Exposition but disappeared under mysterious circumstances by 1925.

The forest of Seward Park fared better because of absentee landlords and Seattle's nascent park movement. The park gives the best picture of what most of Seattle's presettlement forest looked like. Old Douglas-firs are interspersed with younger trees, particularly in openings caused by wind, which either snapped treetops or toppled entire trees. These downed trees have become nurse logs taken over by salal, western hemlock, and sword fern. Western red cedars occur in the wetter microclimates, although they are found throughout the forest, while larger hemlocks grow best at the north end of the peninsula. Other understory plants include vine maple, Pacific yew, Nootka rose, red flowering currant, and Indian plum. It is a wild landscape, populated by trees and shrubs adapted to take advantage of our mild winter climate.

Because Seward escaped ax and saw, it lacks one of my favorite and one of the more widespread clues in Seattle: cut stumps. Logging was the driving force in Seattle's early history and even contributed to the coining of the town's infamous moniker, Skid Road, a reference to skidding the massive trees down to Henry Yesler's mill. Log Boom Park in Kenmore provides another clue to the transport history of logs, which were tied together and floated in a boom out to Puget Sound through the now-dried-up Black River to the Duwamish River. By the early 1900s little lumber remained within city limits; all that we now have are the cedar stumps.

Unlike other big tree species in Seattle, cedar stumps decay slowly and can remain intact for more than 150 years. Many also include an extra clue to Seattle's timber-driven past: wedge-shaped notches, where lumbermen inserted a steel-tipped plank, or springboard, upon which to stand. They did this to get above the buttresses of bark and wood that characterize the base of most cedars and that were hard to cut and mill. Stumps that lack these notches may have been small enough to cut without the extra height provided by the plants, or the tree may have snapped off and decayed enough to resemble a poorly cut stump.

I have spent many hours exploring Seattle for stumps and found them at nearly every park that has untamed woods, such as Thornton Creek parks 1, 2, and 6, Schmitz, Interlaken, Frink, and Discovery. I have even seen them in a few lucky homeowners' yards. The one thing they have in common is moisture; cedars grow best in wet to very wet sites and most likely were the dominant conifer around Seattle's many springs and streams. If you were to put together a map of all of Seattle's cedar stumps, you would begin to get a feel for the greatness and for the locations of the cedars of our presettlement forest.

Carkeek Park, 200-plus acres of ravine, forested hillside, bluff, and beach on the shores of Puget Sound, has the city's best and biggest stumps. I have counted at least three dozen, ranging in size from a few feet wide to a 25-foot circumference titan, which flares below its many springboard notches to probably twice this girth. It stands at the bottom of the ravine, near a seep next to the trail. I am always pleased to see it, but it is not the only stump worthy of appreciation.

I especially like stumps slowly being taken over by hemlocks, which have sent roots slithering like tentacles down the stumps' sides. I marvel at how full of life dead trees can be. I have found stumps colonized by sword fern, salal, red huckleberries, alder, bracken, and vanilla leaf, and a few so encrusted in lichen and moss that I had to wonder how any other plant could get a seed in edgewise. I revel in their ability to hold water, and I like to visit in winter when I can grab a hunk of brick-red wood and squeeze it like a sponge.

Each stump once supported a tree. I know this is obvious but I think it is worth stating because a stump exemplifies the connections one can make when reading the landscape. When I see a cedar stump, I imagine a forest of big trees. I think of the arrival of settlers who needed the trees for home and livelihood and who had an understandable belief that the supply of wood was inexhaustible. I think of the present and how these stumps have become nurseries for plants and animals. And finally, I think of the future and the potential for another forest of giants to come. I read similar connections between

Seattle's glacial past and good, hard bike rides, between a desire for grass-filled parks and too many Canada geese, between a city-leveling fire and 50-million-year-old sandstone building blocks. I read these connections as links between time and topography, between action and end point, between death and life. They are what bind me to this place.

Carkeek is also a fine spot to see false clues, the abundant red alders and bigleaf maples that dominate the park. They grow on the slopes, on the bluffs, and in the bottom of the ravine, and they include what tree expert Arthur Lee Jacobson believes is Seattle's thickest trunk, a 30-foot circumference bigleaf maple overlooking Puget Sound. Bigleafs are the larger and more long-lived of the two species. They normally reach a diameter of 12 to 20 inches within 85 years and rare individuals live for 200 years and grow to 100 feet tall. Bigleaf maples are beautiful trees, and one of the great pleasures of Seattle is when their leaves, some up to two feet wide, turn brilliant yellow in fall. Further beauty comes from the licorice ferns, mosses, and lichens that festoon trunks and branches in a green beard of fertility.

Alders are the sprinters. On a good site they shoot to 30 feet in 5 years, 80 feet in 20 years, and coast along slowly adding girth and height until they max out at about 130 feet. Unusual alders reach a century, with more typical deaths at 60 to 70 years. Their gray bark gives them a birchlike appearance, and a patchwork of mosses and lichens adds additional color. In early spring, thousands of dangling, pollen-choked catkins wave in the wind, a sign of the impending invasion.

Red alders and bigleaf maples are Seattle's two most abundant trees, and therein lies their deception. On November 13, 1851, only small pockets of these species grew here, most likely restricted to seeps, floodplains, and riparian areas, where they were also joined by Seattle's other tall deciduous tree, black cottonwood. Some alders probably sprouted in the burned over areas, too, and the Maple Leaf neighborhood name may reflect an abundance of bigleaf maples (it could also refer to the Maple Saw Mill or the Maple Shingle Company), although neither tree approached the abundance of today.

Alders could not grow well in the shade of the conifers; young seedlings withstand partial shade for a few years but will grow very little and will eventually die. Maples tolerate shade better but still do not compete well against the firs, cedars, and hemlocks. Lumbermen considered both to be weed species, although early settlers planted maples along many Seattle streets until they discovered that the roots destroy sidewalks and sewer pipes.

Alders and maples excel in disturbed habitat, such as landslides, road cuts, and clear cuts. Alders do especially well because they are fecund and precocious, becoming sexually mature at three to four years old. In addition, they can convert atmospheric nitrogen, a dearth of which limits plant growth, into a usable form, so they don't need rich soil. Because of these factors, alders have crawled out of the creeks and now form nearly pure stands across many of Seattle's logged, landslide-prone landscapes. Maples are not as aggressive and rarely form single-species groves, but they still move quickly into disturbed areas, a benefit in Seattle because those same sidewalk-busting roots also help stabilize slopes.

Red alders and bigleaf maples are not the only false clues; the name of one Seattle neighborhood also gives misleading information. In 1856, Lieutenant George Davidson committed a botanical blunder and named the hill north of Elliott Bay, Magnolia. Unfortunately for our curious George, the nearest magnolias grew 1,600 miles away in Arkansas. The lieutenant, of course, was referring to Seattle's only common, nonconiferous evergreen tree, *Arbutus menzeisii*, a name bestowed on two other neighborhoods, Madrona and Laurelhurst (early settlers often called madronas, laurels).

Also known as *madrone, arbutus,* or *madrono*—the name depends upon where you hail from—madrona stands out in an area of outstanding trees. Glossy, dark green leaves, papery, cinnamon-ochre bark, a springtime display of thousands of white flowers, and a late summer explosion of bright orange, warty fruits combine to create a tree that commands attention, as Lt. Davidson observed. Location makes them even more noteworthy; they prefer exposed, sunny sites.

The modern-day locations of larger madrona groves give clues to where they grew historically: the Magnolia bluffs, the south and west sides of Discovery Park, the south side of Lincoln Park, the south end of Seward Park, and the Seola Park/Arroyos neighborhoods. All are south or west facing and all have well-drained soils. In early February I visited the Seola/Arroyos area, the southernmost point in Seattle along Puget Sound.

This little-known section of Seattle contains by far the most extensive groves of madronas.

I started at a spot officially designated the Seola Greenbelt, a small park preserved by the city in 1989. I found a dirt trail that led down into the madronas, through a plant community unlike any I had found in Seattle. Madronas made up the entire slope of tall trees, except for three Douglas-firs; the understory was nearly pure salal, with an occasional brown bracken and fir seedling. The biggest madrona I could access measured 11 feet around, and one nearby that I couldn't measure was easily three or four feet bigger. Most were at least a foot wide, although I also saw many bigger and smaller ones, a good sign of a mature and healthy floral community.

What stood out the most, however, was the open feeling of the trees. Unlike the dense green and brown light of a conifer forest or the pervasive shade of an alder or maple grove, the madrona overstory allowed light to pierce through and illuminate the vegetation, especially the stunning cinnamon bark of the trunks. I felt relaxed, warm, and free, sensations enhanced by my location on a steep, south-facing bluff overlooking Puget Sound. I would not have been able to enjoy this openness 150 years ago, for although these particular groves give a clue to November 1851, they are more likely a modern product. In a natural madrona stand, such as those found at Point Defiance in Tacoma or Deception Pass on Whidbey Island, Douglas-firs are more intermixed and grow much more abundantly than I saw at Seola. They would be prevalent as seedlings and saplings and many would tower over the madronas. Because White Center, the main community near Seola, was built around logging, big firs would have disappeared quickly.

Several large multistemmed madronas, a growth pattern that results when the trees resprout following logging, may give a clue to Seola's past, although multistemmed trees can also indicate fire. If two high intensity burns, spaced 50 to 75 years apart, had hit this area, the first could have destroyed the majority of Douglas-fir, and the second could have eliminated any survivors or new growth. I found no burn marks on any of the large madronas, but I could only get to a few of them. Others can investigate this enigma.

Leaving Seola, I headed north and west about a half mile to access the Arroyos Natural Area, another hillside of protected madronas. I couldn't hike into these trees because of an impenetrable boundary of blackberries, but I could see a good profile of the slope from a ridge on the east side of what had been a sand quarry. Once again the madronas ran from the bottom to the top of the slope, and no Douglas-firs broke through the canopy. Hard to say if fire or logging created these unusual groves but either way the Arroyos and Seola trees are important reminders of the spectacular communities of madronas that once ringed many bluffs of Seattle. Paradoxically, I stood across the street from several madrona stumps, which looked like they had been cut so that homeowners near them would have a better view of Puget Sound and the Arroyos Natural Area.

On my route back north from Arroyos, I decided to stop at the one other location in Seattle that has a place-name that offers a clue to a past plant community: Me-kwa-mooks Park, a small green space created on land donated to the city by pioneers Ferdinand and Emma Schmitz (of Schmitz Park fame), just south of Alki Point. Me-kwa-mooks is a rough-sounding equivalent of a Lushootseed word (written *sbaqwabaqs* and pronounced *SBAH-quah-books*) meaning "prairie point" or "prairie nose." It refers to a grassy, tree-free habitat rich with a brilliant palette of wildflowers. I only wish that someone in the Denny party had been a botanist or artist and had recorded this chromatic interplay of the violets, yellows, and reds of the flowers, and the greens, blues, and whites of the water.

All that remains of this unusual plant community is the name, but good insight can be obtained by searching through UW herbarium specimens. During the late 1800s and early 1900s several botanists collected plants from Alki, 58 native species of which made it into the herbarium. It must have been a spectacular place to collect with rose-colored Hooker's onion (*Allium acuminatum*), golden paintbrush (*Castilleja levisecta*), lilac to pink saucer clover (*Trifolium microcepalum*), white prairie star (*Lithophragma parviflorum*), and violet harvest lily (*Brodiaea coronaria*), the last of which botanist Archibald Menzies saw Natives collecting at Restoration Point on May 28, 1792. None of the above plants now grow in Seattle and of the original 58, an additional 19 have been extirpated and 16 more are considered rare or uncommon.

If you look at a map of northern Puget Sound, you can see why this ecosystem existed: obvious headlands or points jut out into the water.

The most prominent are West Point and Alki in Seattle and Restoration Point on Bainbridge Island, the latter two of which were pushed out of the water by movement along the Seattle fault. Sticking out into the Sound made them inhospitable because of buffeting winds, a high water table of brackish water, and less stable soil due to storm events and periodic extreme high tides.

Unfortunately, these prairies are not the only extirpated plant communities of Seattle. We have also lost our bogs, a habitat that has been called a "history book with a flexible cover." Like prairies, our bogs contained an unusual array of plants adapted to an extreme environment that required tolerance to flood, to drought, and to high acidity. Only one clue to this environment remains, and to see it I had to cheat and go outside city limits.

My destination was a small lake just north of SeaTac Airport. To reach the water, known as Tub or Bug Lake, I parked on Des Moines Memorial Drive, walked east down a narrow path through blackberries, scrambled through a hole cut in a chain-link fence, and continued to a narrow ditch, spanned by a dicey 2 by 10 plank. Such moats are a typical feature of bogs. Vegetation growing along the moat included hardhack (*Spiraea douglasii*) and western hemlock, which are stunted and may be as old as 300 years, even though they are only four inches in diameter.

The plank was surprisingly sturdy, as opposed to the "land" on the other side, which felt like dense foam. I was not actually standing on terra firma but on a thick accumulation of muck—brown, spongy matter technically defined as sphagnum moss decomposed past recognition. As I walked atop the muck, water squeezed out from under my feet and accumulated in low spots in the path. After 25 yards or so, I moved out of the muck onto moss peat, also brown and spongy but less decomposed than muck. I was now standing on a floating mat of sphagnum and peat, and I could make the nearby western hemlocks sway by jumping up and down and sending waves through the mat. After 10 more minutes of jumping and swaying, jumping and swaying, the novelty began to fade.

Just like my encounter with the madronas, I was now in virgin territory, in a plant community unlike any other I had seen in Seattle. The high acidity and permanent water made this environment no place for the usual botanical suspects. Instead, I found bog laurel and Labrador tea, classic bog plants that grow around the northern hemisphere. In spring, the laurels produce spectacular pink blossoms. Labrador tea has smaller white flowers and both have dark green leaves that curl under at the edge. Searching under the shrubby tea and laurel, I also located ground-hugging cranberries, which along with one of Washington state's few carnivorous plants, sundews, only grow in bogs. I was past the sundew season but I know of others who have found them at this bog.

In another 20 feet I was at Tub Lake. I didn't dare jump up and down at this point because I feared my floating mat would break off. Sedges, rushes, and cattails grew at the water's edge and pond lilies floated in the water. If I had enough time, on the order of hundreds of years, I could stand at this point and watch as the sphagnum mat grew out into the water and the lake became a forested meadow growing on top of the peat moss.

Bog formation requires three factors, one related to our damp climate, and the other two related to our glacial history. A surplus of water is the first requirement, met by our maritime-influenced high precipitation and mild temperatures. Second and third are infertility and poor drainage. As many local gardeners know, when the glaciers retreated 13,650 years ago, they deposited low nutrient soils but they also left behind shallow depressions where water could stagnate. In North America, bogs are generally restricted to the north, primarily in Canada and Alaska. The majority of Washington state bogs are in the Puget lowlands. Although Seattle should have been bog-rich, they were never common within city limits.

While searching through the scientific literature, I located descriptions of only six in-city bogs. One was adjacent to Lake Washington, the old Mud Lake at Sand Point. Two have been covered by shopping centers, a 24-acre peat area under University Village and a cranberry bog now paved over by Northgate Mall. The largest one, at 45 acres, filled the depression at what is now Dahl Playfield at 25th Avenue NE and NE 80th Street. Interstate 5 at NE 55th Street covers the smallest one, a five-acre area that disappeared long before the freeway arrived. The sixth Seattle bog was just a mile or so from the Seola madronas and straddled the Seattle/Burien boundary. Others are known to have existed but passed too quickly from bog to home for anyone to write about.

Nevertheless, some modern residents have discovered a boggy clue, in ways that they probably wish they did not have to. In the summer of 2002, people living near N 87th Street and Greenwood Avenue, in north Seattle, noticed cracks appearing in their walls. They also watched as two sinkholes formed, foundations sunk, and sidewalks buckled. In addition, a new Safeway was the third major building project at that intersection in the past two years, and the third major construction site to have to pump millions of gallons of water from the site after discovering peat beds under the property.

I have not been able to determine when Seattle's bogs disappeared, but a landmark 1958 report on peat resources in Washington does not list a single bog within the city. The report, however, does mention clues that residents who lived in Seattle in the first half of the 1900s could have found. If they had visited a local garden store, like Malmo Nurseries, they could have purchased bags of peat moss, which had been mined from the former bogs. In peat mining, sphagnum moss is dug by hand, set out to dry, and then shredded and packaged. Some locals, in particular Japanese farmers, also made use of bogs by draining them and planting them with lettuce, cabbage, and other truck garden vegetables. Now, even these clues are gone. Paving has replaced peat, Canadian sphagnum has replaced local sphagnum, and agribusiness has replaced small farms.

My search for clues ended at Tub Lake. I know I do not have the entire picture of what Seattle looked like on November 13, 1851, but the picture I now possess is far clearer. It is a picture of plants superbly adapted to the specifics of place. To wet soils. To temperate weather. To complex topography. To fire. To slow change.

For me, this exercise has been akin to making a family tree. Since my parents were the first of my family to move to Seattle, I have had to seek out other connections to Seattle's past. Like many people, I seek to know the past because I want good stories to tell and I want to fit into a bigger picture. Finding Seattle's botanical legacy has filled those needs. I feel better connected to this city. I have a richer appreciation of this place. And I like to think I have some good stories to tell.

You may drive out Nature with a pitchfork,
yet she still will hurry back.

HORACE

The pond around which I walk Taylor three or four times a week has become a cherished wildlife haven for me. I have seen great blue and green herons, northern shovelers, cardinal meadowhawk and eight-spotted skimmer dragonflies, western forktail and northern bluet damselflies, garter snakes, killdeer, barn swallows, ring necked ducks, western swallowtails, predaceous diving beetles, and cedar waxwings feeding on nectar, insects, tadpoles, and frogs. I am fond of all of these animals, but my favorite denizens of the pool and its surroundings are the chorus, or Pacific tree frogs.

The first time I saw one I was collecting ripe blackberries in the abundant patches surrounding the pond when what I thought was part of the plant leapt away from me. After stuffing a few more blackberries in my mouth, I nabbed one of these well-camouflaged, golfball-sized hoppers. It was a marvelously handsome green frog with black racing streaks running from its nose through its eyes and randomly shaped, faded bronze blotches on its back. These contrasted with white toe pads, which allow the frogs to cling in gravity-defying positions.

I knew these frogs were at the pond because in the spring the male's call, a two-toned *crick-it* that Hollywood has appropriated as *the* sound of nighttime in the woods, nearly drowns out the noise of I-5 only a couple hundred yards away. I had never seen one, despite innumerable searches, but I had seen the end results of the croaking. Successful calling attracts females and results in gelatinous masses of eggs that hatch as tadpoles in three to four weeks.

One summer hundreds of tadpoles crowded the rapidly evaporating pond. When the water covered an area about the size of a bathtub and was shrinking by several square feet a day, Marjorie and I came over, scooped out bags of tadpoles, and carried them to nearby permanent bodies of water. Many of the tadpoles died, but the following spring noisy frogs again called in the blackberries.

This pond is at the northwest corner of North Seattle Community College (NSCC) and is part of the headwaters of the south fork of Thornton Creek. Over the years I had contemplated walking the length of this creek, which flows south and east to its confluence in two miles with Thornton's northern fork. I had read that Thornton drained more land—7,402 acres or a little under 14 percent of the 84-square-mile city—than any other creek, and I wondered what wildlife I would find if the headwaters were so rich.

I also wanted to examine firsthand a watershed that could be a poster child for both the best and worst ways that we treat streams in the urban landscape. On the plus side, Thornton flows above ground for more than 90 percent of its route, through some of the wildest, least-developed sections of the city. On the negative, fecal coliform counts consistently exceed state safety criteria, while stream sediments contain pesticides, heavy metals, PCBs, and hydrocarbons unsafe to aquatic life.

I am not alone in recognizing this dichotomy. Thornton has three non-profit organizations protecting and rehabilitating it, as well as educating the public about the importance of urban streams. In addition, the city of Seattle has invested over $25 million during the past decade on habitat enhancement, acquisition, and protection. In contrast, Thornton caught fire in 1977 after 300 gallons of gasoline leaked from an ARCO gas station, exploded, and sent 20-foot-high flames down a five-block stretch of creek. I talked with a biologist who wouldn't stick his hands in the water without wearing gloves and a hydrologist who compared the creek to roadkill. "You can tell it's a creek but you certainly wouldn't call it living."

As with the city's other creeks—Longfellow, Pipers, Schmitz, Ravenna, Mapes, Puget, Fauntleroy, and Taylor—Thornton has been transformed over the past 150 years from a salmon-filled waterway flowing freely through stands of black cottonwoods, bigleaf maples, western hemlocks, and western

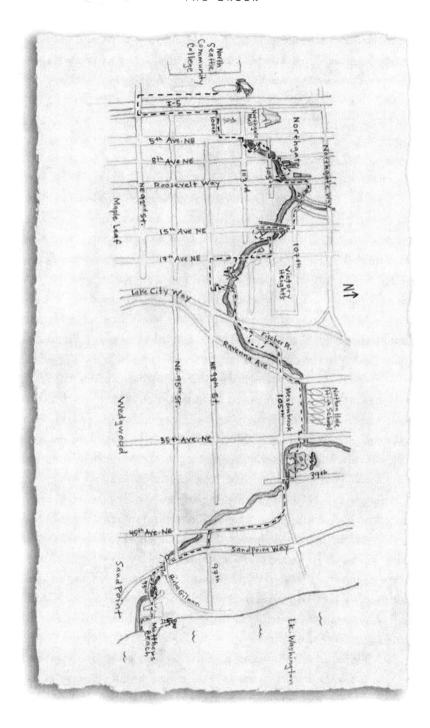

red cedars to an often channelized, mostly salmon-free creek surrounded by concrete-dominated ground cover. This modern terrain of impervious surfaces—such as roads, roofs, and parking lots, which envelop over 50 percent of the watershed—has made the creek invisible to most of the watershed's 75,000 inhabitants, half of whom couldn't name Thornton or its tributaries when asked to identify a creek near their home, according to a 1998 poll conducted for Seattle Public Utilities.

I start my journey down Thornton at the community college in a clearing between a large, densely grown wetland and my little pond. From here, a maintenance road leads to the largest body of water on campus, a surge pond that parallels I-5. The several-foot-deep pool serves as a stormwater detention for NSCC and makes fine habitat for waterfowl throughout the year. I see only mallards on my walk but in winter I have observed buffleheads, wood ducks, gadwalls, common and hooded mergansers, American widgeons, common goldeneyes, Canada geese, coots, and pied-billed grebes. More experienced birders have seen over 95 species on the campus.

A 36-inch-wide pipe drains the pond, carrying water east under I-5 to 1st Avenue NE. The conduit has also allowed upstream travel for at least one beaver who I have never seen, but who has gnawed down several Lombardy poplars on the pond's east side and started to work on several smaller trees at the south end. Since swimming down the three-foot pipe is not an option, I walk south to NE 92nd, east across the freeway, and back north along 1st Avenue to NE 100th and the Northgate Park and Ride, covering about three-quarters of a mile to reach a spot 500 feet from where I started.

A cranberry bog once covered this part of Thornton Creek. Native people, known as *Tu-oh-be-DAHBSH*, or people of the *Tu-oh-bed* (a Native name for Thornton), had a small settlement at the mouth of Thornton and made use of the bog. They called the spot *Slo'q'qed* (pronounced STHLOOKW-keed), which translates roughly to "bald head," a possible reference to the relatively treeless nature of the bog.

No clear record exists as to how large the bog was or how long it survived on this site. Estimates place it at anywhere between 30 and 100 acres, covering land now dominated by Northgate Mall and I-5. One of the earliest known maps of the area, the 1894 McKee's Accurate Road Map of Seattle and Vicinity, shows a wetland on the spot where I stand, across the street from the mall and its surrounding parking lots, but it is not accurate enough to gauge size. The only scientific documentation of a bog in roughly this location uses the lower number and reports that only one acre remained by 1913, the rest having been mined for its peat and drained.

When developers began to prepare the ground for Northgate in 1949, the land was mostly forested with a few remnant wetlands and a pond south of the mall property. Mall owners paved over that last large pond, Square Lake, in 1971, saying, "What we are doing is nothing but a complete improvement for the area." The only bodies of water that testify to the swampy conditions of old are small pools north of NSCC and the wetland at NSCC.

In the last decade the 13-acre wasteland of concrete built over Thornton Creek, known as the south parking lot, has become a point of controversy. In 1998, Northgate owner Simon Property Group—the largest publicly traded retail mall developer in the country, with a market capitalization of over $20 billion in late 2002—proposed to replace the lot with an urban village, including a 30-screen movie theater, a 210-room hotel, two office buildings, and at least 150 apartments.

On the face of it, this plan makes sense. In such a high-density zone people could use their cars less by walking to stores or catching buses to downtown Seattle at the adjacent Transit Center. Instead of a barren lot, developers said that they would create a vibrant community with many urban amenities. Some local residents, however, have a different vision for the parking lot.

Those opposed to Simon's plan do not oppose development on the site but think it could be scaled back to facilitate the creek flowing on the surface instead of underground. Bob Vreeland, cofounder of the nonprofit Thornton Creek Legal Defense Fund, wants developers to free Thornton Creek by removing it from the 72-inch pipe that flows under the south parking lot and restoring the creek to more natural conditions. "If Simon would just look beyond their short-term profit, they could understand that the potential is limitless for regional, national, and international recognition for creating a unique development where people could have fish and housing and offices. They could create waterfront property and give people a reason to be there," he says.

Vreeland and others involved in protecting the creek also advocate returning a key function of the site's historic wetland: water detention. During large rainstorms of the past, water runoff would enter the wetland, slow down, drop sediments, and gradually flow back into the main drainage at a reduced pace and a smaller volume. Now, rain falling on the mall, office complexes, and surrounding parking lots washes directly into Thornton, carrying oil, gasoline, detergents, lawn and garden chemicals, trash, pet waste, heavy metals, and sediments. With no large, spongelike environment to flow through, this stormwater generates greater-than-normal flash floods that scour the stream channel, increase hillside erosion, and wash out gravel necessary for fish spawning. When the sediment settles out it can suffocate salmon eggs.

Since rebuilding the wetland is not likely, some sort of detention pond, which would hold water and release it slowly, is the next best compromise. It could be built either with or without "daylighting" Thornton. Some people consider a detention pond more critical to a healthy creek than daylighting because it will affect more property downstream. Furthermore, city regulations require detention for any redevelopment project at Northgate, but they do not require daylighting.

Detention ponds, however, are not sexy. Nor do they directly deal with the animals that attract the most attention in the Pacific Northwest. Five species of salmon historically lived in Thornton Creek: coho, cutthroat, sockeye, steelhead, and chinook. The Tu-oh-be-DAHBSH probably caught fish at the mouth using a weir, and the 1859 GLO survey records a fish trap just below Meadowbrook Pond. Early day reminiscences, as well as those from more recent inhabitants (up to the early 1960s), describe catching salmon and trout throughout the creek system.

In modern times, only a smattering of individual fish have graced the creek, although annual surveys have found all of the salmon species. In 1997 community members discovered 20 to 30 coho one-half mile above the confluence in the north fork, and a Washington DFW biologist observed searun and resident cutthroat, some up to nine inches long, in the south fork, over 1.5 miles from Lake Washington. In the 2001 survey, volunteers reported more than 70 salmon and more than 40 redds.

During my conversation with Vreeland it was clear that he cared deeply about Thornton Creek and about enhancing its habitat, but it was not until he started to talk about salmon that his passion became clear. "We need to think, MY GOD, here is an animal with a pea-sized brain that survived without its parents, swam hundreds to thousands of miles in predator-filled waters, and returned back to its exact place of birth. If they can do that, then I can press on in the horrible conditions we live in."

Vreeland, a fisheries biologist, recognizes that daylighting Thornton at Northgate would not significantly benefit salmon. Little new habitat would be created and that new habitat would only be at the upper end of the drainage, which means that salmon would only gain additional access to the pond at North Seattle—assuming they swim up the pipe under I-5. Instead he looks at how salmon provide inspiration, hope, and connection. "Without urban salmon, we will have no connection to fish in rural and wilder streams. Fish will become an out-of-sight, out-of-mind situation. It is much better that 10,000 people see 10 salmon than 10 people see 10,000."

When people see a chinook swimming near Nathan Hale High School, near the confluence of the north and south forks of Thornton, I hope they think about how that fish once swam along the coast of Canada, navigated down Puget Sound, through the Chittenden Locks and across Lake Washington to the mouth of Thornton. The local salmon can remind us that wilder places exist and that if we want to continue to see salmon at Thornton we not only have to protect Thornton but we also need to protect those places where the salmon exist in greater numbers.

Daylighting is about more than just salmon, though. It about respecting the fact that a wetland once dominated this landscape and that people once obtained sustenance from these waters. It is about honoring that past and giving people the opportunity to strengthen their connections to the place they call home.

The importance of daylighting and habitat restoration and protection boils down to what vision we want for ourselves and how we want the landscape to reflect this image. This does not mean that no development should occur at the south parking lot or other environmentally sensitive spots, but that many development projects could be done in a manner that takes location into account, as well as how buildings and parking lots affect human and nonhuman neighbors. Not that we should only blame developers such as Simon for Thornton's problems. After all, the creek flows through 700 backyards. Each of us impacts the waterway by using pesticides, by letting oil and antifreeze wash into drains, by adding impervious surfaces at our homes, and by washing our cars in driveways or on streets.

At present, the south parking lot reflects the traditional paradigm of man over nature. Its main use seems to be for used car and RV sales. As I walk by on my downstream journey I see two guys sweeping the lot. One has a normal-sized broom and a dust bin and the other carries a broom and pushes a garbage can on wheels. Each moves slowly, scrutinizing the pavement, periodically sweeping up a cigarette butt or a stray scrap. In the few minutes I watch, neither covers more than a few yards.

Not having time to watch such diligent devotion to cleanliness, I cross 5th Avenue and descend down a bank and under a large laurel, to where Thornton Creek emerges from a pipe that began at NSCC. The water forms a shallow, clear pool in the shade in front of the pipe before heading north and rippling between verdant banks. I follow.

Park 6, as this area is known, has gone through a transformation over the past decade. Park employees and local citizens working with the Thornton Creek Alliance, a nonprofit dedicated to preserving and restoring an ecological balance in the watershed, have cleared out trash, removed alien vegetation, and planted natives, including a grove of firs and hemlocks, known by some as the Conifer Cathedral. Unfortunately, stormwater runoff has damaged some of the plantings, but a path that parallels the creek still winds through a relatively quiet, shrub- and tree-crowded corridor.

The transformation is not over yet. Seattle Public Utilities has a multiyear project planned for further trail development, wetland enhancement, native plant establishment, and creek dredging. Like many people I have met who are involved with Thornton, project director Chris Woelfel gets animated when talking about restoration along the waterway. "Park 6 originally was just one blackberry patch," she says. "The community transformed it and I want to help provide the money and in some cases the heavy equipment to create a place for people and wildlife. Restoration is fun. I think it is here to stay."

Chris refers to her plans as "gentle projects." People can get involved, help nudge the landscape back toward health, see progress, and keep coming back. "If we look at this from a purely environmental outlook, then we miss part of what makes a place special. We can't put a fence around good habitat. We need to combine people and habitat with social values, such as safety, areas for kids to play, and a sense of wildness."

I follow the creek as it flows by willows, maples, alders, and cottonwoods, some several feet in diameter. Nettles, salmonberry, and red flowering currant grow over the narrow walkway, much of it covered in water from seeps dripping off the slopes rising out of the floodplain. Where the path passes along a couple of backyards, two western tiger swallowtails fly in the sunlight. After crossing under an intersection, the creek reemerges into the larger, eastern section of Park 6.

Another trail parallels the water. This section is wider and wilder. Morning glories twist and creep up blackberries in an alien battle for supremacy. Giant skunk cabbage, with their tropical-forest-sized leaves, grow in several seeps along Thornton's banks. Trees have crashed across the creek, forming bridges and dams. Local restorationists call these piles "large woody debris," or LWD for short. In stream restoration projects, LWD is an essential element because it slows down water, traps sediment, and provides habitat for fish and aquatic insects.

The creek disappears into a thicket of impenetrable blackberries just down from the skunk cabbage, so I head to the street, around the back side of an apartment complex, before finding a path under a western red cedar and back into wilder habitat. Paths split off in several directions. Mine leads me down a shallow slope, into an opening under more cedars and eventually to a dead end at the Villa Roma apartment complex, where people have tossed trash over the fence and into an unnamed side drainage of Thornton.

This drainage abuts an historic piece of land: five acres once owned by Edith May Thornton, the eponymous maiden of the creek. Thornton was a first grade teacher at T. T. Minor Elementary School when she acquired this parcel in 1897 for $240. She owned it until her death, at the age of 58, in a car accident caused by a drunk driver near Bellingham, Washington, on February 7, 1927, only one month after she retired as the Whatcom County Treasurer. After spending several days tracking down Edith's life history, I was left with one big question: Was the creek named for her and why? She never lived on the property and only made $100 in improvements to it. Further searching may reveal some other Thornton or some definitive reason for the naming, but until such a time, Edith May Thornton is a good person to be honored by this creek.

After taking several more wrong paths, I eventually find the creek again, but only a short distance before it disappears into another culvert. To reach water again I climb a short, steep slope, run across Roosevelt Avenue, turn right on NE 108th Street, and walk a quarter mile to where another tributary, Victory Creek, flows under the road into Thornton. On either side of the street sit huge stumps of old growth western red cedar, complete with plankboard notches. Young western hemlocks sprout from each stump.

A short walk on sidewalk-free city streets takes me to 15th Avenue NE and a bridge 75 feet above the creek. I enjoy the rare, vertiginous perspective into some of Seattle's taller trees, many of which rise an additional 30 to 40 feet above me. On the other side of the bridge, I climb over a guardrail and scamper down a rough path toward the creek. I can reach the water again but choose to avoid the blackberries and turn down a side street, which dead-ends at the slope I am descending. Another 100 yards further a six-foot-wide path leads into a section of green space called Park 2, which unlike most parks in Seattle lacks the Seattle Parks Department's official wooden, rainbow sign. I only know I have ventured into a designated park because I carry a map of the entire creek produced by the city in 1998.

One aspect of the green spaces along Thornton Creek that I like is this sense of discovery. No signs tell me which trail I am on. Shrubs and spider webs spread over and into many of the routes. Others dead-end in brambles and rarely can anyone walk two abreast. My guess is that kids made the trails while exploring the woods. When they found something interesting they told their friends and they came back and searched more. Few finer options exist for a kid looking for something fun to do.

Upon entering Park 2 I walk about 20 feet along the main trail and then follow one of these unmapped paths up the creek. I am quickly rewarded:

a 9 x 20 x 10-foot boulder is partially buried in duff and soil a few yards from the path. Geologists call huge sore thumbs of rock such as this "erratics." One of America's best-known landmarks, Plymouth Rock, is an erratic. Glaciers moving out of Canada during the last ice age picked up the famous landing point of the Pilgrims, carried it across Massachusetts, and abandoned it when the ice melted. The same happened with the Thornton Creek erratic, probably about the same time. Only a few other erratics remain in Seattle; settlers probably removed or dynamited many more when they cleared the land for fields or homes. The Wedgwood Erratic, 19 feet tall and 75 feet in circumference, may be the best known. Fourmile Rock, sitting on the shore below Magnolia Bluff, is another.

I continue up the path for another minute or so before scrambling down to the water. My first thought upon reaching the creek is "I am not in Seattle." Giant Douglas-fir and bigleaf maple tower over devil's club and lady and sword ferns on the opposite bank. A constant snow of cottonwood seeds drops upon me. I hear no sounds of humanity. Nor can I see any buildings. Not to say that I do not see any invasives, such as blackberry and ivy, but they are rare and easily overlooked.

Downstream I see downed logs and stumps. A quiet pool has formed behind a classic type of LWD, a western red cedar trunk. More snags and tree butts dot the slopes and flats on either side of the creek. Vanilla leaf, salmonberry, and bracken ferns push up out of several stumps. When I turn one decaying log over I find millipeds, spiders, centipedes, pillbugs, earthworms, and snails. Several snags have various sized holes in them, most likely homes for cavity-nesting birds.

Another positive feature of green spaces like Parks 2 and 6 is that plants and animals can decompose naturally. Cityscapes seem to encourage the removal and cleaning up of fallen leaves, broken limbs, dead bodies, rotten trunks, or moldy growths. Part of this is due to litigation. No one wants to be sued because a branch or tree crashed down upon or tripped up someone. In addition, the neighborhood aesthetics encourage people to keep yards orderly and neat.

Decomposition returns essential nutrients to the soil, and moldering limbs and bodies provide homes for the next generation. A case in point is Pacific

Northwest forests and dead salmon. Studies show that salmon may not grow on trees but that trees grow on salmon. Coho, chinook, and sockeye returning from the sea bring back ocean-derived nitrogen and phosphorus. When the fish die, birds, mammals, reptiles, and insects consume the nutrient-rich carcasses. These animals in turn may become food for others that cannot reach the water or they poop out the nutrients. One study in British Columbia found that up to half the nitrogen in old-growth trees came from the sea, transported by salmon and spread by bears.

I understand that urban land managers cannot always leave hazardous trees to die a natural death and that leaves can clog up sewer systems, but maybe they can establish more areas where these processes could occur. At Green Lake, park managers working with neighbors allowed several dead and dangerous alders to remain standing. Initial reaction split evenly between supporters and detractors. Now, five years after the project started, the native plants have filled in the area below the snags, and people support the new look. Local naturalists have noticed an increased diversity of wildlife using the site.

The success at Green Lake has also encouraged the parks department to incorporate this unorthodox idea across the city. "We are not mowing in some locations so we can create tall grass meadows and we have also let native vegetation take over other spots," says Paul West, former Seattle City Parks urban forester. "I think that letting the alder snags stand at Green Lake has helped form a new perception of the landscape." As with the salmon, death brings new life.

After a quiet 30 minutes sitting along this oasis, I return to my trek downstream. I cross the creek and follow a well-beaten path with bleeding heart growing on both sides. Devil's club forms a vicious barrier at an opening where a tree has fallen. The path ends at an S-shaped bend in the creek. As I approach I hear a sound overhead and look up to see a belted kingfisher flying over with a fish in her beak. She lands on a high branch 50 feet away and I watch through my binoculars as she consumes her lunch.

Since no other paths head down the creek, I climb up and out. Several routes end in thickets before I locate a way out of Park 2 and back to pavement. Among the trees I did not realize that it is so hot. My one small water bottle is running low so I quickly move south, turn east on 98th Avenue NE and proceed down to a flight of steps at NE 20th Street, which returns me to the creek, now channelized in a 10-foot-wide, open concrete trough, bordered by blackberry and Japanese knotweed. Private property forces me away from the water and along a road 100 feet from the creek. At Lake City Way, a major north-south corridor, I fill my water bottle in a Les Schwab tire store.

I cross Lake City and walk north by several businesses including one building that houses an insurance agency—*Your Good Neighbor*—and Stan Baker Shooting Sports—*We Buy Used Guns.* A short way past what I can only assume to be gun buyers insured not by Smith & Wesson, a recently cleared path leads back to another section of creek being restored by nearby residents. They have planted the benchland above the creek with vine maple, Indian plum, Oregon ash, Oregon grape, and huckleberry. Chris Woelfel correctly called restoration "fun," but I think another driving force is a sense of empowerment. Most of us do not do things in our lives and work that pay off immediately. We endure meetings, plod through to-do lists, plow through planning documents, and inch ahead. With restoration, on the other hand, positive results appear immediately.

What had been a hillside choked with aliens quickly becomes free of the invaders. A creek filled with trash is now clean. A Douglas-fir strangled by ivy looks healthy again. People and animals can now visit. Restorers then have to wait for new plants to take hold and keep returning to prevent the aliens' reappearance. This may involve years of work, but the initial return is high.

Restoration also confers a sense of connection and responsibility. When I have helped clear out invasives or plant natives, I have felt more attached and protective. I have returned to see my little Douglas-fir or the cedar I saved. I have picked up trash again. I have taken friends to see my efforts.

Volunteers have also planted conifers, which provide nice shade in the heat. These will be important in helping to keep the creek's water cool, a necessity for salmon. This section, now called the Thornton Creek Natural Area, used to be part of La Villa Dairy, a 120-acre family-owned business started in 1921 by Norwegian native Ole R. Blindheim. His son, Alvin, sold the property to the city, saying that he wanted this final part of the Blindheim property, in particular the creek, to remain intact and protected against development.

The creek flows into private property below the natural area and remains in concrete and riprap until it emerges more than 1,500 feet later at Nathan Hale High School. At this point the creek runs straight and shallow, mostly shaded by an allee of Lombardy poplars for another 1,000 feet to its confluence with the north fork of Thornton, just above Meadowbrook Pond. I see several small fish swimming in the creek. I cannot tell if they are young salmon but they are the first fish I have encountered on my walk.

Nathan Hale borders Meadowbrook Playfield, which contains several ball fields and a creek/wetland on its southern border. Across the street sits Meadowbrook Pond, a nine-acre site with a detention pond built between 1996 and 1998 for flood control. Historically a wetland, Meadowbrook housed the Lake City Sewage Treatment Plant from 1952 until the city decided to concentrate all sewage treatment at West Point. The abandoned property and buildings became storage areas for the high school, as well as housing for the students' auto shop. Extra monorail track from the 1962 World's Fair also ended up on the property. In the late 1980s local activists began to push city officials to redevelop the site, leading to demolition of the treatment plant in 1990. Several years of debate and meetings resulted in a plan for restored wetlands, an art garden, a wildlife refuge, and the central feature, the detention pond.

I enter Meadowbrook Pond from 35th Avenue NE, following a paved path past berms covered in lupines and a few salals. Street sounds quickly fade behind the mounds, although a lawn mower run by a park employee reminds me that I am not in a natural setting. Trees shade Thornton Creek, which now contains waters from the north as well as the south forks. I cross an eight-foot-wide metal bridge over the creek and continue toward the pond past several signs describing the natural resources of the location.

Park designers worked hard to create a space for both people and animals. They teamed with artists from the initial planning stages to "focus and connect one physically and emotionally with nature." The path I follow curves and undulates, echoing natural features. It ends at the Sound Sanctuary, a 30- by 40-foot amphitheater-like space, which looks carved out of the landscape. Native plants grow over, under, and on the walls.

Artist Kate Wade's *Water Gate* connects the east end of the sanctuary to the pond. Her art piece consists of an open, hallwaylike frame made from metal beams that extend out into the water. Metal grating leads to steps down into the pond. From the edge I see mallards, killdeer, Canada geese, and crows on a low berm that separates the pond into distinct pools. A rat moves under the grating.

River otters, great blue herons, and red-tailed fox have been sighted around the water, too. From the walkway that spans the entire pond, I see one of Meadowbrook's newest inhabitants, a beaver. It moves quietly through the water for a few seconds before diving under. Beavers moved into the area soon after site construction ended. They have built a small lodge of branches on an island in the pond. To prevent the beavers from cutting down several black cottonwoods and willows at the water's edge and on another island, park employees have put chicken wire around the trees' trunks and planted "sacrificial" trees for the hungry rodents.

Judging from the number of people walking, sitting, and bird-watching at Meadowbrook, it appears that the designers have created a space that people like. I see more visitors here than on my entire walk along the lesser-known and often wilder parts of the creek. People range in age from toddlers to seniors, each enjoying the unique, human-created, wildlife-friendly habitat. Meadowbrook Pond is an evocative argument for creating a similar type of space at the south parking lot at Northgate.

From Meadowbrook Pond, I leave behind relatively wild lands and head onto concrete. Thornton travels underground for a block by several older, unusual houses. On a previous trip down the creek with Peter Hayes, former program developer for the Homewaters Project, a nonprofit working on education in the watershed, he had pointed out that these homes had been built one-half story off the ground so that they would not be flooded when Thornton overran its banks. "You can see that none of the more recent homes took this into account," he said.

The creek emerges just past the last of these flood-prone homes, but I cannot get close to the water because it flows through people's backyards. I even lose my way for a while, getting turned around in a series of dead ends and cul-de-sacs, one of which ends at a house built over the concrete-lined creek. This section of Seattle is the most suburblike I have encountered in my rambles around the city. Every house has a manicured lawn that runs all the way to the street. No sidewalks blight the green expanses.

I eventually find my way out of this disturbingly tidy neighborhood and spend another 10 minutes walking south and east toward the creek, which I pick up at another officially designated natural area just above Matthew's Beach, on the shore of Lake Washington. Willows and cottonwoods dominate this section, where the creek has its last lengthy nonriprap or concrete-lined flow. Volunteers have planted natives, removed ubiquitous blackberry and ivy, and added LWD. This natural area is not quiet—Sand Point Way runs next to it—nor particularly wild, but it is cool and it offers a place to discover insects, birds, fish, and amphibians.

From here until Lake Washington, Thornton runs almost entirely through concrete, beginning with a keyhole-shaped tunnel under the Burke-Gilman trail. I reconnect with the water by going under the overpass, formerly the tracks of the Seattle Lake Shore and Eastern railroad, started in 1885 by Judge Thomas Burke and Daniel Gilman. I walk through a small grove of cedars and firs and find a bird I have not yet seen in Seattle, a pileated woodpecker. At 17 inches in length, it is the largest species of woodpecker in North America. I watch it hop on the ground and pummel a small stump with its beak, in a search for insects. It appears to be successful, eventually leaving after creating a small pile of rotted wood.

This end stretch of Thornton exhibits some of the best and worst aspects of the watershed. About half the length of the final 2,000 feet of the creek passes through a cement channel, in places three feet wide and eight feet tall, no place for any plant or animal. At the tail end of its journey, however, the creek has been given a new lease on life. In 1998 the Seattle Parks Department and the U.S. Army Corps of Engineers started a restoration project at the south end of Matthew's Beach. Construction crews diverted a small runoff- and spring-fed creek, which once flowed directly to the lake, into a new stream channel that feeds a pond before flowing into Thornton. The pond helps improve water quality by allowing sediment to settle before water enters the creek. In addition, juvenile coho and chinook can use the pond and off-channel habitat as a cool refuge from predators.

As in many projects, volunteers drove the process by pushing for restoration. They also improved habitat around the pond by replacing invasive vegetation with native shore pines, cedars, and willows. On the initial day of planting, volunteers worked in sucking mud and torrential rain. They even ignored free cups of coffee while stooping and planting in standing water.

Three years after the project was completed, vegetation has made the beach and creekside habitat wild again. Fifteen-foot-tall alders, spreading wild roses, rushes, and cattails grow around the small pond, where two-inch-long fish leap after insects. The only easy routes through the plants are on the trails. One species is conspicuously absent from this restored zone—Canada geese. They are abundant on the grassy park spaces north of the creek, despite the people sunbathing, tossing a Frisbee, and yelling.

I finally reach the outlet of Thornton, three miles from my starting point, after following a narrow path through the three-year-old growth. A few kids drink beer on the beach. A log floats in the creek's mouth. This quiet, nondescript ending seems appropriate for this little-known body of water.

I am glad I have completed this journey. I knew that I would not experience true wildness on my adventure; I walked by a huge mall, near a crowded interstate highway, and in a drainage with a population density of 6,500 people per square mile. The landscape is not pristine and nonnatives dominate. I had to put on blinders to enjoy this route, but they came easily and with a bit of green tinting. Part of the urban wild experience is recognizing what is here and finding satisfaction in it.

One of the underappreciated aspects of our species is this tunnel vision. I am able to filter out the bad things I don't want to observe or hear. I can compartmentalize and see the trees through the concrete. I may not see the forest—because one does not exist—but I can home in on plants and animals, the intriguing stories they have to tell, and the lessons I can learn from them.

Several of these lessons stand out for me. The first is the resiliency of the land and its inhabitants. Just because a stream is not healthy does not mean that it is dead or unworthy of investment. Given the chance, through elimination of stream barriers, addition of logs, and a reduction in pollutants, salmon can and have returned to Thornton. Native plants also show this tenacity and can survive in the midst of a densely packed, road-filled city, if habitat is protected and alien species removed.

The second lesson involves connection. I don't think that exploring Thornton Creek, or any other urban creek, is an ideal way to develop a connection with wildness, but it is one way that works in cities. The paths I wandered have been used not only as places to smoke cigarettes or drink beer, but also refuges from urban life. People may find solace or develop a passion for wildness in these green spaces. Younger kids may discover who they are as they get muddy, get hurt, get lost, and get away from the ubiquitous stream of electrons from TVs and computers. They can test themselves climbing trees, playing hide-and-seek, probing into birds' nests, coming face-to-face with raccoons or barn swallows.

Children are not alone in finding a connection to Thornton. I have seen the power of this drainage in the eyes and heard it in the words of those fighting to protect the watershed. I have also been influenced by this small creek. All of us recognize that Thornton Creek can help bind the local community together. We understand that a place does not have to be pristine to be worthy of protection and care. We understand that if people are open and observant, wildness is all around us.

I found Rome a city of bricks and left it a city of marble.

AUGUSTUS CAESAR

The character, the sources, and, above all, the behavior in use and durability of the building stones in a large city should be matters of interest to architects and builders, to students of economic geology, and to the general public.

W. O. CROSBY AND G. F. LOUGHLIN,
TECHNOLOGY QUARTERLY, 1904

I majored in geology in college for two simple reasons: physics and field trips. It wasn't that I disliked physics; it was my complete ineptitude—I once got a 16 percent on a three-hour quiz—that forced me to abandon my original plans of getting an engineering degree and designing bicycles and other forms of human-powered vehicles. With the engineering option eliminated, I fell back on my success at field trips.

In the *Introduction to Geology* class I took my freshman year at Colorado College, we had gone on a weeklong field trip through Colorado, Texas, and New Mexico. We visited hot springs, examined 1.8-billion-year-old fossils, crawled through caves, and whacked rocks in some of the most beautiful scenery I had ever seen. I still have two rocks I collected on that field trip. Over the next three years, I took another 10 geology courses, the highlights of which included field trips to places such as the Grand Canyon, Rocky Mountain National Park, and Arches National Park. I found that what I liked most about geology was learning the stories about the planet's past. I liked knowing about ancient rivers and volcanoes, long-dried-up seas, and extinct plants and animals. I liked knowing about the history of the landscapes where I hiked and lived.

After graduation I moved to Moab, Utah, to work and teach in a rock-hound nirvana. For nearly a decade the red-rock canyons, arches, mesas, and cliffs permeated my life. I became addicted to seeing, learning about, and traipsing over rock, particularly sandstone. When I moved back to Seattle in 1998, I went into rock withdrawal. I sought out the closest examples I could find—the building stones of the downtown area.

I began to wander the business district gawking at buildings. I saw granites from Minnesota, Brazil, China, and India; fossils from Germany, France, and Indiana; and rocks ranging in age from 80,000 to 3.5 billion years. I found that several buildings incorporated stones from quarries first used by the Romans over 2,000 years ago and that a controversy in the construction of the downtown Metro bus tunnels forced county officials to return $500,000 in "tainted stone." In learning to read the rocks of building stone, I also developed a new appreciation for the intersection between people and geology.

Like many cities, Seattle can trace its use of building stone to fire. On June 6, 1889, John E. Back, described in the *Seattle Post-Intelligencer* as "a thick-set blond of mediocre intelligence," let his pot of glue boil over and onto the stove in Victor Clairmont's basement-level cabinet store near Front (now First) and Madison. Acting eagerly but incorrectly, Back tossed water on the flames, which spread the fire to wood shavings on the floor. Soon the entire wooden structure was burning.

Flames spread across the business district, which early Seattleites had built out of wood, the most abundant local material. Before Seattle's Great Fire could be contained, it burned more than 115 acres and destroyed the downtown retail and industrial core. The Great Fire clearly showed the drawback of using wood for construction, particularly in a town without adequate water pressure to put out a blaze. Within days the upstart, proud town vowed it would rebuild, but this time with a material that could better withstand fire—rock.

Builders started with local sandstones and granites, but for variety soon sought out rock from Vermont and Indiana. As additional money and people flowed into Seattle over the subsequent decades, owners desired more exotic material and found it in rocks from Italy and Sardinia. As cutting techniques improved and transportation became cheaper, the worldwide stone trade began to resemble plate tectonics, with granites and marbles traveling across the planet, propelled by the demands of builders.

When I need a rock fix, I often go downtown to Pioneer Square, because it contains so much sandstone, some of which I can walk across. From foundations to support walls, grayish green sandstone also dominates the many structures, such as the Pioneer Building, Grand Central Building, and

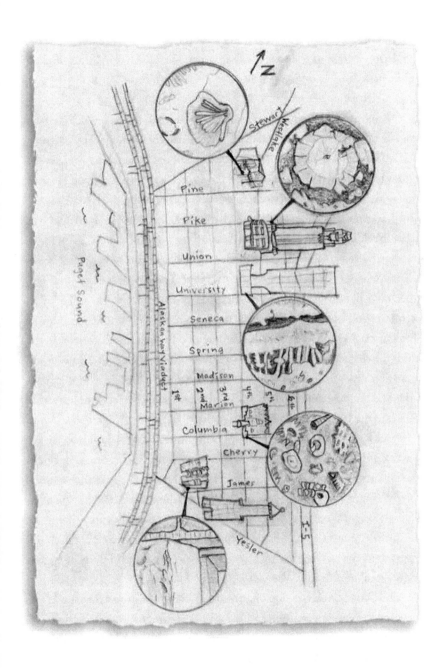

Terry-Denny Building, all of which popped up within a year or two of the fire. Most contain two-foot-thick blocks of rock—thick enough to support a multistory structure and to withstand fire—known to geologists and builders as Chuckanut Sandstone.

On one of my periodic expeditions to explore downtown Seattle's geology, I stop by the striking Pioneer Building, its arched entryway topped by two rows of what look like stacked sandstone donuts. On the south side I find several windowsills where I can peel up an individual, eighth-inch-thick layer of sandstone. This spalling occurs because water penetrating the layers of sandstone has deposited salt crystals that have slowly grown and wedged apart the sandstone strata. Further damage can occur during the infrequent Seattle winters when the temperature drops below freezing and ice forms. When water freezes it expands about 9 percent and has the same damaging effect as salt crystals.

Only a handful of the Chuckanut blocks have layers weakened enough for me to pull off. Building technique plays a role in weathering rates. If a builder stacks sandstone blocks with their beds vertical and parallel to the building's surface, like an upright book face out on a shelf, then the agents of erosion can weaken the stone so that beds peel off one layer at a time. If the beds lie horizontally, like a book flat on a shelf, water does not easily penetrate the layers and the rock deteriorates more slowly. Ledges, such as the windowsills I found, are the most common place for building stones to weaken because they are not protected by other rocks. Stacked blocks generally resist weathering better, but salt and ice can degrade them, too.

Examining my recently detached chunk of Chuckanut with my 15x magnifying glass, or hand lens, I see specks of black, clear, and white minerals—hornblende, quartz, and feldspar, respectively. I rub the chunk between my fingers and minerals break off. If I close my eyes, I can pretend the gritty grains in my hand are from my beloved red rocks of Utah.

The Chuckanut was one of a triumvirate of sandstones that started to appear in downtown buildings in the 1890s. Bellingham quarries supplied the Chuckanut, while other quarry sites near Tenino, 12 miles southeast of Olympia, and Wilkeson, 15 miles east of Tacoma, provided rocks known by their locality name. The quarries succeeded because they combined proximity to water or rail transport with a homogenous, well-cemented, low-porosity rock.

Despite the 125 miles separating the quarries, they share a related geologic history. The great beds of western Washington sandstone were deposited 40 to 50 million years ago in the Eocene Period. Judging from the fossils found within the Chuckanut, geologists believe that a subtropical climate dominated the end of the Eocene. Palm trees, swamp cypresses, and tree-sized ferns grew in the moist (40-100 inches of rain), bayoulike environment. By 38 million years ago, however, cooler conditions prevailed. Willow, maple, and sycamore, as well as temperate climate conifers—trees that could withstand freezing temperatures—had replaced the subtropical vegetation.

The area that would become western Washington lacked the dramatic topography that now dominates. The modern Cascades would not push their way into the picture for at least 15 million years, with most of the big mountains we know forming only in the last few million years. The Olympics did not exist either. Nor did the Olympic Peninsula, Puget Sound, or the San Juan Islands. Instead, a broad, low-elevation coastal plain extended eastward into central Washington.

Waves from an ocean that spread to the west washed ashore on beachfront property, now covered by the urban metropolises along Puget Sound. What mountains did exist rose far to the east along the Washington-Idaho border. Rivers and streams washed out of those mountains and meandered toward a coastal lowland dotted with seasonal lakes, swamps, and lagoons. As the water spread toward the ocean, it deposited bed upon bed of sand, eventually building up several thousand feet of sandstone.

These beds, or strata, are what give sandstones their typical appearance, which many have likened to a layer cake. The layer-cake pattern and subsequent salt- and ice-induced splitting of layers is the main reason why sandstone is no longer a popular building material. Builders still use sandstone, but if you see sandstone blocks they are more than likely on a older building and more than likely a local product.

Sandstone was not the only western Washington rock to become popular after June 1889. Builders also turned to a salt-and-pepper stone known as Index granite, quarried 35 miles northeast of Seattle in the hamlet of Index.

John Soderberg, a Swedish immigrant and founder of Swedish Hospital, opened the quarry in 1893 after the Great Northern Railroad laid tracks along the Skykomish River. Rock from this quarry soon began to appear in the city as structural foundations, paving stones, curbs, lintels, and quoins.

The Smith Tower, built in 1914, is Seattle's best-known building with Index granite walls, although they make up only the first few stories. A two-block walk south and east from the Pioneer Building brings me to this splendid skyscraper, once the fourth-tallest building in the world and tallest west of the Mississippi. Compared with some other granites found in Seattle, the Index granite is more heterogeneous and less flashy. Furthermore, the variously sized blobs of black and white in the Index do not appeal to those who want consistency in their building stone.

Geologists, on the other hand, like these blobs, or enclaves, because of the insight they provide into the formation of granite and other closely related rocks. (Quarry workers called them "heathens" due to their unwelcome presence spoiling the uniform texture of the rock.) White enclaves indicate a gas or water pocket in the magma, or molten rock, that cooled to form the Index. The black ones are pockets of iron- and manganese-rich molten material that moved up through the Index magma, like the movement of colored blobs in a lava lamp. You may also find bits of sandstone that fell off the chamber walls in which the magma crystallized, but they are rarer.

The Index granite formed 34 million years ago, after a wedge of oceanic crust—the Juan de Fuca plate, pushed eastward by tectonic action—bumped into the North American continent. The cold, iron- and manganese-rich oceanic crust then began to dive under the lighter continental material. As the Juan de Fuca slid deeper, it descended into the asthenosphere, the 40- to 120-mile-deep layer of hot, partially molten rock that transports the dozen or so plates that compose the outer layer of the planet. As with a stick of butter thrust into hot water, the leading edge of the Juan de Fuca began to melt, creating magma, which started to rise.

The magma crept higher and eventually pierced the bottom of the North America plate, where it began to cool and crystallize into the Index granite. In some places the magma continued to rise through the plate and burst onto the surface, forming volcanoes. A pulse of Juan de Fuca subduction, which may have started as recently as two million years ago and continues to the present, is also responsible for modern volcanoes such as Mount Rainier and Mount Baker.

Igneous rocks, such as granite and basalt, are the superstars of the rock world. In addition to starring roles in bad, geologically questionable movies (*Volcano* and *Dante's Peak*) or headlines ("A New Eruption Hits 50,000 Feet at Mount St. Helens" and "Pinatubo Lights Up Night Sky"), igneous rocks also played a significant part in the proliferation of stone as a building material in this country.

When architect Solomon Willard walked over 300 miles in 1825 to find the perfect granite for the Bunker Hill Monument, it led to the construction of the first railroad in America. Because the quarries were too far from water, engineer Gridley Bryant proposed a 2.75-mile-long railroad from the rock to the Neponset River. Horse-drawn cars with 6.5-foot-tall wheels carried the loads, which averaged six tons each. More recently, some critics have argued that when Philip Johnson and John Burgee used Connecticut granite on their AT&T Building in Manhattan, they started a revival in stone-covered buildings. Granite dominates the modern building trade because it is hard, colorful, and weather resistant.

From Smith Tower, I walk east and north over to the Rainier Club at Fourth and Columbia to examine one of the earlier nonlocal rocks to appear in Seattle. The club, built in 1904, is mostly brick but also contains white to buff limestone blocks quarried near Bedford, Indiana. The rock is known as the Salem Limestone and is one of the most commonly used building stones in the United States.

In Seattle, one can find Salem blocks at the new Seattle Art Museum (the old SAM is made from Wilkeson Sandstone), the Seattle branch of the Federal Reserve Bank of San Francisco, and the Seattle Times. Other widely known Salem buildings include the Empire State Building, Grand Central Station, the Holocaust Memorial Museum in Washington, D.C., and San Francisco City Hall. Lesser-known Salem structures can be found in nearly every state and as far away as Japan.

Deposition of the building stone section of the Salem Limestone occurred 300 to 330 million years ago in a quiet, tropical sea that spread across an area that would become the Midwest. At that time most of the landmass now known as North America lay south of the equator. As in the Bahamas, where future limestone is forming, the sea was clear and shallow. The warm waters supported a diverse range of swimming, crawling, and bottom-dwelling invertebrates. When they died, their bodies collected in a watery cemetery on the seafloor, eventually solidifying into a 40- to 100-foot-thick stone menagerie.

Getting out my trusty hand lens, I examine the limestone blocks that cap a long wall of brick on Fourth. At 15x magnification, the Salem becomes as intricate as a Pointillist painting except that tiny corpses have replaced the dots of paint. Most of the fossils I find are the remains of shells shattered by long-stilled tidal action. I distinguish many fragments of pelecypods, or bivalves, the animal class that includes oysters, clams, and scallops.

Crinoid stems, one-sixteenth- to one-half-inch-wide discs, are the most common recognizable fossil. They come from animals closely related to starfish, sand dollars, and sea urchins, which lived at the bottom of the sea. Crinoids resemble a wildflower with a rootlike base attached to the substrate, a stem of varying length and consisting of discs stacked like poker chips, and a flower-like or fanlike top. Now much less common than their ancestors, modern crinoids tend to live in inaccessible parts of the sea.

Another common fossil fragment resembles Rice Chex cereal. This was the housing complex of a microscopic, sedentary animal known as a bryozoan. The fan-shaped Salem bryozoans lived in colonies of interconnected rooms. Water flowing across the netlike structure provided food for the hundreds or thousands of organisms that formed the colony. Other fossils include brachiopods (clamlike shellfish), gastropods (snails), and ostracods (minute crustaceans that also resemble clams).

After carefully probing this long-extinct ecosystem, I head north to a building that typifies the modern use of building stone. Unlike Seattle's earliest structures, which used massive blocks of stone for structural support, the City Centre building (5th and Union) is clad in one- to two-inch-thick sheets of rock that hang like skin on the steel infrastructure. This practice of using stone merely for decoration is one reason that so many different varieties of rock from so many different continents can now be used as building stone. And this is why I am so happy to explore downtown buildings. City Centre, for example, uses rocks from Africa, Sardinia, and Finland.

My favorite of the three is the red Finnish granite, quarried about 30 miles southwest of Helsinki. It crystallized approximately 1.6 billion years ago and is known by geologists as a rapakivi granite, and by builders as Porkkala Red. I like rapakivi granites because of the ease of distinguishing them from other rocks and because of their unusual age and distribution. Once you find one in an urban environment, it is quite easy to impress your friends by tossing out a few fun facts.

For instance, I start out by saying, "Few other rocks display the unusual texture of a rapakivi. Most rapakivis have one- to three-inch-long, ovoid, feldspar crystals, either red or pinkish, often rimmed by greenish gray, plagioclase feldspar. The Porkkala lacks the rimming but does display first-rate microcline, a potassium rich feldspar. Another good example is the 1000 Second Avenue building, which uses a rapakivi called Baltic Brown."

Once I have dazzled my friends with a textural analysis, I add a few notes on the unusual age of rapakivi granites. "The majority formed between 1 and 1.75 billion years ago with an average age of 1.54 billion years. No other type of granite magmatism fits in such a tight time frame. So when you see one on a building, you can feel confident that you are most likely looking at rocks that crystallized several hundred million years before the first complex forms of life existed."

And finally, I electrify them by addressing rapakivi distribution. "Although they occur on all the continents, rapakivis are generally restricted to the oldest, most stable part of these landmasses, called the continental craton, or shield. Geologists value these rocks because they are important evidence for how the continents formed, and they aid in the understanding of plate tectonics." When confronted with such fine information, most people get a glazed look in their eyes, which I perceive to be pure bliss.

Leaving the exciting world of rapakivi granites, I retreat south a block to the Rainier Tower and its cavity-filled, oatmeal-colored base of travertine, one of the few building stones in Seattle with which you can interact. Travertine is a type of limestone that lacks fossils and does not form in the sea. Instead, it precipitates from calcite-rich water associated with springs or caves. Mammoth Hot Springs in Yellowstone National Park is a good example. As water spilling out of a spring evaporates, any solids carried in solution settle to the ground, like the settling of spices in Italian salad dressing. In travertine, calcite is the primary solid, building layer upon layer as long as the spring continues to expel water. The holes found in travertine indicate deposition around plants. Millimeter-wide, yellowish calcite crystals fill many of the spaces.

While no one is looking, I take out a bottle filled with Modenaceti balsamic vinegar and splash some of the dark liquid on the calcite crystals. They start to fizz as the acid in the vinegar reacts with the calcite, producing carbon dioxide and water. Passing the fizz test is one of the key indicators of a limestone. Most geologists use dilute hydrochloric acid or even distilled white vinegar for the test, but we in urban environments have to make do with what is at hand.

The Rainier Tower panels are the youngest stone in Seattle—less than 200,000 years old. The stone still continues to form in hot springs, though the time of greatest depostion occurred about 80,000 years ago. The older travertine was quarried near Rome in the town of Tivoli, where people have built structures out of the easy-to-cut rock for over 2,000 years. Well-known travertine buildings in Rome include St. Peters, the Quirinal Palace, and the Colosseum.

Just north on Fifth from the Rainier Tower rises the Washington Federal Savings building, a structure that saddens my geologic heart. Overzealous builders filled in each hole in the building's travertine with some sort of cement or goo. My guess is that the builders were not concerned with renegade geologists wielding salad dressing ingredients but thought that the rock required a bit of preventative maintenance. In a colder location, like Boston, water seeps into the cracks, freezes, expands, and weakens the rock. Seattle's moderate winter climate, however, has little effect on the creamy rock. About the only problem here comes from urban pollution that discolors the travertine.

This oatmeal, black, and green building also displays Seattle's most controversial type of building stone, a rock known in the construction trade as Verde Fontaine. South African quarries produced this pine green rock, which solidified underground over one billion years ago. The green coloration comes from the mineral chlorite, which forms from the alteration of iron- and magnesium-rich minerals within the rock.

The conflagration over Verde Fontaine began in early January 1989. During the construction of the city's underground bus stations, Eddie Rye of the Black Contractors Coalition notified the tunnel builders, Metro, about the planned use of Verde Fontaine in two of the downtown stations. This directly conflicted with a resolution that Metro, which managed King County's bus system and collected, treated, and discharged Seattle's sewage, had passed only 16 months earlier that prohibited the use of materials "fabricated or manufactured" in South Africa, because of apartheid.

After Rye blew the whistle, Metro executive director Alan Gibbs said that even though the use of the rock technically was not illegal because it was only quarried in South Africa but cut and finished in Italy, using the South African granite would "taint the project forever"; therefore, Metro would drop the Verde Fontaine from the project, costing hundreds of thousands of dollars. Citizens and public officials both praised and castigated Gibbs's decision to stop using the green granite. After six additional weeks of meetings, debates, and public input, Gibbs resigned. The tunnels opened on September 15, 1990, with walls covered in less polemical rock.

I am not surprised that contractors may not have known of Verde Fontaine's South African origin. Jerry Williams, an architect with the tunnel's design firm, TRA, said at the time that designers choose a building stone to go with the color scheme and normally don't know where the stone is quarried. I found this to be the case when I was researching this story. Many architects and building managers with whom I talked proudly said, "We used Italian granite and Italian marble for interior and exterior walls," no matter where the rock originated.

I don't think they meant to mislead me; they were just misinformed. Many of the building stones used in Seattle were cut and finished in Italy, regardless of whether they were quarried in Finland, Australia, or South Africa. Contractors often send rocks to Italy because of lower cutting costs and a higher quality product. Therefore, buyers know only the Italian connection and no more. Building stone may also acquire a secondary cachet when processed in Italy. One geologist told me about a white Australian marble, which acquired a new name, Carrara Marble—best known as the marble made famous by Michelangelo—after being cut in Italy. Which would you rather buy: Michelangelo's marble or some Outback rock?

Abandoning controversy and degraded travertine, I continue north on Fifth Avenue to my final destination, the Westlake Center, one of the dullest architectural locations in Seattle. This is one of the best parts of urban geology: even ugly buildings might contain intriguing geology. Upon entering Westlake Center, I get down on my hands and knees. Two people ask me if I have lost a contact lens—Seattle is such a friendly place. I shake my head and return to my perusal of one of the best fossil exhibits in Seattle. The floor of Westlake Center is made from blocks of a red-streaked, tawny limestone quarried about 15 miles south of Dijon, France, which geologists call the Comblanchien Limestone. The fine-grained mud that solidified into the Comblanchien settled in shallow, lagoonlike waters protected by sandbars. The water was an arm of a sea that covered Europe roughly 175 million years ago, during the Jurassic age when dinosaurs gallivanted across the planet.

Bottom-dwelling organisms dominate the Westlake fossils. This includes sponges, small mounds of filter-feeding organisms, which fossilized into dark blobby shapes that stand out from the surrounding ecru matrix, and solitary corals, which from the top resemble a clock face without the numbers and from the side look like an ice cream cone. Brachiopods—marine animals often mistaken for clams—were common in one slab, while another block contained a few snails.

The fine-grained quality and pureness (99–100 percent calcite) of the Comblanchien have made it a popular building stone since the Middle Ages. Like many stones used in the building trade, the Comblanchien's fame spread with the railroad, which reached the quarries during the reign of Napoleon III (1852–1870). The limestone has remained popular in France and is found in Orly Airport, the stairs of Sacre Couer, and the Musee d'Art Moderne, in Paris. Jurassic-age French limestones play another role for some Seattleites. Grapes that make many of the finest burgundy wines, such as Beaune, Nuits St. George, and Chambertin, grow on soils derived from these rocks.

When I asked the architectural firm that designed Westlake about this rock, no one mentioned the fossils. Instead I was told, "I believe we had that rock specially made for us." I have asked other people in the building-stone trade the age of a particular rock and had answers ranging from "a few thousand" to "as old as the hills" to "several billion." The last answer is my favorite even though it is often the most imprecise. At least the person who made this ambitious claim realizes the great age of the Earth and might even believe in evolution.

Lack of geological literacy is symptomatic of our general ignorance about the natural world, though ecological and geological processes affect us every day. When I teach geology programs for schoolkids at the Burke Museum of Natural History and Culture, I like to ask if any students deal with rocks and minerals on a daily basis. Most say "No!" I think that many adults would offer the same answer; yet these students watch their teachers write with chalk, made of microscopic fossils, sprinkle a mineral known as salt on their french fries, swallow calcite-rich Tums, and attend school in buildings made of rock or brick.

Because geology (and all aspects of the natural world) play such pivotal roles in our lives, I think it would be nifty if great works of natural history (or even basic texts) shared space with great works of literature on everyone's personal bookshelves. People could take pride in being able to accurately describe a rapakivi granite, state the age of the Earth, or converse intelligently about evolution. I know that not everyone has had formal training in the sciences, but if they need a place to begin their reading, I can recommend a good building or two.

As the clarion notes float downward on the still night air, who can resist temptation to rush out of doors and peer into darkness for a possible glimpse at the passing flock, as the shadowy forms glide over our roofs on their long journey? Or, even in daylight, what man is so busy that he will not pause and look upward at the serried ranks of our grandest waterfowl, as their well-known honking notes announce their coming and their going, he knows not whence or whither?

ARTHUR CLEVELAND BENT, LIFE HISTORIES OF NORTH AMERICAN WILD FOWL, 1923

I once knew an educated lady, banded by Phi Beta Kappa, who told me that she had never heard or seen the geese that twice a year proclaim the revolving seasons to her well-insulated roof. Is education possibly a process of trading awareness for things of lesser worth? The goose who trades his is soon a pile of feathers.

ALDO LEOPOLD, A SAND COUNTY ALMANAC, 1949

Many Seattleites believe that the city has too many Canada geese. They say that the birds and their abundant fecal matter have ruined picnics, golf games, and sunbathing. They worry that the birds spread disease and create safety problems at airports. To these folks, geese are basically large flying rats, which the government should round up and exterminate by the thousands.

I am not troubled by Canada geese, but I rarely go on picnics, I play only miniature golf, and I don't have property on the water. Nor do I go to beaches to sunbathe or swim. When a skein of geese flies over my neighborhood, I see beauty and feel a sense of freedom. I know their northbound flight ushers in spring and their southbound journey heralds winter's arrival. I celebrate that these symbols of wildness still grace my city, although I have stepped in my fair share of goose poop and have not been happy about it.

Despite my sentiments, the birds have lost out. In 2000, federal agents captured 3,500 geese from around Puget Sound, put them in specially designed trucks, and gassed them to death. The first killing took place in summer, when neither adults nor their offspring can fly and when the birds are most noticeable, hanging around and pooping in parks. It was considered such a success that agents working for Wildlife Services, a division of the U.S. Department of Agriculture, killed 4,200 additional birds in 2001 and had a permit to kill 4,200 again in 2002.

I am disturbed by this turn of events and by how the bird's reputation has plummeted, from revered to reviled. Rarely has any species undergone such a complete reversal of opinion, particularly an animal that is neither a predator nor a threat to our safety. The simple solution of killing the geese reinforces an unrealistic cause-and-effect relationship between humans, animals, and the environment. If we are going to solve this perceived problem of too many geese, then we need to take a look at the bigger picture. Why are the geese in Seattle, why do they thrive here, and what realistic, biologically appropriate actions can we take to limit their numbers?

Seattle's Canada goose story begins in 1968. Before then, geese did not nest west of the Cascades. Lack of habitat had historically prevented the birds from making homes on the wet side of the mountains, although they migrated through. By the early 1960s, however, Seattleites had replaced the primary barriers to geese—big trees and dense understory along shorelines—with lush grassy parks, yards, and golf courses. Paradoxically, while Seattleites were unknowingly creating ideal habitat for the birds, Canada geese populations across the United States had steadily dropped because of overhunting, unrestricted harvesting of eggs, and habitat loss in the late 1800s and early 1900s. Goose numbers had become so dire that the American Ornithological Union considered one subspecies to be extinct in the United States as late as 1957.

When biologist Harold Hansen "discovered" a wild flock of the formerly abundant giant Canada goose in 1962, he started a frenzy among biologists to breed the birds to try and reintroduce them to their former habitats and to place them in new habitats. In the Northwest this rush to save "our grandest waterfowl" manifested itself in a project called Operation Mother Goose. Its goal: save Canada goose eggs from inundation by water rising behind the John Day Dam on the Columbia River in eastern Washington. Biologists would release the Mother Goose hatchlings back along the Columbia to reestablish wild populations. They also planned to introduce goslings to previously goose-free areas in Washington state. As had happened throughout the country, these Johnny Gooseeggs had been driven to manipulate bird communities because of habitat loss. In this case, dam construction had cut in half the number of geese along the Columbia and Snake Rivers, the state's most important nesting areas. The wildlife managers did not trust the population to rebound without intervention.

Operation Mother Goose began on April 11, 1968, 17 miles up the Columbia River from the nearly complete John Day Dam. Early in the morning approximately 25 men from the Washington state Department of Game and the U.S. Bureau of Sport Fisheries and Wildlife gathered at a small island. From this base of operations, crews spread out in powerboats to collect eggs from nests on 25 to 30 islands in the 70 miles of river that would be flooded less than a week later.

Once an egg was collected, it was placed in a cardboard box insulated with goose down from the nests. When enough eggs accumulated, the boxes were lashed onto a rack on the outside of a helicopter and whisked 50 miles northeast to the Kennewick Game Farm, one of several facilities across the state that raised game birds such as pheasants for hunting. Biologists immediately unpacked their cargo, shined a light into each egg to determine the stage of development of the embryo, and placed it into one of three incubators. The entire process took about two hours from collection to safekeeping.

Curt Hedstrom, who managed Kennewick in 1968, told me, "We picked up about 1,200 eggs. They started to hatch immediately and continued for 32 days. I was lucky enough to raise 1,000 of them." Most of the young geese survived at the game farm, although nearly 100 suffocated under their sisters and brothers. Within four weeks, each rapidly growing gosling was eating more than a pound of feed each day.

"The idea was to take the young ones and hope that adults who had been there for years would take them under their wing, so to speak," Hedstrom said. Goslings could learn from and join wild flocks and soon graduate to the twice-yearly migration. Hedstrom coined the project's moniker because of this behavior. "I titled it Operation Mother Goose because of the imprinting. Of course, whoever raises them, they think that's their mother." The first releases of the geese into the wild took place at McNary Refuge and McNary Game Farm at the confluence of the Snake and Columbia Rivers. Biologists released 100 birds between the two sites.

By June 12, more than 900 geese had been distributed, mostly to refuges and game farms near the Columbia, but a few outliers received Mother Goose deliveries, too. For example, Arizona Fish and Game picked up 126 goslings for Phoenix and Flagstaff; Idaho Fish and Game acquired 50 to plant on the Coeur d'Alene River and Spokane obtained 100 birds. "I think the greatest success was around Yakima. They didn't have hardly any honkers there before and there's a big population there now," said Hedstrom.

Operation Mother Goose was front-page news for four days in Walla Walla, sharing space with the search for Martin Luther King's assassin, and the Vietnam War. Most regional newspapers covered the event. Television stations from Portland filmed the operation and the Associated Press picked up the story and distributed it across the country. Of the two Seattle daily newspapers, only the *Post-Intelligencer* carried news of Operation Mother Goose, under the heading "Goose Eggs Saved From Rising Water Behind New Dam." The short article described the event and stated that goslings would be released along the Columbia.

Despite my search of newspapers published in the weeks following the event, however, I could not answer a niggling question: Did biologists release goslings from the John Day eggs in Seattle? Another way to look at this question is which came first, the goose or the gosling? Had Canada geese begun to colonize Seattle prior to 1968 and no one had noticed, or did introduction of Mother Goose youngsters lead to the present-day situation of 25,000 geese? This is a key point. People pressing for protection of a species often use the argument that the animals were here first and therefore we ought to learn to live with them or at least make it possible for that species to survive our intrusion into their territory.

What if people arrived first, however, and the animal second? In urban landscapes we have heavily manipulated the environment and have often brought, either purposefully or inadvertently, alien species with us. People seem to find it easier to justify eliminating "weed" species such as rats, English ivy, pigeons, or dandelions if the offender isn't native. Even now, starlings and English sparrows, the two most prolific and widespread nonnative birds in the U.S., can be killed without a permit.

One of the arguments used during Seattle's first war on geese was that the geese are nonnative birds. In 1987 the Seattle Waterfowl Management Committee formed to try and alleviate health and safety problems and damages caused by geese. Two years later they hired UW biologist David Manuwal to complete a 12-month study of urban Canada geese. Manuwal and his group examined 25 parks in the Seattle area, finding between 3,000 and 4,000 Canada geese around Puget Sound. He traced the origin of these birds to an introduction from John Day eggs, although he neither named Operation Mother Goose nor cited any written documentation for it. Manuwal concluded that the best way to stem the growing population was to capture and ship back across the mountains up to 90 percent of the birds over a five-year period. He wrote, "Do we use preventative management now when it is relatively cheap or do we wait until the population of Canada geese is so large that their numbers must be reduced dramatically?"

When news of Manuwal's report became public, activists gathered signatures, wrote letters to the editor, and protested at public forums. "We think the geese have a right to be where they are. They have just as much a right to be here as the people who use the beach," said Dr. Wayne Johnson of the Northwest Animal Rights Network. "We do not think Canada geese should have to pay with their life because of fecal matter." Johnson also added that park officials had not stressed options such as discouraging people from feeding the geese.

Biologists argued that hand-feeding geese was not a big problem, observing that the number of people who actually feed the birds is insignificant. Many of the people who blame the problem on handouts to geese are park and golf course managers, who feed more geese than anybody by providing manicured lawns. In this sense the activists are correct; we need to stop providing food to geese. However, we also need to look beyond blaming the single person giving out some food at a park.

Countering the sentiments of animal rights activists, biologists in 1991 turned the "native versus wild" point on its head by arguing that removing the geese from the city would be a huge benefit to the birds. "We're trying to put them back in the wild where they can breed, bring up young, and establish a new free-flying population of Canada geese," said Bill Rybarczyk of Idaho Fish and Game. Despite the arguments, public officials agreed with biologists, and goose collection began in the summer of 1991. Federal biologists gathered 2,524 birds and shipped them east. A year later they transported 1,731 more, followed by 519 in 1993. The number dropped not because this action succeeded in reducing overall numbers but because Idaho didn't want any more birds. Our problem had become Idaho's.

Deportation did lead to a downturn in numbers, but not for long. An August 1993 aerial census found only 2,315 geese in Seattle, although biologists predicted that if no further action was taken, the population would double in five years. Urban Canada geese produce up to 15 eggs per nest and can quickly build their numbers again. It is obvious that these biologists were correct.

By the end of the 1990s, the urban goose population had reached critical proportions. Beaches were closed because of too much goose poop and complaints flowed in to park officials. This led to a 1999 environmental assessment on resident Canada geese in the Puget Sound area. Lead author Keel Price, a biologist for the USDA's Wildlife Services, thoroughly examined the purpose, alternatives, and environmental consequences of managing resident Canada geese and concluded that killing 3,500 birds would be the best solution to slow the population growth. Price's report did not stipulate when the killing would end, although it stated that management objectives would be revaluated on an ongoing basis.

As Manuwal had written in his earlier report, Price used the bird's introduction as a justification for his findings. The opening statement of his conclusion reads, "It should be noted that the western Canada goose was not historically found in the Puget Sound area. It was mans' [sic] intervention that accelerated their introduction...." Price also alluded to Operation Mother Goose without citing specific documentation. "Quite frankly, they (DFW) destroyed all their records when it became obvious that they had probably caused this problem (too many geese)," Price told me. "I don't think you can find paper one at DFW that indicates how many they brought or where they brought them from."

Contrary to Price's statement, officials did produce a still traceable paper trail on Operation Mother Goose. A series of annual analyses called the "Small Game Reports" have detailed information about who was involved, how many eggs were collected, how many survived, and where Mother Goose goslings were distributed. Price was correct that none mention any bird releases around Seattle.

The closest locale was the South Tacoma Game Farm, another DFW facility that raised game birds for hunting. Bud Angerman, former head at Tacoma, was the first person to expressly say that Mother Goose birds crossed the Cascades. "We wanted to start a captive program because we had good habitat. We received 10 to 15 goslings from Kennewick. They started reproducing and soon we had too many, so we sent some to Yakima and to Capital Lake in Olympia."

He did not, however, release any in Seattle. "I remember that geese were already there," Angerman said. "I used to see them at Alki and down by Terry Avenue in 1957–58." Most likely they were migratory birds. Angerman suggested that I contact Curt Hedstrom to see if he had sent any west.

"There were some planted near Lake Washington. In fact they are a nuisance there right now. I don't know how many of them were my geese," Hedstrom said. "And that, of course, didn't turn out too good. I don't know if the person who planted them there had permission to do so or not." When I asked him who did it, he responded, "I'd rather not name . . . "

About a week after I spoke to Hedstrom, an envelope from him arrived at our house. He included a short note, which began, "Hope these clippings are a help." The half-dozen newspaper articles contained details on Operation Mother Goose, photos of officials collecting eggs, men in hunting caps boxing the eggs, and several shots of very cute goslings. The short note ended, "Hope this is a positive article about the geese."

I tried Hedstrom again, wanting to find out more specifics on the release around Seattle. "In regard to Lake Washington, I don't think they were planted right on the lake. I can't tell you for sure but I see no reason that they would. I could be mistaken. Maybe they were planted miles and miles away and there were geese there at the time. I kind of assumed that they were planted somewhere near there," he said. "They wouldn't plant an area where people didn't want the geese. They didn't just nonchalantly plant them. They must have had a reason. I just can't come up with it. I wish I could refer you to someone else who would know."

Hedstrom may not have realized it but he did offer the first reason why Canada geese might have been released near Seattle. "The Game Department works for the sportsmen. They're the ones that paid our wages," he said. The geese would help establish a flyway where hunters might have a chance to shoot the birds. Officials probably could not have forecast how the geese would multiply, how they would have to be killed, or who would have to kill them.

Maybe we should let the sportsmen back into the picture. If hunters could hunt Seattle's geese, we might have fewer complaints about the birds, or at least fewer birds. Obviously this won't happen in an urban landscape, but it does point out one of the reasons geese prosper here. No one eats them, and urban dwellers don't allow goose predators to live in our midst. My other fantasy is to reintroduce predators such as coyotes to Seattle. What a treat it would be to see a coyote catch and kill a goose at Green Lake; I suspect though that this would cause even more consternation than our present situation of too many geese.

We should not blame the Operation Mother Goose biologists for our modern-day problem. The biologists thought they were preserving a cherished species. My discussions with Hedstrom and Angerman made it clear they were proud of what they had done. Moreover, they were not alone in their actions; at least 40 states tried to acquire goslings from Operation Mother Goose. The same agency that ran Mother Goose, Sport Fisheries and Wildlife, also encouraged individuals to get involved. In 1971 they published a guide titled *Home Grown Honkers*. It was oriented toward an "interested man or woman [who wanted] to establish small breeding flocks of giant Canada geese in his or her home area." A wholesome activity for any family. Chapters in the 150-page volume included information on habitat requirements, how to incubate eggs, and how to protect goslings from predators.

The authors devoted a long section to urban areas and offered a surprisingly prescient caveat: "We also conclude that, while honkers are a definite asset in many cases, they may become a nuisance in others. In the latter cases, don't blame the geese, someone put them there without carefully weighing the possible consequences or making adequate plans if the venture succeeded. . . . As the population grows, provisions must be made to remove any surplus above a desired level."

We will probably never be able to state definitively the number of Mother Goose goslings released around Puget Sound, but they would not have stayed if we hadn't done such a fine job of altering the landscape. Don Kraege, waterfowl manager for DFW, puts it this way: "Canada geese are opportunistic birds who surely would have taken advantage of the vacant habitat and few predators. Mother Goose merely sped up the process."

The Canada goose population has grown, in part, because the creation of goose heaven has led to a significant change in the lifestyle of urban geese. That familiar flight of honkers crossing the sky is probably a flock of wild geese during the annual fall or spring migration. Unlike their feral relatives, urban geese do not migrate. Why should they? Animals migrate because they need a better place to eat, breed, or live, and no goose is going to find a better spot than Seattle. Since the birds do not leave, their presence is felt year-round instead of only during the seasonal migrations. Urban geese also have a significantly higher survival rate than their wild relatives. Around 90 percent of the birds in a city survive their first year compared with 60 percent for wild populations. Those that make it to their first year also live longer than wild birds, because the main cause of mortality for wild adults is hunting.

It's not that people do not like Canada geese; it's that people do not like what the birds produce. Geese are walking digestive tracts disguised as birds, defecating between 5.2 and 8.8 times per hour, 28 times a day, or up to 92 times per day in winter. A single bird can produce 3 pounds of droppings per day or 1.17 ounces dry weight of material. (Geese, like all birds, combine urine and excrement in one tidy package, which ornithologists call droppings, although poop or feces gets the point across, too.)

Whether fecal output causes diseases, however, is less clear. Dr. Milton Friend, past director of the National Wildlife Health Center, a biomedical laboratory that assesses the impact of disease on wildlife, says geese pose few, if any, problems as a disease vector to humans. In response to a series of e-mail questions, he wrote, "The direct answer is that one does not contract swimmer's itch from contact with geese or their feces. There is little evidence that Canada geese pose a risk for humans relative to transmission of salmonellosis. There is also very little risk of contracting cryptosporidiosis from geese fecal matter."

And yet, the perceived threat of disease drives many of the calls for eliminating the birds. Geese droppings have been blamed for closing beaches across the region, although recent reports show that house pets contribute a significant fecal coliform load and it is hard to pinpoint a single source considering how much material, such as spilled oil, sewage overflow, and road runoff, drains into our lakes and streams.

Science, however, does not play much of a role in the public perception of the goose problems. It is an emotional issue, and for many the simple answer is one once uttered by Arlo Guthrie in his infamous "Alice's Restaurant": "*Kill! Kill! Kill!*" Officials choose extermination because it may slow down the population explosion, as well as temporarily remove the birds from areas with high rates of complaint. Studies show, however, that Canada geese populations can remain steady or increase even with adult mortality rates of 40 percent, which means that public land agencies will be forced to continue to kill.

Opinions and politics notwithstanding, late April and early May are the times to forgive Canada geese who trespass against us. How can you be upset with an animal that produces such adorable young? I saw the season's first gaggle of young geese on May 7 at Green Lake, tightly squished together looking like a hydra-headed rug of yellow-gray fluff. Like the adults, the goslings have obsidian eyes and dull black beaks. Each youngster has small, absurd wings, about the size of an Oreo cookie. Their plaintive peeping completes the picture of cuteness.

Not that the adults are ugly birds. The sleek black neck and head offset by a chin strap of white. A gray to brown body that resembles a wasp nest—intricate layers of gray feathers like lamella of paper. Sturdy black legs and webbed feet covered in reptilian scales. They are also graceful fliers, as anyone knows who has watched a V-shaped skein skirt the sky or who has been transfixed by the ever-present conversation of *qua-honks* and *la-ronks*. Despite the number of times I have watched them, I still stop and stare each time I see a group flying overhead. Few more elegant expressions of freedom exist.

At Green Lake, six adults supervised the 18 youngsters, who ranged in size from a robin to a mallard. Hard to imagine that these nubbins of down could grow into 40-inch-tall adults with three-foot-wide wings that could carry a bird thousands of miles or knock a small child silly. (This does not happen often and generally only occurs when an adult is protecting a gosling, but this danger is a complaint for some people.) By mid-July, however, these goslings will be able to join their parents in flight and in another year they can start adding to the population. But on this warm

Sunday at Green Lake, you wouldn't know the birds' dismal reputation. Their goslings still captivate.

"They are sooo cute!" said a muscular Rollerblader who had stopped to watch.

A woman pushing a stroller added, "The city wants to kill all of them . . . meanies."

"I am going to start a protest and chain myself to a goose," said a young women with various piercings.

One man gave a discourse to his friends, describing how the city wants to kill 3,500 geese. "The geese were here first. Nature right next to the city. This is why I come here."

I partially agree with this guy. I visit Green Lake because I like to see Canada geese, as well as bald eagles, mallards, and pied-billed grebes. Wildlife in the city is crucial to my love for Seattle but I recognize that we cannot allow every plant and animal to proliferate without human intervention. For better or worse, we have become the de facto stewards of the landscape, particularly in urban settings, which is why I am ambivalent about what to do with the geese.

Part of me supports the activists' arguments that we created this situation and should therefore learn to live with the birds and their growing population. Simple nonlethal alternatives to killing exist, such as visual deterrents, dogs trained to harass the birds, and chemical repellents, but most of these methods have not been widely used. The major non-lethal changes we need to make—planting understory species, eliminating grass, creating rock or shrub borders between water and land, and not giving the birds handouts—are hard to execute, but we can begin to implement some of them.

Another part of me says that killing 3,500 birds is good because it may help slow down the population growth, although Seattle's previous experiment proved that killing must occur year after year and not just once or twice. Currently, no one has shown that the birds are doing any damage to other animals or to the environment, but if the upward population trend continues, biologists predict that over 100,000 Canada geese could dwell in Puget Sound by 2014. Who knows what sort of impact so many large waterfowl will have on other species?

Perhaps both camps are wrong, their solutions too simple and disconnected from science. We need to acknowledge that we created this problem. We need to modify not only habitat but also our expectations. Both species want the same things: lawns, parks, golf courses, clear views to the water, and easy access to beaches.

We need a coordinated effort by both camps. Park managers need to work together so that when one park drives out the birds with dogs, those geese will only find another park doing the same thing. Land managers and homeowners need to work together to create less geese-friendly habitat. Park visitors and homeowners need to accept that every visit to a green space may not be as pristine as we'd like.

We also need to create a new model of human-animal interaction in the urban landscape. We must move away from the historic paradigm that dominated in wilder settings: killing animals perceived as threats to safety or lifestyle cures our problems with that animal. The management of wolves, mountain lions, and grizzly bears exemplify this negative standard. By the early 1900s, ranchers' concerns about these predators killing their sheep and cattle had led to the virtual elimination of these icons from the American west. Since then we have reintroduced grizzlies and wolves, with surprising success, but now we hear renewed calls for eliminating legislation that protects them. Lions, who have come back on their own, are still hunted in most states.

A similar approach is being taken with urban Canada geese. If we cannot learn to live with these relatively harmless and rather handsome animals, whose only problem is that they poop too much, I wonder how we will ever live with species whose impact may be far less benign. Maybe instead of deriding Canada geese we should honor and study the bird. How do they survive and thrive in a landscape so altered, mismanaged, and generally maligned? It is a question that our species will have to address more carefully in the future, if we are unwilling to change how we treat the planet. If we want to continue to see wildlife in urban settings, or in other landscapes, we must be more willing to be inconvenienced by animals like Canada geese. Stepping in poop is not a call to arms.

Ultimately it should not matter who came first, the geese or us; we are here together now and must deal with it. Though most folks still seem to want a quick fix to the abundant geese, the goose problem did not appear overnight and will not disappear easily. I hope that the mass killing of geese makes it clear that we must take responsibility for our actions. Complex natural history problems such as urban Canada geese can only be solved through long-term, biologically appropriate, and sometimes challenging solutions.

It astonishes me how little the ordinary person notices butterflies.

VLADIMIR NABOKOV, *SPEAK MEMORY*, 1947

If spiders did not occur in our fauna, and if the keepers of a zoological garden were to bring from some remote part of the world living examples of the little animals that spin from their bodies threads of silk of different kinds, . . . and with these threads construct snares of surprising regularity for trapping their prey, the presence of such marvelous animals would attract greater attention, and we would make long journeys to see them. Fortunately, however, this marvel can be seen at home by any one that has eyes and will look.

JOHN HENRY COMSTOCK, *THE SPIDER BOOK*, 1920

When the warm days of summer approach, the competition for insects in our house becomes fierce. The killers include Taylor, several carnivorous plants, a plethora of spiders, and, to a small extent, me. My role might more accurately be called a gofer; I often catch flies to feed to the plants. My job, though, requires utmost care. I need to disable the fly but not kill it. Like other predators, Venus flytraps require movement to trigger their deadly embrace.

Unlike many hunters, I met with success on my first pursuit of game. We had just purchased a group of insectivorous plants, known to its seller as the Carnivorous Combo, and had set it in a south-facing window, when I heard a potential meal buzzing about the house. I quickly picked up my weapon, the previous day's business section of the *New York Times*, and headed out to locate my quarry. After an exhausting five-minute search, I debilitated a housefly with a precisely controlled whack, scooped it up, and deposited the meal in the flytrap's waiting jaws of death. The trap snapped shut within a second of the fly's first movements. I took a victory lap around the couch.

The other insectivorous plants, sundews, lack the drama of the flytraps, but they still have healthy diets. When I discovered a cache of aphids on our hibiscus, instead of cutting the leaves off I gently removed the wee green bugs and fed them to the sundews. Unfortunately, the aphids eventually overwhelmed and killed the sundew. I later read that aphids are one of the main pests of sundews.

Taylor, while not a true insectivore, also likes to chase insects, particularly airborne ones. She does not discriminate and will chomp after any that disturb her personal space. I have not seen her catch one, although I often hear the clattering of her jaw as she tries. One summer she successfully made contact with what I suspect was a yellowjacket. I was working out in the yard when Taylor appeared at the back door, the entire left side of her face swollen. When I sat down with her she just rested her face in my lap and looked up at me with one good and one swollen eye. I have rarely felt so helpless.

By the time we got to the veterinarian most of the swelling had dissipated. Denise, the vet, said that dogs have allergic reactions to stings and can go into anaphylaxis just like humans. Taylor's reaction, while severe, was not life threatening. Denise suggested that I give Taylor two antihistamine tablets, which I supplemented with a new dog bone. The next day she continued chomping at low-flying insects.

Despite the efforts of myself, Taylor, and the plants, we pale in comparison to our home's premier insectivores—the spiders who inhabit every room in the house. Without them, our home would not be as pleasant a place to live. The ubiquitous cobweb spiders live in the ceiling corners. Their drab brown coloring seems to suit their quiet lifestyle. I rarely see them moving about, but invariably I find wings or legs from previous visitors dangling from webs. I then realize how little I see of the travails of life and death in our house.

The other main group of spiders I notice inside are the jumping spiders. Unlike their sit-and-wait cousins, these quarter-inch-wide, spring-loaded beasts actively search for their meals. Jumping spiders are constantly on the go and will even track my movements if I get too close. When they patrol the windowsills, their blue, green, and black bodies iridesce in the sun. Camouflage is not their forte. Jumping spiders rely on their excellent eyesight, considered the best of any animal their size, for locating predators and prey. When stalking, they approach slowly and then leap onto their meals. I consider it to be a good day when I see this true predator on patrol. I can only hope that I catch my flies with such panache.

Cobweb spiders and jumping spiders are not the only spiders that live around us. I once read that in an urban environment you are rarely more than six feet from a spider, certainly comforting news for those who feel lonely in our chaotic world. According to local spider expert and curator of arachnids at the Burke Museum, Rod Crawford, at least 200 spider species live in Seattle, 25 of which may take up residence with us. Over 800 species inhabit the state. Their habitats range in elevation from the summit of Mount Rainier to sea level. Their sizes vary from 1 mm to 95 mm. All are predators. All are poisonous. But like the proverbial dog, their reputations are far worse than their bites.

Those in the know, in particular Mr. Crawford, only consider three species relatively abundant and venomous to people; the other 800 or so are generally shy, did not evolve with humans in mind and therefore have no desire to bite us, and are too small or have poison too weak to do us any harm. Further reducing Seattleites' reasons to worry about this plenitude of generally eight-eyed, eight-legged predators is that one of the venomous species, the western black widow, *Latrodectus hesperus*, only occurs east of the Cascades, except for some on the San Juan Islands. They prefer unoccupied rabbit holes, where females can build messy-looking webs.

One note of lore before abandoning black widows: the plight of black widow males is not as bad as generally reported. Yes, they occasionally get eaten, but in a study on the courtship behavior of black widows, researchers found that the twofold larger females do not actively attack and eat their partners after mating. Instead, males crawl away from females and go to another part of the web to spend their final days. Because their sperm transfer appendages break off after mating, they complete a lifetime's worth of amorous activities in one quick burst. I like to think that male black widows are one of the world's most liberated beings, for how many other males would provide food for their progeny by letting themselves be eaten by their mate?

The other medically significant species, hobo spiders, *Tegenaria agrestis*, does live in Seattle, although like most of us, they are not natives. Harriet Exline, a world renowned arachnologist, made the first collection of this spider in the United States on November 20, 1930, on the embankment of railroad tracks (now the Burke-Gilman Trail) that pass what is now Husky Stadium. The spiders probably arrived on a boat from Europe and spread via transportation corridors, hence the common name. Hobo spiders are one of a triumvirate of arachnids known as European house spiders that live in the Pacific Northwest: the smaller (legspan of .6–1.4 inches) *Tegenaria domestica* arrived in Port Angeles in 1923 and the larger (legspan 1.6–3.7 inches) *T. gigantea* first appeared on Vancouver Island in 1929 and Seattle in 1960. They are probably the most seen or at least the most noticed spiders in the city.

Each is common around houses, generally building funnel webs in basements, sheds, garages, and barns. (Hobo spiders need contact with the soil for their webs; therefore their webs are adjacent to or under buildings.) Hard to tell apart (brown with gray markings) except by size, they move quickly, up to 20 inches per second, and because of bad eyesight they can appear to run aggressively at a person. I still remember several childhood encounters with these spiders scurrying across the floor while I watched TV in my parents' basement. I admit I didn't take the time to look closely, only long enough to verify that my foot stomping had killed them. I am sure they were the biggest of the three species and probably record-size specimens at that.

One, two, or possibly all three of these spiders—I believe it is the smallest of the three—lives in our garage, where they build numerous webs in the corners of windows and walls. These airy graveyards contain more detached body parts than a Sylvester Stallone movie. Moth wings predominate but I have also found yellowjacket bodies, sectioned and whole, various spiders, housefly heads, and legs galore of many unidentifiable species. (I am quite a fan of spider webs. In Utah, I found a black widow web with a mummified red-spotted toad dangling in midair and another with a dead scorpion and a dead black widow.)

Judging by the parts shop in our garage, European house spiders are doing me far more good than bad. I don't mean to imply that I like spiders more than these other species or that I rejoice in knowing that insects and other arachnids are getting eaten, but spider predation is key for keeping down the populations of other terrestrial arthropods. Their predation helps keep the balance in nature.

Predation is one of the great aspects of the urban world of bugs. We all know it is a bug-eat-bug world out there, but except for rare spectator sports such as Wall Street and reality TV, we rarely get to watch firsthand. If you go out into your yard or local park, you can find predator-prey interaction all around you. It is quite fun and occasionally a bit gory to watch.

Dragonflies are the largest and most spectacular insect predator in the city. The larvae eat crustaceans, mosquito and black fly larvae, fish, and tadpoles, and adults consume mosquitoes and other insects, including other dragonflies. Their eating style is not for the faint of heart. In the summer of 2003 I was fortunate enough to watch a western pondhawk devour a common spreadwing. The pruinose blue dragonfly began by severing the smaller damselfly's blue-eyed head and eating it in a few quick chomps. A few more bites and the blue-black thorax disappeared, followed by the 10 segments of the abdomen. All that remained were the wings, fluttering to the ground. I know someone else who once watched a dragonfly hit a moth over open water. When my friend retrieved the moth, he found that the larger insect had merely snipped off the moth's abdomen and kept on flying.

What we call dragonflies are scientifically known as odonates, the order of insects that also includes damselflies, which have thinner bodies and usually rest with their wings closed over their backs. The 54 species found in King County are black and red, black and yellow, black and blue, emerald green, bright red, sky blue, and various combinations of this palette. Some have blue eyes, others green. They fly forward and backward at speeds up to 60 mph. They hover. They mate in midair and can remain attached even as the female deposits eggs. One species, the green darner (*Anax junius,* which means Lord of June), is the Washington state insect. Common species in Seattle include blue-eyed darner, western pondhawk, cardinal meadowhawk, and eight-spotted skimmer.

Odonates can be found near any body of water in the city, especially small ponds with aquatic vegetation. Like most insects, they prefer the warmth and sun of summer. I see them every time I walk Taylor around North Seattle Community College from about late May to mid-September and have even caught a few in my butterfly net. I usually just look at them in the net but one time I decided to look more closely. Once I had scissored the wings near the body between two fingers, I could see the dragonfly's red abdomen expand and contract as it breathed. I also peered into its huge eyes, said to be the most acute of any in the insect world. I wondered what it would be like to have the world's largest dragonfly, a 29-inch-wingspan giant from Kansas, stare me down. Of course, I was born about 280 million and 38 years too late to meet what has been dubbed the "world's largest ever insect."

Ladybugs are another easy-to-watch predator. To attract them to your home, simply don't use insecticides. If you are lucky, aphids will appear on your plants. Soon hoards of adult and larvae ladybugs, which resemble minute black-and-yellow alligators, will attack and consume the aphids. It is almost exciting enough to set up lawn chairs and cheer on the little carnivores. Sure, some plants won't "look" as good during the invasion, but most aphid infested plants still produce flowers, put on leaves, and set seed.

Ladybugs may be "cute," but not if you are a mite, scale, or mealybug—other menu items in the ladybug diet. Their rapacious habits have been known since at least the Middle Ages, when their common name first appeared. The lady in question is the Virgin Mary and the name alludes to a time when ladybugs appeared after desperate wine growers prayed to the Virgin for help from crop-consuming aphids. They are also known as lady beetles or ladybird beetles. More than 75 species live in Washington state. More than half have a range that includes the Puget Lowlands. The smallest lady beetle, *Microweisia misella*, is about a third as long as a grain of rice, and the largest, *Anatis labiculata*, is about the size of a pinto bean. Some are solid black, brown, or red. Others have various blotches in combinations of yellow, red, orange, black, and cream, and one even looks like a well-armored, miniature Jersey cow.

When I go out into my yard to watch lady beetles munch aphids, I usually find only one species dining. A recent introduction, they did not appear in Seattle until 1991, 10 years after 37,852 specimens had been released in eastern Washington. Generally red, an eighth of an inch long, with up to 19 black spots and a white M-shaped mark on the forward part of the body, they are known as *Harmonia axyridis* and are native to western Asia. (A native species, *Hippodamia convergens*—the convergent ladybug—is the variety sold in stores as aphid eaters. They do eat aphids, but when released, generally disperse immediately.)

Harmonia is now the most abundant ladybeetle in the area, as well as one of the most widely distributed and abundant species in the country. Whether it has displaced other species in its conquest of America is a question open to debate, but former UW zoologist Peter Karieva found *Harmonia* and one other nonnative composing more than 80 percent of the ladybugs found in a survey of 24 localities in the state, including remote spots in the Cascades.

Ladybugs are a member of the order Coleoptera, a group so diverse that British biologist J. D. S. Haldane once said God has "An inordinate fondness for beetles." They are the most diverse group of insects in Seattle. Melville Hatch, a world-renowned beetle expert who worked at the UW from 1927 to 1972, estimated that there were 1,500 beetle species in the Seattle area, and this in a region with a paucity of beetles.

Beetles, of course, are insects (class Insecta) animals characterized by six legs, a head, thorax, and abdomen, and mostly two pairs of wings. Four of every five species on the planet is an insect. To give an idea of diversity in Washington state, where few, if any, systematic insect surveys have been done, there are at least 800 solitary bee, 71 stonefly, 39 ant, 49 mosquito, and 1,300 fly species.

Only a few people have made extensive studies of urban insects. A study by Rod Crawford at the Montlake Fill in 1976 estimated the number of arthropods at between 40,285 and 82,110 per square meter. In 1941 Frank Lutz wrote a book about his backyard in New York, where he tallied 1,402 species in four years. Jennifer Owen in England has also written of her garden collecting for 15 years, during which she found over 1,600 species. The leader, though, is Gary Hevel, an entomologist at the Smithsonian. He collected insects for two years in his two-acre backyard in suburban Washington, D.C. With help from fellow Smithsonian curators, he has catalogued over 2,700 species and expects to reach at least 4,000.

Hevel's total is impressive, but he didn't even seek out the other well-known group of multi-legged organisms, arachnids. This class, Arachnida, includes spiders, harvestmen, mites, scorpions, pseudoscorpions, and wind scorpions. All have eight legs, external skeletons, and grow by periodically molting and renewing their exoskeletons. Arachnids also include the one group of bugs that gives me the willies. I have little compunction in killing ticks I find in the house, on Taylor, or on me. Beyond their propensity to spread disease, which includes Lyme, tularemia, and Rocky Mountain spotted fever, I find their ability to balloon up with blood, particularly my own, rather disturbing. It's as if every time a person ate a meal they inflated to gargantuan proportions. This would not be a pleasant sight and I will not dwell on it any longer.

In contrast, I like harvestmen, the one arachnid that other people tolerate and also like. More commonly known as daddy longlegs, harvestmen are not spiders, which have two main body parts, the cephalothorax and abdomen, and eight eyes. Harvestmen lack a constriction between the head and abdomen and only have two eyes. The common name comes from the tendency of several conspicuous species to congregate in fields at harvest time. They are predators, but rumors aside they are not remotely venomous to people. In fact they have neither fangs nor venom.

Because of the harvestmen's popularity, kids, and at least one Seattle-based writer, try to pick them up, which often results in the loss of one of the arachnid's legs. Oddly, this is supposed to happen. A harvestmen's first line of defense is to detach a leg or section of one, which drops to the ground and begins to wriggle, drawing the predator's attention away from the escaping prey. Legs are also a harvestmen's primary sensory organs. Next time you see a daddy longlegs, which despite the name can be female, watch how it raises its second pair of legs to taste, smell, and feel the world around it. If you want, pick it up, but be careful.

Fewer people observe our other local arachnids, mites, but that does not mean that they do not live in our vicinity. The mite ecologists I consulted, all of whom prefaced their answers with "This is only an educated guess," speculated that mite species diversity ranged from 2,300 to over 10,000. Several even call us home. These include such well-known skin irritants as chiggers, the larval stage of a family of red mites, and sarcoptic itch mites, the little beastie that causes scabies. While these mites do not live permanently on us, at least two species do, and they have set up home on our faces. Known scientifically as *Demodex folliculorum* and *D. brevis*, they live in pores and hair follicles.

My guess is that most of us have not noticed them. Fortunately, they are not terribly large, about a quarter the size of the period at the end of this sentence. A follicle mite looks like a toothbrush with four pairs of legs for bristles and a long, handlelike tail. A female can lay up to 25 eggs, which mature in the follicle before heading out to start their own family of face feeders. They spend most of the time head down in a follicle, tail waving in the breeze, munching away on our skin cells. Other good places to look for mites include your bed, the bag of dog food in your kitchen, or the soil in your yard, where densities have been reported as high as a million individuals per square meter.

Not all of the multi-legged critters in our houses and yards have only eight legs. A handsome milliped, *Harpaphe haydeniana*, sports the most legs of any terrestrial animal in Seattle. They use their 31 pairs of legs to penetrate rotten logs and soft soil, where they shred, crush, and consume detritus. Ecologists estimate that *Harpaphe* process between 33 and 50 percent of all leaves and needles that fall to the ground in Pacific Northwest forests, making them one of the most important components of a healthy forest ecosystem. Like harvestmen, they need a moist habitat.

I have only found them in our yard a few times, but I will never forget the time I saw several hundred *Harpaphe* in a bathtub-sized area on a trail in Redwood National Park. Each of the mobile beasts was black with yellow lateral racing stripes, like a tiny section of uncontrollable road in a transportation engineer's worst nightmare. Ecologists call this type of coloration "aposematic," a term that refers to vivid colors used by animals to advertise their bad taste or poisonous nature, basically the animal-world's equivalent of teenagers' clothing.

Harpaphe are aposematic because they produce hydrogen cyanide when threatened. The milliped survives by reducing its metabolism and closing its breathing pores. Whenever I find a *Harpaphe*, I like to pick it up, put it in my hand, shake it slightly, and take a whiff. They produce too little cyanide to harm a big strong guy like me, but they also produce benzaldehyde, which as everyone knows has a distinctly almondesque aroma. Other millipeds produce chemicals that put an attacker to sleep or cause it to lose its appetite, seemingly two good ideas for some entrepreneur to exploit.

No one knows exactly how many milliped species are out there. Of the estimated 80,000 varieties only about 8,000 have been described and none have 1,000 legs. A California species, *Illacme plenipes*, is the present record holder with 750 legs. Richard Hoffman, who wrote the *Checklist of Millipeds of North and Middle America*, speculates that between 80 and 100 inhabit our fair state, but unfortunately no myriapodologist has conducted an intensive study of them. The number is probably higher.

The other group of animals known for its legs is the centipedes. The two groups, which are less closely related than one might think, are easy to tell apart. Centipedes have one pair of legs per segment and millipeds have two. In addition, centipedes are predators and have a pair of claws on the segment behind the head. None of our 20 or so species can inject a venom poisonous to people, but you do not want to be bitten by some of the larger ones in the tropics, which probably won't kill you but will make you unhappy.

We have one very common species of centipede in Seattle, *Lithobius forficatus*, the garden centipede, which unlike *Harpaphe* is not native. I see them almost every time I am rooting about in our yard. They live under boards and flowerpots and in the soil. While writing this section of this chapter, I went out to locate a *Lithobius* to describe; I found several under the first board I turned over. The rusty orange, one-inch-long 30-leggers scurried in a mad dash to get back into a moist, protected spot. I was not quick enough to catch one but I did nab three species of crustaceans that lived under the same board.

Known scientifically as terrestrial isopods, these land-based relatives of crabs and lobsters have more common names than any bug I know. A list compiled in 1935 consists of 66 names, including bibble bug, coffin-cutter, God A'mighty's pigs, slater, woodlice, little old woman of the wood, tiggy hog, and sow-bug. People I talked to seem to know them as pillbug, potatobug, and roly poly. Our most common backyard species, the sowbugs, *Porcellio scaber* and *Oniscus aselus*, and pill bug, *Armadillidium vulgare*, were the ones I caught. They are gray, have 14 legs, and eat decaying plants and animals. The main difference to nonscientists: pillbugs can roll themselves into a ball and sowbugs can't.

Ecologists call our particular isopods "synanthropes," a term used to refer to animals that live in close relationship with people. Without us, our most common roly polies would not be here; all three came from Europe and have been in this country since at least 1818, when entomologist Thomas Say first described them. They probably arrived in Seattle in ballast on ships. A total of 16 species of woodlice live in Washington, half of which are native.

Like most people, I like tiggy hogs. They don't bite or sting. Their legs are hidden so you don't generally see all that itch-inducing movement. They neither stink nor squish when you crush them. They stay out of the sun and prefer a maritime climate, such as we have in Seattle. In addition, they have many splendid, less obvious features. They brood their young in a kangaroo-like pouch, known as a marsupium. They can reproduce parthenogenetically, Latin for "virgin birth," and if infested by the bacteria

Wolbachia, males function as females. They are good conservationists, eating their own feces as a means to retrieve extra nutrients. Finally, sowbugs can drink water through their rear ends using two appendages known as uropods. Pillbugs, however, lack this equipment, a loss that enables them to roll into a ball, to avoid predators.

As you may have surmised, I like many bugs besides sowbugs, thus putting me in a category with about 10 other people in this country. In a poll conducted by the University of Arizona in 1984, only 6 percent of the respondents said they enjoyed urban arthropods in their yards. The number dropped to .7 percent if the critters were inside their homes, with nearly 90 percent replying that they disliked or were afraid of indoor bugs. When asked how much they liked certain arthropods versus other animals, interviewees rated four of the bugs even lower than the most disliked mammal, skunks.

The situation is so bad that even entomologists suffer, a subject explored poignantly in entomologist May Berenbaum's collection of essays, *Buzzwords: A Scientist Muses on Sex, Bugs, and Rock'n'Roll.* For example, in a world populated with bug-related superheroes, how can no entomologist be the alter ego of these arthropod-enhanced superbeings? They fare no better in literature, where H.G. Wells described an entomologist as "a man of dull presence . . . in shape not unlike a water-barrel," or in Hollywood, which depicts them as evil, inept, or merely fashion-challenged. Berenbaum even cites a study claiming that entomologists earn less than their counterparts in 17 other life-science disciplines, which may account for why they don't have time to save the world.

One of the big questions that long-suffering entomologists ask is why so many people fear bugs. Historically, people believed that if something or someone, be it bug or beast, frightened a pregnant woman she would pass this fear on to her unborn child. Freud interpreted animal phobias as a stand-in for a child's jealous and hostile feelings for his father. A more modern, sexually enlightened approach blames arachnophobia on a "childhood inability to separate mother from self and is tied to our urban, capitalistic society." Still others take the long-term, biological view that we have an innate fear of objects that can harm us. The "run-away, run-away" theory holds that early humans who avoided danger gained a selective advantage.

Or maybe we develop fear from a bad encounter or because someone taught us to avoid bugs.

Entomophobia and arachnophobia, as these fears get classified, appear most often between the ages of one and seven in both sexes. As they get older, however, a female's tendency toward entomophobia becomes much higher. One reason cited for this discrepancy is that males may not admit their fear. Most people lose this phobia by their teenage years, although residual fear probably exists throughout our lives. As one researcher asked, "Is there a little Miss Muffet in all of us?"

Our fear of most insects and arachnids does not make sense. As Sue Hubbell points out in her excellent book, *A Book of Bugs: Broadsides from the Other Orders*, "The majority of bugs neither help nor harm us. They are indifferent to us and our doings, whether we like them or not." We benefit from bugs through their consumption of other bugs, speeding decomposition in forests, and pollination of plants. And who would like a world without honey?

Hubbell admits that some spiders and insects bite, sting, and spread disease; that some people are allergic to the venom; and that the venom can kill. Fewer than one percent of the population, however, is allergic to bees and wasps, and in the United States, few people get life-threatening or death-causing diseases from arthropods. When a bug-related disease does make it into the headlines, it often gets blown out of proportion. Judging from the press coverage in 2002, I would have thought that anyone who ventured outside east of the Rockies, and especially in Michigan or Illinois, the two hardest hit states, would be lucky to escape the teeming swarms of mosquitoes carrying West Nile Virus. Yet only 4,156 people were infected with West Nile and only 284 people died from it around the country.

I do not mean to belittle those deaths and illnesses, but I am not sure that it means we should indiscriminately spray malathion and other insecticides in an attempt to kill every mosquito we can. Of the nearly 50 species of mosquito in Washington state, only nine have been found elsewhere in the country to carry West Nile Virus and not all of these are competent disease vectors. Lab tests indicate that only two readily pass the disease. One is moderately efficient, two inefficient, and the remaining four have not been tested.

Despite our general overreaction, it is important that we be aware of this and other bug problems—stings, bites, allergies, diseases, and poisons—that Hubbell notes. I favor a practical approach to bug management. Be aware and react if they threaten you. Destroy the wasp nest if it is built in an area that you use regularly; otherwise leave it alone. If you go hiking in tick country, wear long sleeve shirts, pants, and check yourself when you get home. Capture and carry outside the spider you find in your house. Give ladybugs and lacewings time to eat your aphids. Don't buy a bug light, unless you want to attract mosquitoes and kill beneficial insects. Rushing out with pesticides and insecticides is shortsighted and potentially dangerous.

I know that not all of these solutions are easy and workable. I have killed my fair share of mosquitoes and yellowjackets. However, I know that most invertebrates I encounter don't want anything to do with me, and so I try to not go into hysterics when I feel threatened.

Two groups of insects garner popular support, despite the near-universal dislike for bugs. Ladybugs and butterflies share a common reputation for beauty, bright coloration, and gentility. Butterflies also have one additional attribute: a nonspecialist can easily identify many butterfly species. Over the last couple of years I have joined a growing number of people known as "butterflyers." It began when I took a class on how to identify local butterflies. I then joined the Washington Butterfly Association and started to go on field trips to exotic places, such as eastern Washington, to look for butterflies. I bought a butterfly net, special butterfly-oriented binoculars (they focus to about five feet), a bug box, and a shelf of butterfly field guides. I have now seen about a third of the state's 140 or so species.

Marjorie and I have also dug up our front lawn and tried to replace it with butterfly-friendly plants. This includes flowers for nectar, but also shrubs and flowers where larvae can eat leaves and adults can lay eggs. It was on one such plant that I had my greatest thrill as a friend of bugs. On May 15, 2003, while trimming one of our ocean sprays (*Holodiscus discolor*), I noticed what at first I thought was bird poop. When I looked more closely, I discovered that the poop was moving and that it had two yellowish humps, two black horns, and a white and olive body. I eventually figured out that it was the larva, or caterpillar, of a Lorquin's admiral, a black, white, and orange butterfly that I had seen in our yard several times the previous year. Lorquin's are fun butterflies to watch because the territorial males will perch on a plant until an intruder, any species from a bumblebee to me, passes by. He will then fly after the invader, often returning to the same perch after successfully defending his territory. My caterpillar's only movements were to go from leaf to leaf, munching tip to stem.

I continued to watch the larva until May 22, when it attached its rear end to a branch of ocean spray. When I looked two days later, a chrysalis, or pupa, had replaced the caterpillar. It was about one inch long, whitish with brown patches where its wings were developing, with a brown knob sticking out opposite the wing cases. I cut the branch where the pupa hung and took it inside to a cardboard and screen box I had made for holding insects.

On the morning of June 7, I carried my bug cage from the kitchen to my office. During transport the pupa twitched back and forth like a swing. It continued to do this off and on for another hour or so, until during one short period when I was working on my computer, the butterfly emerged. I must have missed the emergence by about 10 minutes, because the wings had mostly inflated when I first noticed them. The butterfly's beauty stunned me. The colors looked alive, especially the wingtips, which seemed to dance like the flames they resembled. On the undersides I could trace each black vein as it passed by pumpkin blotches, white ovals, and gray-blue chevrons. This was not the first time I had seen such a fresh butterfly. Nevertheless I marveled at the intensity of the colors, as if they had been mixed and displayed for the first time. I am always tempted to freeze and kill butterflies, to preserve this moment, but I never do. Despite my ability to withstand *Harpaphe* cyanide I am a big softy.

Since the butterfly did not have flight-ready wings, I nudged it off its abandoned chrysalid onto my index finger and carried it outside. As I sat in the sun, I thought that something was right with the world. I had planted a native shrub, a native butterfly had found it, and its offspring now crawled across my hand. I couldn't ask for a better way to spend my morning. Unless I had been hunting flies.

Much ignorance, not unmingled with some prejudice and incredulity, existed abroad for many years in regard to the climate of Washington. And this not withstanding the earnest efforts of the first settlers and the pioneer press to enlighten the outside world.

CHARLES PROSCH, *REMINISCENCES OF WASHINGTON TERRITORY*, 1904

All took shelter in it (a cabin) from the rain, which was falling more or less every day, but we did not regard it with much concern and seldom lost any time on that account.

ARTHUR DENNY, *PIONEER DAYS ON PUGET SOUND*, 1908

Sunshine in Seattle is a funny thing. During the first clear days of spring, I almost hesitate to go outside for fear of the euphoria. The path around Green Lake, which had been pleasantly quiet for the past few months, now teems with people. Everyone sports goofy grins. They wave at each other. Friends stop and chat in the middle of the trail, as if they have not seen each other in years. And where did all those dogs come from? I rarely see more than a dog or two on my thrice-daily neighborhood walks, but on sunny days everyone seems to have one.

Bike riding can be hazardous, too, dodging pale people on their rusty Rollerblades and squeaky bikes. I can't count the number of times I have nearly been run over by cars turning one way with the driver gawking in the other direction at fellow sunseekers. Once people find a coveted parking spot, which they can't seem to do without swerving in front of me, they then like to sit or stand in the bike lane fiddling with gear they haven't used in six months. It is enough to make me wish for clouds.

Despite my hesitancy to go out, I feel that I must. If not, I might be berated by friends. They will remind me that it has rained nearly 20 inches in the first four months of the year. They will accuse me of squandering the day. "You have to go out right now. This is Seattle. You must get some sun while you can," my friends will say.

In contrast, the sun of summer leads to another odd reaction from locals. Seattleites can get too much of a good thing. At my brother's outdoor wedding, in early September on a classic warm, dry day, my wife overheard an elderly, native guest say, "I can't take this sun anymore" before she scampered inside. The temperature peaked at 71 degrees that day.

I am not sure if this woman was referring to the sun on that particular day or to the previous two and a half months of clear weather. Summer is Seattle's little secret, our reward for a seemingly endless winter. We consistently get dry, warm weather from July through September, the result of a high-pressure cell lingering off the coast, which blocks maritime weather. Our average rainfall during this three-month period is less than half of Tucson, Arizona, about three inches compared to the desert's six-plus.

At the time of my brother's nuptials, Marjorie and I lived in Moab. I was used to extended periods of 100 degrees or more. On several days during my nine years in the desert I endured temperatures of 113 degrees, made worse by the polyester-knit National Park Service shirt I had to wear. I scoffed at the wedding guest's heat and sunlight aversion. Wimp! You don't know true heat.

Now, four years after moving back to Seattle, I react in a similar manner, shying away from our occasional heat wave. I do have an additional excuse: in 1996, I had a small speck of skin cancer removed from my neck, but regardless I think I would have adopted a preference for temperate over hot. Interestingly, my skin cancer may have developed in my youth in Seattle, when I never wore sunblock, rather than in Utah.

I like the gray in part because it does keep many less adventuresome folks indoors and because I don't have to feel guilty if I stay indoors. I also get bored with Seattle's summer weather. Endless days of clear, low-humidity, 75-degree weather may make many locals happy, but by mid-August I am ready to don a sweater, get pelted by rain, and go on walks without the crowds.

Despite our beautiful summers, Seattle has a reputation as a dreary, rainy, gray place. And we are defensive about it. Although I and many other locals may joke about our weather, we do not appreciate others denigrating our soggy climate. When pushed, which usually requires only a simple slight, we immediately rattle off the one vital weather statistic taught to every child in Seattle schools, worshiped by members of the Seattle Chamber of Commerce and inscribed on the city seal: "Seattle gets less rain than New York!" End of discussion. What else needs to be said?

Northwesterners have been hauling out similar statistics since meteorologists first began to tally such numbers. Although the earliest-known
scientific report on Oregon and Washington weather, written in 1888 by General
Adolphus Washington Greely of the Signal Service, did not specifically compare numbers, it did observe that "contrary to the generally-received opinion"
enormous amounts of rainfall only dropped on six percent of the region. In
1893, Beamer S. Pague, head of the Signal Service's Portland office, did list
numbers and favorably compared Portland's rainfall to New York and 36 additional cities. He concluded that "On the face of this, it is sure that the term
'Webfoot' . . . is truly a misnomer."

The comparison became so ingrained in our character that in his 1972
history of Seattle, longtime resident Nard Jones opened his section on
weather with an apocryphal account of how locals earn a few bucks with this
statistic. Jones wrote that the scam generally works this way: Local goes to
bar. Man sits next to him. Local, being the typically friendly Seattleite, starts
a conversation, slowly turning it toward weather. Local mentions aforementioned
statistic. Man guffaws. Local asks if man wants to make a wager. Sucker agrees.
Local calls weather bureau. Man asks question and learns the truth. Man shells
out for next Rainier Ale.

I don't know when I first learned this fact, but I do have memories of citing it to friends in college who derided our fair city's infamous weather. Yes,
it rains in Seattle but you should see New York. Or what about New Orleans
or Miami? At 62 and 59 inches, respectively, these are dens of soggy iniquity
compared to our practically arid 38 inches or so. Like many Seattleites I acknowl-
edged our dreary image but wanted to show that it really wasn't so bad. Hey,
we are nice folks up here and people shouldn't poke fun at us. Being an
honest sort I did not make any bets myself.

Even those who admit that Seattle can be wet and cloudy turn this toward
an advantage. We like to say that our mild, maritime climate translates to good
growing conditions, healthy skin, and low mental stress. A 1924 pamphlet
distributed by the Chamber of Commerce labeled the weather "filtered
sunshine" and described how it is "best for all, and vital to the development
of the most energetic peoples." Others, such as Archibald Menzies, botanist
on George Vancouver's 1792 exploration of Puget Sound, and Walter Rue,

former weather columnist for the *Seattle Post-Intelligencer*, simply summed up the local weather as "salubrious."

I also like to remind the less fortunate that Seattle lacks the extremes that make other spots miserable. Official records list only one day, January 31, 1950, when the thermometer hit zero—at SeaTac airport—nearly 35 degrees below the average monthly low. In the city, the scientifically verified record stands at 3 degrees, although Arthur Denny reported –2 degrees in January 1862, when ice formed six inches deep in Lake Union.

We have peaked at 100 degrees only twice, on June 9, 1955 and July 16, 1941, and once at SeaTac on July 20, 1994. Unofficially, and universally not believed, our record high came in June 1866, when the temperature hit "114 degrees in the shade," according to author J. Willis Sayre in his 1936 book, *This City of Ours*. Otherwise we average 75 degrees for our monthly highs in July and August, our warmest and driest months.

Of course, I fail to tell dubious friends all the statistics. For instance, Seattle's three inches of rain from July through August represents less than a tenth of annual precipitation, while Tucson's six equals more than half its yearly total. We average 201 days of cloudy weather per year. From October to March, the unofficial wet season, the sun shines on only 30 percent of the days. Rain falls 150 days of the year. Summer weather does not truly begin until July 4. During the weeks around the shortest day of the year, the sun creeps above the horizon for only about 8.5 hours per day. It rained 39 inches from November through March of my first winter back to Seattle.

Despite the months of wet grayness, the number one weather complaint that I heard from friends who knew I was writing about local weather was not about Seattle's rain but about Seattle's forecasters. How come those folks can't get it right? You would think that with all the advances in science over the past few years they could at least correctly tell me whether it is going to rain. Even with new data-gathering technology and better computer models, predicting temperature, winds, precipitation, or cloudiness in Seattle still presents a significant challenge.

Modern-day weather forecasting relies on complex computer models to generate accurate predictions. Feed data—which comes from weather balloons, released twice a day around the globe, satellite images, surface weather stations, aircraft, ocean buoys, and radar—into the equations and out pops a forecast, generally reliable out to about three or four days. The more numbers plugged in, the better the prediction, with each model building off of the previous one.

In the Northwest, though, we run into a snag because most of our weather comes from the Pacific Ocean, where weather data are sparse. Only one location between Seattle and the ocean, Quilluyute, releases weather balloons, an essential data provider because they show a vertical profile of atmospheric conditions. Satellites help by showing ocean cloud cover but they cannot directly measure surface conditions, vertical changes, temperature, wind speed, or relative humidity. Boats, buoys, and airplanes add more observations, but compared with Kansas, for example, where forecasters often have more than a 1,000 miles to track, analyze, and understand a system, our forecasters are the proverbial blind men at the elephant. They only see a small part of the weather and have to use their best judgment to decide what will happen.

Topography adds another layer of uncertainty to the equation. What starts as a quasi-in-balance weather system moving over the relatively slick ocean surface changes dramatically when it hits the coast. A front may get stuck on the Olympics or be cleaved by them. Terrain may enhance or shadow precipitation. Once a storm system flows around the Olympics, it may drop rain along the waterfront, snow at higher elevations, or dissipate completely. Nearly any day of the year, I can pass in and out of sun, fog, rain, headwinds, and tailwinds in a single, one-hour-long ride across our hill-and-trough topography.

In contrast, topography also removes some degree of freedom. Meteorologists know that most storms will be stopped and/or stalled by the Cascades, channeled by Puget Sound, and split by the Olympics. For the careful observer then, topography can provide a level of predictability, although not one to place big bets on.

Two studies in the late 1980s reveal the complexity of local topography and how it creates microclimates. The first, led by Mark Albright, a UW research meteorologist, set out 95 gauges around Seattle to collect precipitation from September 1, 1986, through May 31, 1987. Albright discovered that Seattle has a banana belt that runs along the Ship Canal from the UW across the lake to Hunt's Point. Only 33 to 36 inches of precipitation fell in the nine-month period compared to the veritable rain forest that stretches from Vashon Island through White Center to about Highway 99, where 45 to 50 inches fell in the same period. Montlake and the east end of the 520 bridge also had the highest temperatures in surveys conducted around the county on November 28, 1987 and February 24, 1988. Other wet spots include Lake City, Queen Anne, and Capitol Hill, which received up to 11 inches more than the UW campus.

A lack of data and topographic challenges make our local meteorologists and atmospheric scientists the butt of more ire than any other scientists, in part because their field is one of the few sciences exposed to the public. No one expects physicists or chemists to predict the future, especially on a daily basis. "If they did, they would appear just as stupid as a meteorologist," says Brad Colman of the National Weather Service.

Seattle's milquetoast weather creates a third challenge for forecasters, especially when predicting snow, which requires adding cold to our normal, nearly constant winter flow of mild, wet air from the Pacific Ocean. Freezing temperatures, however, rarely occur in winter, primarily because the Cascades block chilly continental air from flowing west and south into Puget Sound. Snow only falls when arctic air moves down from British Columbia (the coldest of this air sneaks in through the Fraser River Valley) and collides with a Pacific system.

The difficulty for forecasters lies in that even when these arctic flows reach Seattle, the temperature can be so close to the freezing point that a degree or two difference means snow or rain. Mix in Puget Sound and Lake Washington—both usually warmer than the surrounding air, and hilly topography, which results in vertical temperature gradients—and precipitation may fall as snow inland and at higher spots, and as rain along the water. In addition, if forecasters predict one-quarter inch of rain and a half inch falls, no one complains, but that quarter-inch difference translates to over two additional inches of snow.

A fine manifestation of this scenario occurred while I was at work on this chapter. The weather forecast for March 7 called for snow in Seattle. I ran outside to see the first flakes but when I looked up I saw snow dropping out of a clear blue sky. The only cloud was a thin white smudge hovering high to the southeast. Several more tantalizing interludes of falling snow did pass over the house, but it did not begin to stick until around 10:00 P.M.

I awoke the next day to an inch of accumulation in our yard but none on the roads or sidewalks. Residents of Beacon Hill, south Capitol Hill, and points east, received up to six inches of snow. They were also treated to thunder and lightning, a rare event for Seattle snowstorms. SeaTac Airport had a strange snow distribution, too, with four inches accumulating at one end of its 6,000-foot-long runway and no snow at the other end.

Because of its scarcity, snow, like those first days of sunshine, gives Seattleites an excuse to be exuberant. In the four years since we moved back to Seattle, I have only experienced one good snow. Seven inches fell on February 16, 2001, in what local media boldly proclaimed "Snow Storm 2001!" My early morning walk with Taylor was great. No cars. No trash. A hushed silence. (A mild panic did occur, however, because our electricity was out and I couldn't grind our coffee. Nor could our neighbors. I ended up walking a mile or so to a friend's for a cup. Desperate times call for desperate acts.)

When I went out later, a carnival atmosphere had spread around the neighborhood. Work had been cancelled for many. Kids were out sledding with their parents. Neighbors greeted each other in the streets. Mass snowball fights erupted on car-free roads. Snowmen dotted yards, parks, and school grounds. Cross-country ski tracks cut across the field near our house. People were out walking, many with their dogs.

Although I thoroughly enjoyed that storm, a lack of snow does create several positive effects. Our budget-strapped city does not have to spend money on snow removal. Schools stay open when they are supposed to be open and kids get their full dose of summer. People don't get heart attacks shoveling snow and they don't drive their SUVs in conditions they can't handle, a problem that would be enhanced by Seattle's hilly topography.

Seattle's lack of snow is another weather phenomenon that frustrates both meteorologists and friends with whom I talked. Several friends wanted to know why we were getting less now than when they were young and others wanted more snow to fall in the city. Data does show that less snow dropped in the 1970s, 1980s, and 1990s than in previous decades, but with our parsimonious annual average of 10.7 inches, saying that more fell in one's youth does not mean much; it would only take one big storm to push us over the average.

Seattle gets these big storms rarely. The last came in December 1996, when up to a foot of snow accumulated. Unfortunately, above-freezing temperatures and precipitation followed immediately, which led to hundreds of landslides around Puget Sound, most the result of soil saturation and slippage along the Esperance Sand–Lawton Clay contact. Other big snow winters hit Seattle in 1969, 1950, 1916, 1893, 1880, and 1861–62. February 2, 1916, holds the record for most snow in 24 hours with 21.5 inches, although six-foot drifts accumulated "unofficially" in the Big Snow of 1880.

My snow-loving friends, however, might get their wishes answered. Research shows that we may have entered a phase of wetter and colder weather. Scientists term this phenomenon, only discovered in the past decade, the Pacific Decadal Oscillation (PDO) and describe it as a hemisphere-scale, decades-long climatic regime. Like El Niño, the PDO is cyclic, but instead of lasting a year or so, it can affect climate for 15 to 25 years, producing either cold-wet or warm-dry phases. Intriguingly, most of our big snow winters coincided with the cool PDO regimes, which occurred from 1890 to 1924 and 1947 to 1976.

PDO scientists cannot say for certain that we have emerged out of a warm-dry regime (the 1976–77 shift took a decade to recognize), but they would not be surprised if the winter of 1997–98 marked the change to cool and wet. If we have entered this new regime, then we can expect significant changes not only to snowfall, but also to marine ecosystems. For instance, a cool phase favors higher production of salmon stocks in Washington, Oregon, and California, with the opposite effect in Alaska. We may also see spring flowers blooming later, a drop in Pacific halibut production, increases in Alaska shrimp, herring, pollock and capelin, and a corresponding rise in marine birds and pinnipeds, which rely on these prey.

One question that arises out of PDO research is how we will respond. For the first time in history, we may have the knowledge to recognize that we have entered a temporary period of good snowpacks, above-average stream flows, and increased salmon stocks. Will we exploit these surpluses to the maximum and forget about the resource depletion of the warm and dry regime, or will we scale back our consumption accordingly and realize the need to tread more lightly, knowing that what goes around comes around? I can only hope that our newfound knowledge will make us wiser.

A better understanding of the Pacific Decadal Oscillation and El Niño is helping weather and climate forecasts, but on a day-to-day basis many challenges still exist, particularly in spring, the hardest time to predict. Spring's biggest challenge is the precipitation-producing Puget Sound Convergence Zone (PSCZ). The term first appeared in print in 1969 in an unpublished internal National Weather Service document and become popular in the 1980s when UW atmospheric sciences professor Cliff Mass published the first detailed paper on it. Mass's paper describes the phenomenon as a "band of enhanced cloudiness and precipitation in the central and northern Sound with clear skies to the north and south." This results in concentrated zones of rain or snow, which often migrate up and down the Sound.

The Puget Sound Convergence Zone has come to be one of the best known of our local weather events, with most people simply calling it the Convergence Zone. One local paper, however, did refer to it as the Puget Sound Conversion Zone. I did not see the article but I have it on good authority that they were talking about weather and not a particularly successful area of proselytizing.

Topography controls PSCZ formation. In certain conditions, coastal surface winds moving on shore split in two around the Olympic Mountains, and flow down both the Strait of Juan de Fuca and through the Chehalis Gap, a glacial-outwash-carved lowland between the Olympics to the north and the Willapa Hills to the south. Enhanced precipitation occurs where the split fronts reunite, usually around Everett. The Convergence Zone most often forms two to four times per month between April and June and less frequently but evenly throughout the rest of the year.

The PSCZ also reflects another weather phenomenon in Puget Sound: the diurnal change in winds. Wind results from the uneven distribution of pressure, which itself reflects the weight of the air above, and flows from high to low pressures. In western Washington, the daily variation of temperature between land and water creates a conspicuous and consistent set of pressure changes. In spring and summer, typical early morning (3:00 A.M. to 6:00 A.M.)

winds push weakly toward the central Sound from the north and the south. As the land begins to warm, however, wind speed increases—land warms faster than water and creates less dense air that expands and rises—and the wind, known as a sea breeze, flows off the water, upslope toward the mountains. By late afternoon, when winds are generally strongest, air flows counterclockwise on the east side of the Sound and clockwise on the west side, producing our typical northerly late-day winds. The wind switches direction again around 9:00 P.M. as the land loses heat faster than the water and the dense air drops toward the Sound.

Because of this diurnal circulation pattern, the Convergence Zone tends to form early in the day in the northern part of Puget Sound. It moves south throughout the day, dropping moisture, and, if land breezes are strong enough, moves back north in the late evening. This occurred on the day that I wrote this section, the weather report describing it as "Convergence zone marching up and down the Sound." The big challenge, and one that no models can accurately predict, is how fast and how far the band of moisture will travel.

Summer exhibits another consistent but less well known weather phenomenon, termed the "onshore push" or "surge." We feel the push when dry, hot weather gives way to cool days with persistent low clouds. The driving force comes from our old nemesis, California. Initially, a low-pressure system or trough of warm air from California's central valley begins to move north into Oregon, pulling a band of low-level gray clouds along the coast with it. The trough generally pushes into British Columbia by the third hot day in Washington and leaves a ridge of high pressure off the coast.

The pressure gradient between the coast and inland forces air to flow toward Puget Sound, bringing cool, moist marine weather. Depending upon the gradient, we can get anything from clear skies to low clouds between 2,500 and 4,000 feet, temperature drops of 9 degrees to 18 degrees, and strong surface winds. Because the pressure gradient can vary widely and because a subtle contrast can be the difference between clear and cloudy, forecasting this event can challenge even the best prognosticators. One nice feature, however, is that if you can get above 5,000 or 6,000 feet in the Cascades, you can escape the onshore surge of gray.

The Weather Service's Brad Colman calls the push "our regional air conditioner." "We cannot get long-term heat waves because the onshore push always develops during our periods of high temperature and low humidity," he says. And for that, many locals, including me, are thankful. We certainly don't want that heat wave to go on too long. One of the fine paradoxes of life in the Emerald City is Seattleites complaining about too much sun and heat.

I have had some friends tell me that Seattleites are weather wimps. A Vermont-based buddy laughed when I told her the local National Weather Service office holds press conferences to announce that snow is a possibility. My Utah pals chide me when I describe the anguish caused by a record-breaking heat wave of 90-degree days. We may not have temperatures that require our own ice-making machines or that would lead us to round up our Canada geese and pluck them for their feathers but we do have conditions that many so-called weather studs cannot handle, monotonously gray, sprinkly, and temperate.

I ask my hardy friends, "If we are such wimps, then why do you always paint a picture of how bad our weather is and question how anyone can live here?" I wonder how many of them could survive a winter where it rained 90 out of 120 days. Or how about spring temperatures that persist into July? They are merely weather sprinters, having to survive a few days of –30-degree temperatures, storms that drop two feet of snow, or a week of 105-degree-plus weather. We are the marathoners, enduring months of rain and weeks where the sun is only a rumor.

One aspect of other people's weather of which I am jealous, however, is their local language. When we lived in Boston, we were lucky enough to see a "nor'easter" drop nearly seven inches of rain in under 24 hours. During my college days in Colorado, I remember many Chinooks raging down the Rockies, burning through snow like a supercharged blow dryer. Traveling around Washington, one can feel similar winds: the Palouser, or "cow killer," east of the mountains, and the Coho, in the Columbia River Gorge. In Australia, they call an onshore surgelike event a "southerly buster," while South Africans call their warming winds "the Cape Doctor." California has fire-breathing Santa Ana winds, the northeast has the bone chilling Alberta Clipper, the Great Plains has sky-darkening Black Blizzards, and Texas has the numbing Blue Norther.

I am surprised that for such a weather-focused, as well as book-oriented, population, we have few, if any, indigenous weather terms. One might think that in a location where precipitation falls in many guises for nine or ten months a year, a vocabulary would have developed, but Seattle's self-generated, rain-related language is as dry as Phoenix.

Instead we borrow terms from elsewhere. Light rain, shower, intermittent rains, heavy rain, thunderstorm, sprinkle, mist, mizzle, drizzle, fog. I like drizzle—the word and the weather. The susurrant *Z*s float lightly from my lips, an onomatopoetic expression of the mildness of our weather. The word, whose exact etymology is cloudy, first appeared in the sixteenth century in England. The *Oxford English Dictionary* (OED) defines drizzle as "very fine, dense, spray-like drops." Both Shakespeare and Marlowe incorporated the young term, although they could not agree on the spelling, which ranged from *drizled* to *drissels* to *drizzle*.

Phillip Church, former chair of the UW Department of Atmospheric Sciences, also favored the word, especially in his landmark 1974 article "Some Precipitation Characteristics of Seattle," which I subtitle: "One Man's Valiant Attempt to use Statistics to Point Out to the World that Weather Here is Better than You Might Think." Numbers were Church's forte. He looked at annual and monthly amounts, but his real insights came from examining hourly records, which NOAA began to record in October 1948. From the hourly data, Church determined that "it rains a mere 11 percent of the time." January was the peak month, with more than .01 inch of precipitation per hour falling during 22 percent of the hours of the month. July and August both received rain only three percent of the time. I wonder how much lower the numbers would have been if Church had examined a warm-dry PDO instead of a cool-wet one.

Church also derived a table of intensity, which he broke into six categories: light, moderate, and heavy drizzle, and light, moderate, and heavy rain. The three drizzle levels accounted for 72.5 percent of the precipitation with "light" drizzle (less than .01 inch per hour) falling over half that time. He concluded with a statement that would make any gadfly proud: "Because of the preponderance of 'drizzle' intensities one might truthfully say that it rarely 'rains' in Seattle." Or as one pioneer woman put it, "our rains are dry rains."

The English also gave us another weather-related word, but one less familiar to those outside certain special climates. In 1826, Plymouth, England-born poet Noel Thomas Carrington coined the then-hyphenated phrase "sun-breaks," a term the OED defines as a "burst of sunshine." Carrington, who had been a seaman before starting a school in his hometown, wrote a flowery paean to the landscape of his coastal home. He penned his less-than-famous line "O Plym, beloved to thee I owe the few bright sun-breaks, that cheer'd My toilsome pilgrimage!" in a book-length poem titled "Dartmoor."

Sunbreak is not a term I ever heard in Moab; it is a descriptor best applied to overcast places, places that need the optimism of potential sun. (As opposed to my Tucson-based brother-in-law who said, "Yeah, we can use a break from the sun," when I asked if he knew the term.) Like many others since then, Carrington recognized the symbolic importance of these momentary glimpses of sunlight, using his beloved river Plym as a metaphor for hope and salvation.

In the interests of language, I would like to propose a few Seattle-specific weather terms. We could refer to June's non-summerlike cool, overcast days as *iced-decaf Americano* weather. Take a normal drink, black coffee, or weather, sunny and warm, remove the essential elixir, chill, and then add water. I must admit I can tolerate the weather more than the drink. Or how about *Indian* or *Duwamish days*, for the one surprisingly good week of weather that generally occurs in February. We could also refer to our six-month-plus winter as *Windows* weather; it's not that pleasant and we wish it would improve but at least everyone else is in the same boat.

No matter what the language, our weather has made me an optimist, or at least a realist. I know it's going to rain but we might have a few dapples of sun breaking through. Either way I can still bike, garden, walk Taylor, or go backpacking. If it's really raining hard, I can always relax at home, go to a movie, or read a book.

And we are virtually assured of dry, sunny days in the summer, when most people have the time to get out and enjoy it. The days are long and we revel in temperatures hot enough to savor but not too warm to force us to spend money on air conditioning. The long, warm days also come when our gardens need the heat and sunlight. It's not like we can't grow tomatoes in Seattle.

Seattle is a city of hills, and the Seattleite who has been inoculated with the Seattle spirit is just as proud of his hills as he is of his Puget Sound, his lakes, and his parks.

SEATTLE POST-INTELLIGENCER, JULY 23, 1905

The Hill (Denny) was too high and too steep to be utilized for business purposes, so that inevitably the Hill had to be removed.

VON TARBILL, HARVARD BUSINESS REVIEW,
JULY 1930

"Seattle's hills have been its pride and they have been its problem; they have given the city distinction and they have stood in the way of progress," wrote Sophie Frye Bass in her 1947 memoir, *When Seattle Was a Village.* As the granddaughter of city founder Arthur Denny, Bass was in a good position to witness the early history of Seattle, and her book is often credited with popularizing the sentimental notion that Seattle was built on seven hills, just like ancient Rome.

I have heard this topographic claim for as long as I can remember. During my youth, I liked the sound of it; I thought the comparison gave the city an air of distinction. As I matured and became more skeptical, I began to question the details—hills seem to be everywhere—and wondered if some early marketer had invented the idea. Besides, I now viewed the world through my geocentric eyes and had to look for a more coherent story of Seattle's underlying topography. When I moved back to the city, I decided to try to test the theory of the seven hills. Had I been misled as a youth or did we share this hilly quirk with that other city well known for its espresso? Which ones were the magical seven, and could I conquer them in a single, possibly never-before-attempted bike ride?

My initial task of naming the seven seemed simple but proved more challenging than I expected. My friends and family said they had heard the claim but few agreed with Bass, who listed Beacon, Capitol, Denny, First, Queen Anne, Profanity, and Renton. Bass's first five made most lists but only my mom had heard of Profanity and Renton, also known as Yesler and Second, respectively. Some pinned their hopes on Magnolia and West Seattle, but others favored Mount Baker Ridge, Phinney Ridge, Sunset Hill, or Crown Hill. One overachiever even declared that Seattle is blessed with fifteen hills.

I also talked with someone who questioned the entire debate on the seven hills. Brewster Denny, a family friend, is Arthur Denny's great-grandson. He expressed a good-natured bias toward his aunt and said, "I don't see what the controversy is, Sophie was right." Denny sees the seven hills idea as part of the whole picture of commerce and growth. "If you look at the early developments—the university, the opera house—it is clear that the seven hills idea fits in with the early inhabitants' dream of the region's destiny for development and fame," he said. "After all, Arthur Denny recognized how poor a site Alki was and purposely set out to find a location suitable to develop a great city built around a great harbor."

Right or not, Aunt Sophie was not the first to call attention to the hilly heptad. The earliest mention that I could find of seven hills came from a 1906 issue of *Washington Magazine*, a short-lived periodical oriented toward history, architecture, and community. A piece titled "A City for Tourists" contained the line "From a thousand points in the city, that like ancient Rome was founded on seven hills. . . . " Like many early histories, articles, and personal reminiscences, the *Washington* article cited only Seattle's topographical plenitude, and did not name an ideal seven.

These early voices mostly moan about the problems associated with hills. For example, two early engineers thought that people shouldn't have to trouble themselves with walking. Instead they proposed escalators to ferry people and beasts up the slopes. Legendary city engineer Reginald Thomson also had a skewed view of the topography. "Looking at local surroundings, I felt that Seattle was in a pit, that to get anywhere we would be compelled to climb out if we could. I resolved to persevere to the end," Thomson wrote in his memoir, *That Man Thomson.*

Perseverance translated to regrading for Thomson. He authorized hill sluicing, gully filling, and tideflat raising, which led to the relocation of 50 million cubic yards of material, roughly equivalent to a traffic jam of dirt-filled Ford Expeditions stretching from Seattle to Boston and back twice. Local newspaperman Wilford Beaton summed up the historic viewpoint on the topography in his history of Seattle, *The City that Made Itself.* "The hills raised themselves in

The Seven (or Nine) Hills of Seattle

the paths that commerce wished to take. And then man stepped in, completed the work which Nature left undone, smoothed the burrows and allowed commerce to pour unhampered in its natural channels."

Early citizens may not have cottoned on to romantic notions of rocky knolls offering scenic views of majestic mountains, but by Aunt Sophie's time it had become a raging issue. A letter to the *Seattle Times* on March 13, 1950, asking for names of the fabled seven, prompted a rain of responses. Hill advocates listed anywhere between 5 and 10 hills, including long-lost favorites Dumar, Boeing, Nob, and Pigeon Point. Adding a ray of government clarity, the City engineering department officially recognized 12 hills. They included Sophie's original seven plus West Seattle, Magnolia Bluff, Sunset, Crown, and Phinney Ridge.

For most modern Seattleites, West Seattle and Magnolia have moved into the pantheon of seven, substituting for Profanity and Renton. Some local historians quibble with these two because Magnolia did not officially become part of Seattle until annexation in 1891 and West Seattle until 1907. Despite this "technicality" and the fact that Denny has been regraded to a mere blip, conventional wisdom now lists Beacon, Capitol, Denny, First, Magnolia, Queen Anne, and West Seattle as the Seven Hills of Seattle.

Now that I had a good list, I wanted to see if I could conquer them. The spirit of Mallory runs through my veins; the hills were there and I would stand atop each one.

I begin my expedition with Magnolia for the simple reason that it displays the underlying geology better than any other hill. I want to see evidence of the great sheet of ice that covered the Seattle area between 15,000 and 13,650 years ago, the last of at least six periods of glaciation over the last two million years. Geologists call this final cool cleaver of land the Puget lobe of the Cordilleran ice sheet. It was the southwesternmost extension of the epic mass of ice that covered nearly all of Canada during the last ice age, which lasted from 25,000 to 12,000 years ago.

Not wanting to be accused of taking the easy route, I start at sea level at the South Beach section of Discovery Park. The high tide is rising and I can just barely scramble around a low cliff of finely laminated layers of mocha- to cappuccino-colored silts and sands, known as the Olympia beds. In another hour, waves will start to beat against the rock, continuing the eternal battle between stone and sea. A 1994 study found that the sea has the upper hand; these cliffs may retreat as much as 80 feet per century.

The Olympia beds are the lowest and hence oldest layer, deposited by rivers washing onto floodplains in what geologists call an interglacial period, roughly 25,000 to 60,000 years before present. We are in an interglacial now, with a fairly similar environment to the previous one when streams also meandered out of the Cascades through forests and grasslands. The climate was a bit cooler and wetter, with animals such as mammoths and VW Beetle–sized ground sloths living in the area.

High tide is not the only agent of erosion to attack the Olympia beds. Someone has carved JESUS and JEHOVAH in 10-inch-high, 1-inch-deep letters a few feet above high-tide line. I doubt that these two were here in person, but whoever inscribed their names was not alone; Buddy, John, Cliff, Jody, and David, to name just a few of the other graffiti scalawags, also added their marks.

Water from above has also battered this bluff at Magnolia. Blue-gray ooze washes over the Olympia beds, in several spots running as rivulets. More often the muck looks like lumpy shaving cream spread across the lower cliff face. Winter is an especially good time for erosion, and recent storms have generated this mud from the rock unit above the Olympia. Known as the Lawton Clay and named for the military base that originally occupied this site, Fort Lawton, it consists of bands of blue-gray, relatively impermeable sediment, deposited in a glacier-produced lake.

As the climate cooled and the Puget lobe spread south around 17,000 years ago, it dammed the Strait of Juan de Fuca, forming a lake in the lowlands around what would become Puget Sound. Streams gushing out of the glacial mouth deposited fine-grained material into the water. When I find chunks of Lawton Clay near the cliff, I can see distinct, thin layers of silt and clay, which break easily along bedding planes. The small particle size indicates the clay formed in a relatively stable lake environment.

The ice did not tarry in the north, and soon the 4,000-foot-thick ice sheet was nearly in Seattle, plowing south at speeds in excess of 500 feet per year.

Rivers continued to wash out of the glacier but now they deposited sands and silts over the filled-in lake in broad swaths across the landscape. This layer, called Esperance Sand, reaches depths of over 300 feet, although it is only 80 feet thick in this cliff. Esperance sediments are tan and gray with occasional river-channel deposits of gravel and cross beds, inclined layers of sediment formed by water currents pushing grains over ripples.

From the shoreline, I clearly see the contact zone between the Esperance and Lawton, the broad tree- and shrub-covered bench about halfway down the cliff face. The interplay between these two layers causes more consistent problems in Seattle than any other geological phenomenon.

Although the Esperance may look formidable, geologists know it as a weak, not-to-be-trusted unit—at least on steep bluff faces. When wet, the Esperance acts like a giant sponge, soaking up water that gets trapped atop the underlying, impervious Lawton Clay. This reduces soil strength and allows the sand to glide along the slippery clay, sending cliffs, mud, trees, houses, bridges, and cars downslope. Sliding may be slow, called "creep," which is happening to the bench of trees at Magnolia, or quick, as with the winter of 1996–97, when above-normal precipitation led to catastrophic landslides around Puget Sound.

On my ascent up the bluff, I see how the trees battle creep. Most of the alders and maples on the bench lean toward the cliff, as if somebody has tossed a giant lasso around them and is pulling them up the steep face. A few have escaped the noose, however, and now point outward in a slow somersault to the sea. I suspect that another winter or two will send a few more to the shore, as the cliff inexorably loses its battle to the watery agents of erosion.

This contact layer occurs across the city. One of the best ways to find it is to look for landslides and slumping ground, such as the slump on Lakeview Boulevard East, which destroyed several new homes, or the landslide at the west end of the Magnolia Bridge. Landslides have been part of the city "from a time to which the memory of man runneth not back," wrote Thomson. They contributed to peoples' early dislike of the hills and led to a Works Progress Administration project employing over 700 men to work digging trenches, tunnels, and drains, and building footings and retaining walls. Between 1935 and 1941, workers dug over 20,000 feet of drainage trenches.

Springs and seeps are another sign of the Esperance/Lawton contact. They used to occur on every hill in Seattle and were important sources of drinking water, such as the Union Water Company on Queen Anne hill and downtown's Spring Hill Water Company, both of which I describe in my chapter on plants. Their unexpected flows are yet another testimony to the subsurface geology.

Scrambling up the final beds of eroded Esperance Sand, I reach the top, but I have yet to encounter the sedimentary evidence created by the Puget lobe plowing through Seattle. To see the one layer of rock lacking from this bluff, I ride my bike about 1.5 miles south to a small park and walk down 140 steep and often tilted steps to Perkins Lane. After reaching Perkins, I walk out to the end of the road, drop off the edge of the broken asphalt, down and around a dirt path, and end up at the steps of a house, or what is left of it. Torrential rainstorms in February 1996 and December–January 1996–97 generated eight landslides that damaged at least 50 homes along the road. The worst landslide sent five once-permanent houses and the road next to them cascading to the Sound. The cause for this landslide was a weakness in the rock deposited by the glacier passing over Seattle.

Radiocarbon dating shows that ice reached Seattle 15,000 years ago. It continued to move south to about Olympia, where it stalled for 500 to 1,000 years and then retreated to the north, migrating back through Seattle no later than 13,650 years ago. As the ice moved south it ground to bits anything in its path, producing a concretelike layer of rock filled with gravelly sand and scattered cobbles and boulders. Builders know it as "hardpan," while geologists call it Vashon till. It usually caps the Esperance and most of the hills of Seattle.

Leaving the destroyed homes, I walk up to several large Vashon blocks looming above, their sharp edges cleaved from the cliff. Several trickles of sand pour out of one-inch-wide holes that dot the blocks. These pockets and the clean breaks surprised geologists who studied the landslide. Hardpan usually refers to well-cemented, fine-grained sediments, which act as barriers to water and/or roots. The Perkins Lane hardpan, however, contains vertical cracks, which allow water to penetrate the rock until it reaches a sand-rich horizontal layer. Water then flows along the sand lens, creating zones of weakness.

Two other geologic features also play a role in the Perkins Lane landslides. First, Vashon till sits directly on Lawton Clay, which provides a slicker sliding surface than the Esperance. Second, the houses were built at the edge of an older, significantly larger landslide block. Combined with the vertical fractures and horizontal water conduit, this creates an unstable slope, which means that even with good engineering, including hundreds of feet of WPA trenches, pipe, footings, and retaining walls, geologic processes could not be derailed.

Abandoning this sad but impressive spot I climb back up the tilted stairs, which display none-too-subtle evidence that the hill is not as stable as it may look. I get on my bike to continue my noble effort and within five minutes I have reached my first summit—Magnolia. I stand about 50 feet east of the intersection of W Barrett Street and 39th Avenue W. The great massif of Mount Rainier, only 14,004 feet higher than I, rises to the south; Mount Baker dominates the north, and the Olympics and Puget Sound define the west. Crows and starlings cavort noisily on the house closest to me. Sunlight warms my back. The land slopes off in all directions. I am 407 feet above sea level and I am proud.

I also see what geologists call "the most prominent single landform of the entire Puget Lowland." If you look out from this point, and many others around the Sound, you can see that the vast majority of the major hills, both on the islands and on the mainland, top out at roughly the same elevation, around 350 to 450 feet above sea level. For example, Bainbridge Island's high point is around 350 feet, a knoll near Port Gamble rises to 400 feet, and the high spot near Poulsbo is 460 feet.

Geologists hypothesize that just prior to the first arrival of the Puget lobe, a flat plain stretched from the foothills of the Cascades to the Olympics and gently tilted south to around Olympia. No Puget Sound. No big hills or even ridges. Just a Kansaslike planar surface of sand and silt with an occasional high point jutting above the monotony. Streams washing out of the snout of the glacier deposited this plain of Esperance Sand. Then the ice sheet arrived and began to make Seattle out of Kansas.

Early geologists thought that ice carved the dominant features of the landscape, but they were wrong. The accepted theory is that water flowing under the ice in 8 to 10 channels carved the topography of Puget Sound, Lake Washington, Hood Canal, and Lake Sammamish. This may seem implausible, but consider that the Puget lobe was several thousand feet thick, easily enough ice to provide both water and space for sediment-laden rivers the size of the Skagit, which could act like giant belt sanders to cut down through the sand and silt.

After taking a few photographs for posterity I ride north a couple of blocks to Dravus Street and head down to and across a low section formerly known as Pleasant Valley. A short climb brings me to the top of the eastern side of Magnolia. The descent down the east side is steep and fast and soon I am crossing Interbay, once the site of a notorious dump, fabled for fires, gulls, and rats. Before this area became a trash heap and before its life as a navy pier and a rail yard, marshy tidal flats covered most of Interbay and only a narrow isthmus connected Magnolia to the rest of Seattle.

Although I could make a gentle ascent of the west slope of Queen Anne, I decide to ride around the base of the hill, so that I can attempt its south face, better known as the Counterbalance. My best friend lived on Queen Anne when I was younger and it had been a point of pride to ride up the Counterbalance to see him. I want to see if I still can make the ascent. The hill is so steep that when trolley cars ran up it in the first half of the twentieth century they utilized a 16-ton weight on an underground car to help pull the trolley up and slow it going down. When the 32,000-pound counterbalance moved down, the trolley traveled up. The process was reversed for the trolley's descent.

I shift into my "granny" gear and start the slow climb. My little bike computer shows that I am speeding up the hill at about five mph, only three miles per hour slower than the counterbalance-assisted trolley car. At the top I am only a block from the summit but have to detour north, east, and back south to bypass the shortest route, a flight of stairs, to reach Queen Anne's peak at Lee Street and Tower Street.

A laurel hedge and a fire station block my views from this high point of 460 feet, officially called Observatory Park for the views one once could attain by climbing the older of the two water towers that dominate this site. The ladder that wrapped around the handsome stone-and-brick tower, built in

1902, is long gone, and I doubt that in our litigious age Seattle Public Utilities would let anyone ascend. A fence further discourages access.

I like this spot because Lee Street, between First and Tower, is made of sandstone cobbles, a popular road-paving material in Seattle from the 1890s to the 1910s. The most commonly used varieties came from the same quarries as the building stones, particularly Wilkeson, and are about 50 million years old. Street pavers also used Index granite for roads and curbs, where it can still be found on many corners in older parts of Seattle, but they preferred sandstone because it cut easier and provided better traction for horses. Even though rain, wagons, and shoed hooves wore down the stones, they were better than the mud or wood of the past.

Brick was another important paving material and can still be found on a few Seattle streets. In circumstances similar to the emergence of building stone, brick became popular after the Great Fire of 1889 and by the early 1900s local manufacturers could produce 70,000,000 bricks a year. According to John Davies, marketing manager for local brick maker Mutual Materials, nearly 300 brick companies dotted the greater Seattle landscape in the early 1900s. "At nearly every early twentieth-century Seattle job site, which used brick, a little brick company, however temporary, popped up, especially with the abundant supply of mini clay deposits all over the area," he told me.

In addition to the small brick bakers, at least six large factories were situated along the Duwamish River. Most merely scooped Lawton Clay off the bluffs in the valley for source material to make products including building brick, sewer tile, conduit, terra cotta, chimney flu lining, fire brick, drain tile, and flower pots. By the mid-1910s, King County led the nation in producing paving brick. The Denny–Renton Clay and Coal Company made 250,000 paving bricks a day. Local bricks covered streets in Portland, San Francisco, Tokyo, and Los Angeles, as well as Chile, Argentina, and India. Nearly all of Seattle's brick streets used Denny–Renton material.

Only a handful of these historic streets remain in Seattle; most have been paved over, their stories lost to drivers who don't want the jarring ride. I do not mind them. I like the connection to the past and consider it a privilege to drive over the ancient cobbles and rustic bricks, although I try to take these roads when no else is in the car with me.

Another short, quick descent takes me back down the Counterbalance and south on my journey to the lowest of Seattle's seven summits. To city engineer Reginald Thomson, Denny Hill was *the* hill that stood in the way of progress. In his memoir he called Denny an "offense to the public." It rose to a height of 240 feet and made access to northern parts of the city a formidable challenge. Thomson's solution was simple: remove the hill. Regrading began in 1903 at Second Avenue between Pike Street and Denny Way. Stewart Street lost 56.5 feet. Lenora Street dropped 52.3 feet. Later cuts lowered Fourth Avenue and Blanchard Street by 107 feet and Fifth and Blanchard by 93 feet. By 1911 the west side of Denny was gone.

To cut down Denny, contractors used water enhanced by modern technology. They built pumps at Elliott Bay and Lake Union to supply 23 million gallons a day of water (roughly the volume of the Volunteer Park reservoir), which was shot through a 2.5- to 3.5-inch-wide nozzle. This provided enough force to move 2,500-pound boulders. The water jet undercut slopes, creating a slide consisting of a soupy mix of clay, silt, sand, and gravel. Workers put the slush in a flume or conduit and dumped it in Puget Sound, or used it to fill in ravines, such as the ones at Westlake and Fairview avenues. What better way to eliminate a hill in Seattle then to wash it away with water?

Thomson did not stop at Denny. He regraded Jackson and Dearborn Streets between 1907 and 1912, cutting down Jackson by 90 feet and severing the ridge between Beacon Hill and Capitol Hill. The steel bridge on Twelfth Avenue provides the connection now and crosses the gap created by the regrade. Acolytes took up Thomson's credo to get Seattle out of its pit and in 1928 and 1929 contractors leveled the east half of Denny, creating the flatlands that make up Belltown.

Seattle's early engineers may have sluiced away what they believed to be offensive, inappropriately placed land, but I wonder what we gained. Highrise condos and townhouses now compete to provide better views of the Sound and city. It looks like developers are trying to assemble a steel and glass framework to support a new Denny Hill. Thomson and his ilk were lucky; they had easy material to cut through. If the city sat on bedrock, sluicing would not have been so simple. Once again the vagaries of geology not only shaped the city but allowed the city to reshape itself.

Denny Hill's high spot is now only 137 feet, at Second Avenue and Virginia Street. From my venue at the northwest corner of the intersection, I have uninterrupted views of traffic, department stores, and low-rise office towers. Thomson would be proud of what has become of the pits.

It seems only natural that I should head from the lowest high spot to the highest high spot. I ride south along the waterfront, by Seahawks Stadium and Safeco Field, across the Seattle fault, over the Duwamish River and Harbor Island, and around the north end of West Seattle. Over the last few years condos and townhomes have sprouted along the base of the hill. They may be the most expensive and only rentable landslide barriers built in Seattle. Numerous signs of weakness—shear, barren faces of rock, 10-foot-high retaining walls anchored to the hillside by long steel bolts, and tilted trees—dot the slopes behind these new structures, which will prevent any debris from hitting the roadway. I hope the slopes do not slide, but the evidence all points to an eventual failure. As usual, the question is when.

I applaud the optimism of these buildings' inhabitants. When it comes to geology, we in Seattle have to live as optimists. On a long-term scale we have to believe that the Seattle fault and the Cascadia subduction zone will not move and that Mount Rainier will not blow. In the short term we have to trust that precipitation will not be enough to grease the skids of the Lawton Clay or widen the cracks of the Vashon till. Or maybe Seattleites will rely on that age-old pacifier—ignorance. Either way, at least geology makes our lives interesting.

Otherwise we live in a pretty safe place, from a natural disaster point of view. We do not get hurricanes or tornadoes. It can get cold enough to drive people into shelters, but for the most part few people would call Seattle an icebox. The occasional snowstorm causes a few problems, but "blizzard" and Seattle are not usually linked terms. Our fair share of rain generally means a lack of droughts, at least the kind that changes our livelihoods. Despite the rain, flooding is virtually nonexistent, except in a few low-lying spots. Sleet and freezing rain are rare, as are dust storms or hail. And few people have suffered from sunstroke in Seattle.

Nor do we have to worry about plants or animals attacking us. There are no cactus, agave, yuccas, or ocotillo to skewer or scratch our skin. We don't have killer bees, black widows, brown recluses, or scorpions to bite or sting us. Large trees can fall on us but those trees lack big cones, such as 18-inch-long sugar pine cones or two-pound digger pinecones tipped with spiny bracts. Poison oak is native to Seattle but you have to go out of your way to encounter what may be our only dangerous flora.

Geologic-related phenomena are the main natural problems we have to fear. I do not worry constantly about plate tectonics and gravity affecting my daily existence, but I recognize the pentimenti upon which we have constructed our city.

I return to my bike after exploring a few more retaining walls and continue past the monument to Seattle's birth, around Alki Point, and south along Puget Sound. At Lowman Beach I turn east and ride up or next to a series of old landslides, ending up near two more water towers. In only 10 minutes I have ridden from sea level at Lowman to Seattle's highest point, 512 feet above sea level in an alley between 35th Avenue SW and 36th Avenue SW, and SW Myrtle Street and SW Othello Street. I now know how Hillary and Norgay felt. I have conquered the top of the heap, climbing over 2,300 feet in 22 miles.

I look at the Olympics and the northern Cascades. I watch crows play near the reservoir. I eat a Clif Bar, stretch, and drink water, but I know I should not tarry. Three summits await my conquering.

I descend the east side of West Seattle to the Duwamish River flats. After a few mistakes I cross the river into the heart of industrial Seattle, an area mostly ignored by urban renewal. I am fond of this area, another reminder of the city's past. I would like to explore further but my destiny beckons some 300 feet higher in the Jefferson Park golf course at the summit of Beacon Hill.

I reach the 18-hole course, lock my bike, and head out onto the greens past a couple groups of golfers, in search of the highest point I can find. I end up settling on the par three, tenth hole. It seems the highest spot, at 362 feet, and I can use the conveniently located bathroom next to the tee. This is the first summit not located on a street and is the quietest and greenest, with a manicured lawn that would be the envy of any lawn-mower aficionado. I hear car noises but rows of Lombardy poplars block most of the sounds, as well as the views. The ubiquitous crows are the only native species I see.

Time is running out in my day but I decide to raise the bar and add the older, original members of Sophie's Seven—Yesler (a.k.a. Profanity) and Second—during my sprint to the finish. Back on my bike I ride north from Jefferson and cross over the Twelfth Avenue bridge. A short climb and I reach the summit of Yesler Hill at Harborview Hospital, elevation 319 feet. I am not sure that *summit* is the right word for this location, as the land continues to slope upward to the northeast. It does, however, drop off in the other directions.

Yesler honors Henry Yesler, who created Seattle's first paying jobs with his sawmill, built in 1852. The lesser-known moniker comes from the colorful, less-than-official language uttered by lawyers who had to climb a 20 percent grade, pre-I-5 hill, which connected downtown to the courthouse that stood on the hill from 1890 to 1916.

My next summit, a mere five blocks away, also bears two names: First and Pill Hill. Once the location for the houses of the city's elite families, First Hill is now home to many of the city's finest hospitals. I am 360 feet above sea level at the corner of Broadway and James, a far cry from the tranquility of Beacon, but I still see my friends, the crows.

The next hill to the east is one that few people have heard of. Second, or Renton Hill, was named for Capt. William Renton, who logged the hill in 1888. (The city of Renton is also named for him.) I reach its so-called summit by riding down Madison Street by Seattle University and then climbing up to Seventeenth and Madison. I have gained 52 feet but again do not feel like I am at a summit. The hill does slope down to the west and east but runs north and south at about the same elevation, even gaining height to the north.

With one hill left to go, I begin to feel that I have, indeed, been misled as a youth, mostly because from a physiographic point of view the term *hill* is an overstatement for some of the fabled septet. They could better be described as ridges, narrow bodies of land dropping off in steep angles. A map given to me several months before my ride by Tom Nolan, the city of Seattle's GIS manager, had revealed this trend but I had not understood it. The maps showed Seattle topography using color-coded elevations. It translated the rasping path of the glacier into a series of brownish ridges and orangish valleys trending like a needle on a compass. I could now see that Renton connects with Capitol Hill, that First and Profanity should be described as one topographic structure, and that, if not for Thomson's gouging at Dearborn, Beacon would connect with First, too. Only Queen Anne and Magnolia strike me as true rounded hills.

Until this ride I had not realized I had been experiencing the ridges and valleys for years as I biked around Seattle. It had not dawned on me that when I rode north or south I was usually riding on flats or slight inclines but when I traveled east-west I was climbing and dropping, as if I were on a great roller coaster. For example, when I bike over to the Burke Gilman Trail from our house near Northgate, I ascend to Maple Leaf, drop down to Lake City Way, climb up to View Ridge, and plummet down to the lake. Once there, my ride north is flat again.

Only a gentle incline separates me from the apex of Capitol Hill. I am tempted to ride down to Lake Union and make my final ascent a challenge, but I am getting tired so I simply ride north on the spine of a ridge for the last leg of my Seven Summits expedition. In only a few minutes I reach the base of the water tower at Volunteer Park, just a half mile from where I grew up. Also known as a standpipe, the brick tower was erected between 1906 and 1908 by contractor Timothy Ryan, who also built the state's first brick highway, between Tacoma and Kent.

It feels anticlimactic but I am thrilled to be 454 feet above sea level at my seventh (or ninth) summit of the day. I do not know how many before me have attempted such an adventure or whether they completed it. During my grand tour I have ridden almost 34 miles and gained over 3,000 feet in elevation. I have also gained another perspective on the importance of geology to Seattle's past, present, and future. Historian Will Durant summed up my sentiments when he wrote, "Civilization exists by geologic consent, subject to change without notice."

If you have to hate anything, let it be this slug, a cruelly destructive pest if there ever was one.

EUGENE KOZLOFF, *PLANTS AND ANIMALS OF THE PACIFIC NORTHWEST*, 1976

Even the irrepressible, gadabout dandelion, which we vainly try to eject from the lawn, was not a native to Puget Sound but was actually planted here. The great, gloomy forest was no place for the sun-loving little flower but, after a clearing had been made, Mrs. Maynard planted it for medicinal purposes. I reluctantly write this for fear that every time you see that unconquerable weed fairly daring you to dig it up, you may harbor an unkind feeling for the one who planted it.

ROBERTA FRYE WATT, *FOUR WAGONS WEST: THE STORY OF SEATTLE*, 1931

I have a confession. I have transported aliens into the United States. In March 2001 I carried a six-inch-long branch of an acacia tree from El Salvador to Seattle. I collected the dead branch because it bore three seed pods, each about an inch wide and shaped like a slightly less-than-gibbous moon with inch-long thorns protruding from the ends. The stick came from one of the country's few remaining tropical forests, which we explored on a walk with a Salvadoran naturalist.

During our tour we had stopped at the tree to look at ants, which lived on the acacia and protected it from invaders. Our guide had explained that the ants had a nasty bite and swarmed when disturbed. While standing at the tree I noticed the branch on the ground. After the guide continued up the trail, I carefully picked up the branch, made sure no ants clung to it, and stuck it into my field bag. When we got home from the trip I put the stick in a nook in our bathroom with other items we had acquired on our journey.

About a week later I noticed an ant in our bathroom. It was the first one I had seen inside in the four years we had lived in the house. Normally I just carry bugs outside and let them go on their merry way but for some reason I decided to squish this ant. A few days later I saw another one and yet another the next week. After killing the third ant, I began to wonder if my acacia branch was the source for the sudden appearance of the ants. I removed the stick from the bathroom, placed it in a plastic bag, and put it in the freezer, knowing that cold would kill any insect that had traveled in the seedpods from El Salvador. When I opened the bag a few days later I discovered several dead ants.

As far as I know, I got all of the ants that lived in the seedpods. Or at least that's what I like to think. I don't want to go down in history as some modern-day Leopold Trouvelot or Eugene Schieffelin, the men responsible for introducing into the United States the gypsy moth and starling, respectively. More important, I did not want to inadvertently contribute to what has become one of the most important concerns for ecologists around the world. I did not want to be responsible for introducing an invasive species.

Ecologists define invasives as plants, animals, or pathogens that proliferate, spread, and persist to the detriment of the environment. Not just a non-native or exotic species, invasives are the dandelions that take over your yard, the starlings that kick other birds out of their nests, the zebra mussels that clog pipes, the rats that spread the plague. After habitat destruction, invasives cause more harm to natives than other major threats such as pollution, disease, or overharvesting. They alter habitat, drive native species to extinction, reduce water supplies, and threaten agriculture. A 2000 study placed the annual economic cost of invasive species in the United States at $137 billion.

Paradoxically, invasives may also be the species best known to urban dwellers. All I have to do is walk around my neighborhood to find that most houses harbor several invasives. House sparrows and rock doves that flock on my neighbor's green grass are both European natives. The ancestors of the squirrels sprinting across the street have a less exotic, but still nonlocal origin: Minnesota. England gave us the ivy creeping up the Douglas-fir in the backyard of the house on the corner, as well as the Norway rats that I occasionally see scurrying around garbage cans. The butterfly bush blocking the sidewalk across from Licton Springs came from China and the ants clamoring over a rotting apple in a yard two streets over descended from ants that entered the United States from Brazil.

Although no one knows for sure, we can probably assume that a few invaders, such as Norway rats and their close cousins, black rats, arrived in Seattle on some of the earliest ships to dock in the city, followed closely by pigeons. Such undocumented introductions are typical for many invaders; they hitch a ride with somebody (I won't mention any names) and arrive with little fanfare. This is particularly true of aquatic invaders, many of which arrived in ship-ballast water or with shipments of nonnative foods.

Other species, however, came at specific times and places. Hoping to have a more attractive bushy-tailed rodent than the native Douglas squirrel, the Seattle Parks Department imported seven pairs of eastern gray squirrels from Minneapolis and released them in Woodland Park in 1920. Workers have planted ivy for erosion control in Seattle parks since at least 1891. California naturalist Tracey Storer made the first known collection in the western United States of *Arion rufus*, the well-despised, generally brown slug that ravishes our gardens, on June 24, 1933, in Laurelhurst. Fishermen and the fish and game department introduced many of the invasive fish found in Washington lakes so that people would have more recreational fishing options.

Most invasive plants' origins stem from the horticultural trade. One study found that 82 percent of the 235 woody plants identified as invasive originated through nurseries, botanical gardens, or individual horticulturalists. For example, plant propagator Luther Burbank, whose name graces one Mercer Island park, introduced the Himalayan blackberry, from Europe not Asia, in 1885. A Capt. Walter Colquhoun Grant, who was sent seeds by the British consul in Hawaii, planted Scots broom on his 30-acre farm on Vancouver Island in 1850. Not to be outdone, the U.S. Department of Agriculture can claim responsibility for bringing over kudzu and tamarisk, both of which rank high on a recent list of Washington state's 100 worst invaders.

Nowhere is the appeal of nonnative plants better seen than at Heronswood, Dan Hinkley's celebrated nursery near Kingston. On a visit there in late May, I felt transported back to the Permian Era, when all the continents were joined together. In one patch grew black-violet Chinese irises. In another, a Costa Rican giant with six-foot-wide leaves towered above me, and yet another garden featured plants from South Africa, Turkey, and Korea. The shades of green alone would fill the largest box of Crayola crayons, and the different shapes and colors of wildflowers felt like a kaleidoscope. I can understand why people want exotic plants in their gardens.

In an e-mail conversation Hinkley added another reason why people want nonnatives: "It makes our lives more interesting and the world more understandable. I believe with thought it can be a safe and respectful process." As part of the process, he makes his buyers aware of the risks of bringing in plants from other countries. His catalogue contains a concise, thoughtful essay on the dangers of invasives. He also has an invasive-plant specialist review his plant list to remove serious invasive species and highlight those plants with a potential for invasion.

Part of the challenge of invasives, however, is that some species take decades to become a problem. Known as "lag time," delays are a typical behavior in invasives; a plant arrives, grows where it should for years to decades, and then explodes uncontrollably. Ecologists hypothesize several reasons for a species' sudden change from benign little garden plant to native-killing invasive. The plants may have evolved a new genetic makeup that facilitated their spread. It may be a matter of perception or, more likely, there may be enough small patches in enough places that the species reaches a critical mass and becomes cancerous.

A long lag time appears to be the case for one of Seattle's up-and-coming invaders, herb Robert, a rank little red-stemmed, lavender-flowered plant. No one knows the origin of herb Robert in Washington state because it has long been used in herbal medicine in its native habitat of Europe and immigrants probably brought the plant with them. Unaffectionately known as stinky Bob due to its musky aroma, plants can produce 3,700 seeds per square yard. Stinky Bob doesn't just drop these seeds, it shoots them up to 20 feet away, where they can find new terrain or latch onto animals to travel even further. Unlike most natives, herb Robert can also germinate in the fall. In full shade this fecundity can result in as many as 300 plants per square yard, a density thick enough to prevent native wildflowers from growing.

Stinky Bob grows readily in the underbrush in city parks, along roadways, and in backyards. It has also appeared in wilder spots, such as Cougar and Tiger mountains and Olympic National Park. Its one saving grace is that it is easy to pull up, which almost seems to be a front for the plant. I have spent hours at our house clearing out patches of herb Robert, smugly reveling in my success at ridding the yard of this pernicious stinker, only to find them growing back again, even if I cover the ground several inches deep in leaves and needles.

Herb Robert ranks near the top of many people's list of worst invaders. "What separates the bad from the very bad is the ability to invade undisturbed natural areas. I have seen pristine habitat where stinky Bob literally took over in only a couple of years," said Sarah Reichard, an assistant professor of eco-system sciences and environmental horticulture, based at the Center for Urban Horticulture in the School of Forest Resources at the University of Washington.

Sarah is part of a growing movement of scientists who are studying how invasive species impact native ecosystems. Fortunately or unfortunately her walk to find invasives is even shorter than mine; she only has to go out her back door to see the detrimental effects of plants gone wild. In 2001 she and her husband bought a house on Crown Hill, just a few minutes from where they lived on Phinney Ridge. Although larger and with a better view, the new house's most attractive feature was the half acre of land, dominated by a lush ravine, where the previous owner had spent time and money on landscaping. "I sometimes think we are insane for getting this property but I wanted a big garden," said Sarah, when I visited her in July 2003. The problem was not what the previous owner had planted but the invasive plants that had taken over the slopes.

As we walked along a narrow path on the steep hillside, Sarah showed me where invasive clematis crept up massive bigleaf maple stumps like the gnarled green fingers of some subterranean beast. In another corner, ivy and blackberries had taken over, creating a menacing green wall of tangled, thorny vegetation. A few feet further she yanked out some herb Robert that sprouted in teeming masses. She also told me how when another botanist visited he discovered an invasive that no one had ever seen in North America.

Although Sarah leads the fight against invasives, she likes ornamen-tals and has plans to establish a plot of plants from Chile, where she worked on her master's thesis. She also buys nonnatives from the nursery near her house. She has removed invasives so that exotic shrubs can survive and her front yard contains many trees and shrubs that did not originally make their homes in Washington. What they all have in common is their low invasive potential.

Sarah got her start in the very trade that has done more to bring invasive species into the country than any other. In 1988, while working on her master's thesis, she traveled on a seed-collecting trip in Chile for the UW Arboretum. "When I got back I started to wonder whether any of these seeds could become invasive. I was shocked that I found virtually nothing on how to predict if a plant had the potential to invade," she said. Her thesis included one section on the invasive potential of her Chilean seeds. Since then she has expanded her work to create a litmus test for any introduced plant.

"The best way to prevent a plant from becoming an invader is to prevent it from ever entering a country," she emphasized. She found that the single best predictor of successful invasion was previous invasion by that species somewhere else in the world. Other factors that indicated high potential included similar climate, native distribution from a wide latitude range, high seed production, and long flowering and fruiting periods. The model she helped develop correctly classified 86 percent of past species that invaded but it does not answer the single biggest question: Why do some plants become botanical cancer, reproducing uncontrollably and damaging their host environment?

Ecologists have offered several hypotheses to answer this question. One is analogous to a teenager going off to college and getting in trouble because the calming influence of family is now gone. With plants, the theory is that invasives do well away from home because they no longer have predators or pathogens keeping them in check. A lack of enemies leads to increased reproductivity and wider distribution.

Another theory focuses on an invader's ability to hybridize. Researchers have found that the most invasive forms of tamarisk, or salt cedar, considered to be the second-worst offender in the country after purple loosestrife, were hybrids of two species that did not have overlapping ranges in their native environments. Plant expert Arthur Lee Jacobson believes that one such example in Seattle is the hybrid Japanese knotweed (*Polygonum x bohemicum*), a combination of Japanese knotweed (*P. cuspidatum*) and giant knotweed (*P. sachalinense*) that invades more successfully than either parent.

The most recent discovery has found that the evil invader spotted knapweed kills off competitors by releasing a toxin into the soil around its roots. When other plants absorb the chemical, catechin, it triggers a genetic response that causes the plant's cells to die. Researchers also discovered that soils in Colorado and Montana, where knapweed invaded, had levels of catechin four to five times higher than soils in Europe, where spotted knapweed is native.

In the Pacific Northwest, invaders are aided by the mild climate. As we all know, plants thrive in the temperate rain-soaked environment. They don't have to adapt to freezing temperatures and rarely have to survive a prolonged drought. If an invader gets established during typical weather conditions, then it may be able to survive the rare extremes. On a climatic plus side, many gardeners know that our dry summers can cause problems and do keep some plants, particularly woody deciduous ones, from getting a seed-hold.

"I don't think there is a single answer to the question of why," said Sarah. Around Puget Sound, she and other Center for Urban Horticulture staff and students are trying to address this question by focusing on some of the area's better known invaders. Two factors stand out to predict invasive success: high tolerance to stress and high reproductivity. Scots broom, for example, germinates best in dry sandy soils in full sunlight, such as roadways, where it often forms extensive stands. The seeds remain viable for up to 80 years. The plants can fix nitrogen and endure drought and they can tolerate soils with a wide range of pH, sprouting on dunes, heathlands, and acidic grasslands. Although many people appreciate the brilliant yellow spring flowers, one writer considered Scots broom a poster child for the problems that invasives cause. "It is very aggressive, spreads rapidly, growing so dense that it is often impenetrable. It prevents reforestation, creates a high fire hazard, renders rangeland worthless and greatly increases the cost of maintenance of roads, ditches, canals, power and telephone lines. . . . "

Blackberry takes the path of fecundity. A thicket can generate 8,300 to 15,500 seeds per square yard and because so many birds and mammals eat them, the seeds get dispersed widely. In addition, passage through an animal's gut enhances germination by scarifying seeds. Blackberries also spread without sex. When a cane grows long enough to bend over and reach the ground, it can take root and send up a daughter cane. Canes only live a couple of years but can grow 23 feet in a single season and reach densities of over 600 per square yard.

Such fecundity has allowed blackberries to become ubiquitous across Seattle, particularly in disturbed habitat. I have picked them while exploring local parks, biking along the Burke Gilman, canoeing down the Duwamish, and walking in my neighborhood. Like many Seattleites I have been scratched and punctured in pursuit of the fruit, but once I get the sweet, succulent berries in my mouth I know that blood is a small price to pay.

Ecologists don't like Himalayan blackberries because the dense thickets block light to other plants, reduce animal habitat, and hinder access to water in riparian zones, another area where blackberries flourish. With their rapid growth they can quickly outcompete natives and turn a diverse field into a monoculture. Himalayan blackberries, however, do have several features that make them less heinous than other invasives. The most obvious is the edible berry. Blackberries also do not grow well in shade or in undisturbed habitat, which from an ecological standpoint makes them less troublesome than other invasives, in particular the city's worst offender, English ivy, *Hedera helix.*

A native to Europe and the Mediterranean, English ivy arrived in the United States in the early 1700s as an ornamental. The earliest record of ivy for sale in the Pacific Northwest is from Marion County, Oregon, in 1864, where a William Simmons offered Irish ivy in the catalog for his St. Helena Nursery. The oldest known ivy in the state is one planted in 1864 by pioneer Eliza Jane Meeker in Puyallup. It is still growing at Pioneer Park. By 1891 Seattle Parks was growing ivy in its nurseries. Quick growing, hardy, and handsome, ivy could make the worst gardener look like a green thumb. All you had to do was plant it, water it occasionally, and it would spread and, like stinky Bob, move into undisturbed habitat.

And spread it has in Seattle. Ivy battles blackberry in Frink Park, chokes maples in Carkeek Park, strangles Douglas-firs in Seward Park, covers acres of Discovery Park, creeps up buildings at the UW, proliferates aggressively along I-5, and smothers native shrubs in Schmitz Park. It was the first plant I removed from our yard when we moved into our house. It is the only plant that I rip out of the ground and off trees on my walks around North Seattle Community College. Ivy is so successful at invading that Sarah refers to invaded locales as "ivy deserts" because they lack any other plants.

In Seattle, as in many places, ivy's leading attribute was and is its perceived ability to control surface soil-erosion. During the juvenile stage, which can last up to 10 years, plants reproduce asexually by generating adventitious roots at leaf nodes. These minute roots latch onto the soil and allow the plant to spread, with growth rates of up to three-quarter inch per day. If you have ever tried to pull out ivy, a surprisingly easy task, you will realize that these roots only loosely bind together the upper layer of soil and do not penetrate down into an erosion-resistant weave. The dense growth also blocks out other plants that might stabilize slopes.

For those who want to see how well ivy actually does at stabilizing slopes, I recommend a trip to Kinnear Park, to see the landslides that ivy didn't prevent. Or go to Interlaken Park on Capitol Hill, where you will find the same lack of tenacity. What works is what came before, a multilayered forest of ground-covering ferns, kinnikinnik, and salal, understory shrubs, and well-rooted Douglas-firs, cedars, and western hemlocks.

If ivy stayed on the ground, it would be merely an ideal home to rats, a shader of wildflowers, and a strangler of seedlings, but the adventitious roots also allow ivy to climb structures, shrubs, and trees, where its dense growth does more damage. By adding additional weight to trees, particularly when coated with rain or ice, ivy makes trees more susceptible to blowdown. Ivy is especially damaging to native deciduous trees such as bigleaf maple, black cottonwood, and red alder, because it can grow during the winter, spread into the canopy, and block sunlight to leaves below, as well as to understory plants. Death often follows to the weakened host.

In the adult phase, characterized by a change from lobed, youthful leaves to unlobed, leathery, adult leaves, ivy no longer produces adventitious roots. Instead plants put their energy into producing greenish white flower clusters. Six months later purplish black drupes appear. High in fat and nutrients, the berrylike fruit is mildly toxic, a rather nifty feature because birds can't consume very many seeds from any one spot before getting ill. Furthermore, the toxicity forces seeds to move rapidly through a bird's gut, creating more viable and widely spread seeds. Key consumers include house sparrows and starlings, both natives of ivy's native habitat.

Ivy's very success may be its downfall. As more and more people recognize that ivy is one of the leading threats to Seattle's urban forests, they have begun to fight back. City, county, and state agencies are spreading the word about the damages of invasives such as ivy and have even banned many species from being sold in the state. Groups are forming, such as Portland's Ivy Control

League (formerly the NoIvyLeague), to actively rid areas of ivy. In Seattle, EarthCorps, Marjorie's employer, works with 18- to 24-year-olds from around the world to remove invasives and restore habitat in parks and green spaces in King County. EarthCorps also organizes volunteer events, one of which attracted over 200 people to Seward Park on a cool, foggy Earth Day in 2003. Despite its magnificent forests, Seward also suffers from invasives. Creeping buttercup and herb Robert spread in the shade. Thirty-foot-tall English laurels and English hollies grow under bigleaf maples. Bindweed climbs up the tallest trees and the ever-present ivy and blackberry thrive.

The Earth Day crews had come to battle ivy, some of whose vines were inches thick. Clad in Gore-Tex and Carhartts, dirt-covered jackets and torn jeans, young and old volunteers spread across Seward carrying rakes, pruning shears, and thick gloves. Their main method: tromp into a patch, grab the nearest ivy, yank, wrap into a ball. Repeat. They emerged from the park at the end of the day dirty, scratched, and sweaty. They had removed an estimated two acres of ivy.

"I am always amazed to see how these volunteer events make an impact on people's lives," said Liz Stenning, director of field operations at EarthCorps. "It's hard to make people understand the problems of invasives until they get out there and start to rip up plants." I did not participate on Earth Day but have pulled up ivy at other volunteer ivy-pulls and know what Liz is talking about. Removing invasives is both enjoyable and satisfying. You get mucky. You wear macho gloves and rip out plants. You may even get to wield a Pulaski. You do something good for the planet. You are part of a movement.

But the movement has created a backlash. It is not necessarily a backlash against the ivy pullers but against those who think that invasive species are a problem. Naysayer's arguments take two tacks: emotion and science. They claim that the anti-invasives movement promotes a xenophobic, nativist argument, akin to that practiced by the Nazis. Proponents point out that the Nazis established rules for the exclusive use of native plants, which would help guard against "unwelcome alien influences." Writing in the *New York Times*, Michael Pollan, author of *Botany of Desire*, asserts that "It's hard to believe that there is nothing more than scientific concern about invasives species behind the current fashion for natural gardening and native plants in America—not when our national politics are rife with anxieties about immigration and isolationist sentiment."

The anti-invasives movement, however, is not about purity—native versus nonnative—and closing our land and water to all foreign influences. It's about recognizing that some introduced plants and animals have the potential to damage natural ecosystems, and it's about trying to determine which those are before they invade. By giving short shrift to the argument that invasives cause damage and questioning whether "kudzu and its noxious cronies" truly represent what can be expected from imported plants, Pollan and others fail to acknowledge the serious environmental problems of ignoring that potential. Furthermore, the specter of lag time means that some species that arrive innocuously may be the kudzu of the future. We have to make intelligent evaluations, especially as the world's species get flung across oceans and continents ever more quickly.

This is the evolutionary point that many writers, including Pollan, dismiss. They correctly observe that migration is natural, that environments change, and that species respond and adapt. What they ignore is the rate of change. Pollan writes, "Evolution will draw no distinction between the migration of species by wind and birds and ice floes and the migration of species by 747." How then do we contend with someplace like Hawaii, where the rate of introduction has changed from its historic pace, an estimated one plant per 100,000 years, to the modern 22 per year? With just .02 percent of the U.S. landmass, Hawaii is home to 75 percent of the historically documented plant and bird species extinctions in the United States. Is this natural?

The 747 comparison raises another difference between what has occurred over geologic time and what is occurring in human time. In an article for *BioScience*, Sarah Reichard and her coauthor, biologist Peter White, observe that natural migrations, at least for plants, occur on small geographic scales, what they call "natural barriers in the 'coevolutionary envelope.'" Within the envelope, migrators would include the natural enemies, such as pathogens or herbivores, that might keep an invader in check. I suspect that few modern migrators check through their enemies when traveling.

Some ecologists further contend that even if invasives cause some extinctions, so be it. This unfortunate but natural phase will eventually end, and new, well-adapted species will survive, evolve into new forms, and become the new natives. In his thought-provoking book, *Future Evolution*, paleontologist Peter Ward, working with illustrator Alexis Rockman, imagines what some of these future species might look like. My favorite is the drawing of dandelions that have evolved into cactuslike, arboreal, aquatic, carnivorous, and epiphytic forms. Instead of traipsing through a forest of Douglas-fir, future generations might be able to hike through groves of 100-foot-tall dandelions.

The problem with invasive-caused extinctions is homogeneity; if the proliferation of invasives continues, we could well end up with a world dominated more and more by a handful of very successful, very common species. In his book, which focuses on mass extinctions such as the one that ended the reign of the dinosaurs 65 million years ago, Ward drives home this point with a quote from an article in *Nature* magazine: "Thus, today's anthropogenic extinctions are likely to have long lasting effects. . . . Even if *Homo sapiens* survives several more million years, it is unlikely that any of our species will see biodiversity recover from today's extinctions."

Other ecologists further question the idea of natives, asking, "Who is to decide what is the date we pick to define native?" In North America, is it 1492, or do we go back to the Ice Age, when humans first arrived on the continent? And why are natives better than nonnatives? Stephen Jay Gould argued that natives are those organisms that happened to arrive first and stay put; they are not even the plants or animals best adapted to their place, as shown by invasives that move in and outcompete the natives.

Gould also offered a counterpoint to this concept, at least when it comes to invaders. "[W]e know that well-established natives are adequately adapted, and we can observe their empirical balances with other local species. We cannot know what an exotic species will do. . . . " Natives have evolved to live in a checks-and-balances system where extremes do not last long, or, as Gould wrote, they "grow appropriately."

Most nonnatives do grow appropriately in their new homes and no one is calling for a return to some prelapsarian environment. Part of what makes an urban landscape interesting is the diversity of life, whether human, plant, or animal, native and nonnative. We probably cannot eliminate any of the invasives, no matter how hard we try. Furthermore, many people like them. I enjoy seeing squirrels chattering in the park, house sparrows flitting about bird feeders, and golden yellow Scots broom ribboning a roadside. I also recognize that these plants and animals are making their new homes less hospitable to many other species.

We can say that species have always moved around the planet, that such migrations help drive evolution, and that natives just happened to arrive first and stay put, but we can also concede that we are changing the planet at an unprecedented rate, and that we do not know what the full consequences will be. We have made mistakes, some advertant, some inadvertent, and we can learn from them.

"People are the key to invasives because it is as much a social issue as a biological one," said Sarah. We cannot solve the problem simply by pulling out plants or through government regulation, although both help. "People need to realize that plants that grow in their own garden can spread easily. They need to ask nurseries to stop selling certain plants and ecologists need to better understand the mechanisms of invasion and to find alternatives for these popular plants. It is a long road but I am pleased with how far we have progressed."

For my own part, I only hope that I got all those ants.

Every hillside had its spring, and in
the beginnings the settler took his water
where he found it. If there was no spring
in his own yard, he gouged out a log, or
bought some boards from Yesler's mill and
fashioned them into a V-flume, to bring
his water supply close, for a house or a
community.

MARY MCWILLIAMS, *SEATTLE WATER
DEPARTMENT HISTORY,* 1955

Millions of men have lived without love.
None have lived without water.

TURKISH PROVERB

When I turn on the tap at my house, clear, potable water pours forth. I don't have to worry about pollutants or chemicals. I don't have to worry that water won't come out. I don't even have to pay much for this service.

At the other end of the cycle, when I flush my toilet or let water go down a drain, it disappears without any effort on my part. I don't have to worry about polluting someone downstream. I don't have to worry that the system won't work. I don't even have to pay much for this service.

At first glance, this seems like a simple story. Water comes to my tap from a source in the Cascades, either the Tolt or Cedar Rivers, and then flows out of my house to the sewage treatment facility at West Point in Discovery Park. Looking more closely at what might be termed the urban water cycle, however, I began to see a microcosm of the much larger global water cycle, which includes precipitation, evaporation, transpiration, storage, runoff, and recharge. It is a cycle that humans affect through logging, fishing, damming, and polluting. It is a cycle that we depend upon daily for our existence.

To better understand the water cycle, I decided to try and trace my drinking water from forest to faucet, the input flow of the cycle, and from sink to Sound, the output flow. I wanted to see how the different parts of the water cycle manifest themselves in the urban environment.

I started my journey between two high ridges in Yakima Pass, at an elevation of 3,575 feet, about five miles south and slightly east of Snoqualmie Pass. Twilight Lake, which I could almost throw a stone across, sits in this low pass and is the headwaters for the Cedar River, which provides 70 percent of the water consumed by Seattleites. It has been the city's primary source of drinking water since inadequate water pressure during Seattle's Great Fire of 1889 led to a 1,875 to 51 vote to approve a $1 million bond to form a publicly owned water system. After an additional 12 years of haggling, planning, and construction, water from the Cedar reached Seattle on January 10, 1901. The remaining 30 percent comes from the South Fork Tolt River Watershed, 28 miles east of Seattle, which the city first tapped in 1964. (People north of the Ship Canal generally get Tolt water, although water gets mixed in the system, particularly at the Maple Leaf reservoir, so a tap could deliver pure Cedar, pure Tolt, or a mix of the two.)

From Twilight, the Cedar, at this point more creek than river, drops down a steep, glaciated slope into a valley dominated by second-growth Douglas-fir. I could not follow the creek because soon after the water exits Twilight it enters what is known as the Cedar River Watershed, the 90,546 acres of city-owned land that drains into the Cedar. Seattle is the only large municipality in the United States that owns its entire drinking-water watershed. In addition, Seattle is one of only five cities in the United States with a population of over 500,000 people that does not have to filter the drinking water of its primary source. (The Tolt, on the other hand, suffered worse logging and does have a filtration plant.)

Despite a Seattle Public Utilities (SPU) prohibition against entering the watershed, I have taken several tours, twice to look at plants and once on a guided tour offered by the Cedar River Education Center. On these tours, I have visited a lush bog teeming with flowering bog laurel and bog rosemary, seen meadows resplendent with wildflowers, and stood under several-hundred-year-old western red cedars, Sitka spruce, and noble firs so big that two people together could not wrap their arms around them. But the two communities that stood out most were second-growth Douglas-fir groves and clear-cuts.

Each type is easy to pick out. The second growth, consisting mostly of trees between the ages of 40 and 80 years, makes up over 50 percent of the watershed. It looks like most other Cascade forests, healthy but homogenous. In the groves I visited, the trees were uniformly tall and close growing. Little sunlight reached the ground and few understory plants grew. The clear-cuts, of course, had lots of sunlight, but little else. I was amazed to see steep barren slopes, denuded ridges, and butchered valleys, the results of the final years of cutting old growth in the watershed. In contrast, in the one old-growth grove I explored, I saw sword fern, trillium, wild ginger, vanilla leaf, and devil's club. I walked through broad openings filled with seedlings, saplings, nurse logs, and snags. It was cool and comfortable.

Although city officials recognized the importance of protecting the land surrounding Seattle's drinking water, they still permitted logging companies to strip the forests. Logging within the watershed took place most intensively between 1900 and 1923, with few regulations and little regard for sanitary conditions around logging camps, many of which let food, animal, and human waste drain directly into creeks that flowed into the Cedar. I shudder to think what exactly Seattleites were drinking in the first half of the twentieth century. Land managers did begin an extensive replanting program in the 1920s, but from 1945 to 1985 the city still permitted an annual take of up to 35 million board feet, basically all clear-cuts in old-growth forest. When logging finally stopped in the watershed in 1997, about 83 percent of the total forest cover, or over 5 billion board feet, had been cut, roughly enough to build housing for every modern Seattleite, assuming a family of four, in a 2,000-square-foot home.

Money was the driving force behind cutting. When the city started to acquire land in the watershed, it usually did not buy timber rights because it lacked the money to do so. Another land acquisition tactic let a company buy and log a property before deeding the denuded land to the city. Even as Seattle became wealthier, it sold timber and used the money to keep water rates low.

This harvesting of the original Cedar River forest has had a significant effect on the water cycle. Tree removal meant that winter snows melted more quickly and water ran off instead of soaking into the ground for later use. Water retention is also a problem in second-growth forests because the branches of close-growing trees capture snow, which evaporates more quickly than if it landed on the ground and melted slowly. In old-growth forests, snow reaches the ground via the relatively open canopy but it is also protected from melting by this same canopy.

Replanting and natural reforestation have helped return the water cycle to a more natural condition, but an important and potentially costly challenge remains: turbidity. High turbidity, or dirty water, results from high sediment load, generally produced by runoff from road building and tree cutting. In addition to a distasteful appearance, high turbidity often indicates increased levels of disease-causing microorganisms such as viruses, parasites, and some bacteria, and it requires additional use of chlorine, the cheapest and easiest method of killing pathogens in drinking water.

Turbidity is generally not a problem in the watershed, mostly because the heaviest logging ended 50 years ago, but occasional spikes do occur. If these high turbidity events become more consistent, Seattle would have to build a filtration plant, which would cost at least $200 million and hundreds of thousands more a year to run. The best way to remain in the exclusive non-filtration club is to eliminate roads and prohibit logging in the watershed, two practices which SPU has recently embarked upon, due primarily to the Endangered Species Act (ESA), which mandates habitat protection if a listed species is taken (defined as harassing, harming, killing, etc.).

In response to the listing of the Chinook salmon under the ESA, Seattle adopted a Habitat Conservation Plan (HCP) for the Cedar River in April 2000. The 1,000-plus-page document governs management decisions for the next 50 years and allows the city to continue to divert the Cedar for drinking water. More than $90 million has been set aside to fund the HCP. Seattle and Tacoma are the only large cities with HCPs governing their watersheds. In addition to the chinook, the HCP lists 13 other species potentially present within the watershed as Species of Greatest Concern, including bull trout, wolf, and peregrine falcon. Another 69 species, known as Species of Concern and ranging from big brown bats to blue-gray taildropper slugs, must also be monitored and protected.

I was lucky enough to see one of these species on my guided tour of the watershed with education-center staff. We had crossed a small bridge over the Cedar at the one large lake in the watershed, Chester Morse Lake. Originally smaller, it had been dammed in 1904, raising the lake level from 1,532 feet to 1,546 feet. Since it was midsummer, lake level was not high and much of the shoreline near the outlet was treeless beach. We continued across the bridge and around to a small picnic area, where we could walk out to the water.

Through my binoculars I could see a common loon swimming and diving about 100 yards offshore. Our guide, Ralph Naess, education coordinator for SPU, explained that up to four pairs of loons have nested in a single season at Chester Morse, more than any spot in the state. One of only five places in the state where these haunting birds nest, Chester Morse will only become better habitat under the HCP.

To meet the demands of the HCP, SPU has to address forest protection and restoration. Plans call for the removal of 38 percent of the 620 miles of roads that crisscross the watershed, and replacement of damaged or poorly functioning culverts. Timber harvesting for commercial gain will be eliminated. Second-growth forests will undergo restoration thinning to more closely resemble old-growth stands, with openings, large woody debris in streams, snags, nurse logs, and trees of different ages.

The HCP is a landmark document because the city of Seattle will have to manage the land for ecological priorities instead of economic ones. Employing a 50-year timescale, managers have to consider the long-term consequences of an issue. They will have to plan for communities of species, not just for a two-legged one. They will have to manage for the full water cycle and not just for the urban arc. This change in management will benefit not only other species but us, by providing cleaner drinking water and, I hope, by eliminating a costly filtration plant.

After visiting Chester Morse Lake, we headed about a mile and a half down the Cedar River to the largest man-made structure in the watershed, the Masonry Dam. The 795-foot-long mass looks like any other dam curving against the onslaught of billions of pounds of water, except that it does not block all the water; some escapes through glacier deposited sediments, known as moraine, on the shrub and tree-covered slope on the north side of the river, a problem that led to one of the monumental engineering errors in the history of Seattle.

Not content with the wooden 1904 dam at Chester Morse, city officials decided in 1910 to build a concrete dam a mile or so below what was then known as Cedar Lake and increase its storage for drinking water and electricity generation. City engineer Reginald Thomson, of hill-sluicing-away fame, chose a narrow chasm 7,000 feet downriver from the first dam, and voters approved $1.4 million in bonds for construction, despite three reports by geologists and engineers that warned of potential leakage through the moraine. Proponents countered that the reservoir would eventually "seal and become much less pervious than it appears to be now. . . . "

Their optimism was put to the test with completion of the dam in October 1914. By the time water reached a depth of 80 feet behind the thick concrete wall, the skeptics had their Pyrrhic victory. Springs in the gorge below the dam had started to discharge at an unprecedented rate, and in 30 days nearly all the water in the pool disappeared, seeping out at an estimated volume of 30 million gallons a day. Engineers tried again in April, and spring discharge again increased. In addition, the level of Rattlesnake Lake, 1.5 miles northwest, 670 feet lower, and not in the Cedar River drainage, began to rise steadily, from 868 feet on May 1 to 881 feet on May 8, resulting in the eerily slow flooding and eventual relocation of the town of Moncton, which had been built on the lake's shore.

Between 1915 and 1918, engineers, including Thomson, now retired, and William Mulholland (infamous creator of Los Angeles' water system, who later built the St. Francis Dam in southern California, which failed in 1928, killing 511 people), drilled holes, made contingency plans, and tested sealants. Finally, in the fall of 1918, after Thomson and Mulholland's plan for "sealing" the lake had been tried, water began to refill the pool behind the Masonry Dam and rose from 1,484 feet on December 2 to 1,556 feet two weeks later. It remained at this level until the night of December 23, when a flood of water escaped through the moraine and shot out into Boxley Creek, 6,000 feet north of the dam and also not in the Cedar's drainage.

The Boxley Burst, as it came to be known, destroyed tracks on the Milwaukee Railroad, sawmills at the North Bend Lumber Company, and the small town of Edgewick. No one died because an observant night watchman, Charles Moore, noticed the rising creek and alerted townspeople to the impending catastrophe. An analysis in 1941 concluded that "The failure of the Cedar project must be ascribed directly to the almost complete disregard for geological conditions by the builders."

The Masonry Dam fiasco highlights one of the key challenges of the water cycle: storage. Because the dam cannot be filled to its planned capacity, SPU cannot store as much water as it would like. Nor can it increase the storage at other reservoirs, such as the ones in Seattle or at Lake Youngs (formerly known as Swan Lake and altered in 1922 by SPU to create a reservoir capable of holding four billion gallons of water, about a three-week supply).

Water storage is especially critical in Seattle because our heaviest water use, jumping from about 125 million gallons per day (mgd) to almost 225 mgd, comes in summer, when we have our lowest rainfall. Our passion for green lawns drives this summer profligacy. One study found that a typical household (consisting of 2.7 people) uses 117 gallons per day (gpd) during the summer watering their yard, 10 gpd washing a vehicle, and 6 gpd on children's toys. An average Seattleite uses between 103 and 117 gpd throughout the year, most of which goes to indoor usage, with 18 gallons flushing down the toilet, 15 cleaning clothes, 13 cleaning us, 11 flowing from the tap, and 10 leaking somewhere.

To counter this summertime need, SPU has begun to promote a method that increases storage outside the watershed while also allowing individuals to take a personal role in the water cycle: collecting precipitation in rain barrels and cisterns. "It's appropriate technology. All it requires is a 50-gallon barrel collecting runoff from your roof. Just think how much storage we could have if 100,000 people had them," says Naess. Seattleites obviously agree with him: when SPU offered rain barrels for sale, they sold the entire supply of 1,500 in only a few hours.

King County has taken this a step further at its King Street building, where it collects rainwater to use in toilet flushing. The system saves an estimated 1.4 million gallons per year. Several community gardens, the Growing Vine Street Project in Belltown, and many individuals have already realized the importance of conservation and collect water in cisterns around Seattle, saving tens of thousands of gallons of water and reducing the amount of street runoff that has to be treated.

Even in a city that gets 36 inches of rain per year and in a watershed that receives 102 inches annually, collecting precipitation is a logical way to save water, especially with a major challenge to the water cycle looming in the near future: global warming. Most Seattleites, except for those lucky enough to live on the shores of Puget Sound, don't have to worry too much about one of the better known aspects of warming, a rise in sea level. Instead, we face a short-age of snow, one of the most important units of storage in the water cycle.

During a typical Pacific Northwest winter, snow falls, accumulates, and creates a giant reservoir of water. When temperatures rise in June or July, the snow begins to melt and fills rivers, right at the time when water use starts to rise and precipitation starts to drop. Warmer temperatures caused by global warming, however, will alter this scenario because more precipitation will fall as a liquid instead of as a solid. Recent models by UW researchers predict that by 2020, 17 to 29 percent of snow will fall as rain. Smaller snowpacks will melt away more quickly and not be available in the summer, affecting irrigation needs and electricity production. Earlier runoff will also affect salmon, which have evolved for later summer peaks. Increased rainfall could also force dam managers to further lower their reservoirs to prevent flooding. We have already seen this phenomenon in 2001 and 2002, with subsequent increases in water and electricity rates, and we can expect more increases in the future.

Despite its problems, Masonry Dam stores huge volumes of water, which leave the reservoir in three places. Water still seeps through the moraine, some escaping into Boxley Creek and eventually the Snoqualmie River, and some percolating back to the Cedar. On the day I stood on the dam, a small flow trickled from the base, where it disappeared into a narrow wooded chasm. Most of the water, though, flows through two 78-inch-diameter steel penstocks, gushing 7,500 feet to a Seattle City Light power-house, which can generate a maximum of 30 megawatts, or enough energy to run four buildings the size of the 76-story Bank of America Tower during peak needs. It is the oldest municipally owned hydroelectric plant in the country.

I picked up the trickle again at Cedar Falls, a half mile or so below the dam. The falls consists of two successive jumps pouring into a basketball-court-sized pool colored like a mixture of sky and sea. It reminded me of Lake Louise, near Banff, Alberta, and of the intense blue of ice caves on Mount Rainier. The falls historically prevented fish movement between the upper and lower sections of the Cedar and is the last spot one can see the river until it emerges out of the woods below the Landsburg Diversion Dam, another 12.4 miles closer to Seattle.

This dam has been one of the most important impediments to the natural water cycle of the Cedar River for the last 100 years. Built of wood in 1901 and reconstructed in concrete 34 years later, it has prevented salmon from returning to the final stretch of the river, as well as to three large tributaries. The Diversion Dam is undergoing a retrofit under the Habitat Conservation Plan. Roughly $9.3 million of the $90 million HCP is being spent on altering the Landsburg Dam and one small dam below it to allow salmon to reach the relatively pristine section of Cedar River and its tributaries between Landsburg and Cedar Falls. (The one feature the Cedar lacks is large woody debris, which will be added to the river under the HCP.)

I visited Landsburg with SPU's Ralph Naess on a typical spring day, overcast and drippy. After checking in at a security gate, we drove about a quarter mile up to a small park, where a six-foot-high dam once stood. SPU completed removal of the blockage in October 2002. Instead of replacing the dam with big steps or a ladder, which would have been easier and cheaper, engineers created a series of six short steps. From a viewing platform, I could not tell that a dam ever blocked the river. Water pooled and cascaded around debris and boulders, many of which had been placed strategically for fish. Kayakers had set up gates for a slalom course. Salmon will now be able to get over the first hurdle on their return up the Cedar.

They cannot yet get by the second hurdle, but work is progressing quickly. Naess began by leading me into a baby blue building where screens sweep debris from the water before it enters pipes bound for Seattle. "This method wasn't set up for fish because they cannot escape the screens," he explained. "In the new screening system, water will flow down V-shaped channels through a sieve network that stops but does not injure the fish, which can then be removed and put back into the water below the outtake."

In addition to changing the screening process, designers had to reengineer how water flowed over the dam at Landsburg. In the old system, water merely shot through four fish-unfriendly gates and over a steep lip. In the new system, most water will go through one gate designed to accommodate fish on their way out to the ocean. The HCP requires that a certain percentage of the Cedar River, dependent upon water conditions and season, flows past Landsburg, down through Maple Valley, and into Lake Washington at

Renton. The volume is determined by requirements for salmon habitat and for keeping an adequate amount of water in Lake Union for proper interchange of salt- and freshwater at the Chittenden Locks. The HCP also requires a minimum flow for water below Cedar Falls, to ensure good habitat for the salmon that get above Landsburg.

The biggest change is the fish ladder, which lets Chinook, steelhead, and coho (but not sockeye) back into the Cedar above the Diversion Dam. Because of concerns that dead, rotting carcasses would adversely affect water quality, which was the reason the original dam blocked fish access, only 46,500 pounds of fish—about 1,000 Chinook, 4,500 coho, and unlimited steelhead—will be allowed to go upriver. Biologists want to restrict sockeye because there are too many of them and historically they did not inhabit the Cedar. They will do this by first mechanically separating large Chinook from small Chinook, Coho, and sockeye (there are so few steelhead that biologists will let all of them through). A "pescalator" then lifts the fish to sorting tables where SPU staff further separates different species of salmon by hand. The sockeye win a free trip back downriver.

Because of the way the city now manages the Cedar River Watershed, the water that leaves Landsburg is extremely clear and clean, probably more so than at any time in the previous 100 years. The only additives are between .5 and 1.5 ppm of chlorine gas and one ppm of fluoride. Chlorine has been added since 1911 and fluoride since 1970, after voters, who had rejected previous proposals in 1952 and 1963, finally approved its addition. Before reaching Seattle our drinking water makes one final stop at Lake Youngs, flowing 10 miles northwest by tunnel. Two other additives go into water leaving Lake Youngs, lime and soda ash, which help reduce corrosion in pipes. This is particularly important for homes built with copper piping soldered together with a tin-lead mix, popular from the 1950s to 1980s before the city and county banned the mixture.

In a report released in June 2003, the Natural Resources Defense Council cited lead as one of two reasons that Seattle had poor-quality drinking water. The other reason was high levels of haloacetic acids, a by-product of the chlorine added to the water to kill pathogens. These two issues are now mostly moot because of new treatment plants at Lake Youngs (completed

June 2004) and on the Tolt River (completed January 2001), both of which use ozone and UV light to kill pathogens such as *Cryptosporidium* and *Giardia*. They should help make Seattle's drinking water some of the cleanest in the country.

Lake Youngs' water then flows to one of several reservoirs around Seattle and finally to residences and businesses. Total time in the water cycle from Chester Morse Lake to tap is between two and three weeks.

Part of what makes this system so nifty is that it relies principally on gravity to move water from forest to faucet. Landsburg was chosen because its elevation of 535 feet is higher than any point in Seattle, particularly the first reservoir that water originally flowed to, in Volunteer Park. Lake Youngs is slightly lower than Landsburg but still allows for water to flow by gravity into the city. Water from the Tolt has an even bigger drop, starting at 770 feet.

In my Seven Hills chapter I discussed standing near a water tower, stand pipe, or reservoir at the summit of several hills. (I didn't mention the towers at Beacon and Magnolia but they were nearby.) From these high points, water drops to homes and businesses around the hill or to lower points, such as downtown or along the Duwamish flats. The Lake Forest Park Reservoir and Bitter Lake Reservoir, at 550 and 509 feet respectively, serve most of the north end of the city. The water at our house, however, comes from the Maple Leaf Reservoir, dropping about 150 feet in elevation.

When we have finished using it, water enters the output part of the urban water cycle and leaves via gravity down a six-inch-diameter pipe connected to a sanitary sewer pipe running down the middle of our street. This pipe takes sewage down toward Green Lake, where it enters the 90-inch-diameter North Trunk line, which carries water under Ravenna, down toward Union Bay and along the ship canal out to West Point. The water travels at about two feet per second.

Along the way to the West Point Treatment Plant, water from our house mixes with another 125 million gallons of sewage water and enters the plant surprisingly clear. I discovered this on a tour of West Point with a group of Boy Scouts that I horned in on. The tour leader began by asking us what we hoped to see. "Poop," exclaimed the giddy youngsters. "You've come to the right place. We *so* have poop here," responded our equally enthused guide.

After a quick discussion of facts and figures—the plant was built in 1966 and upgraded in 1991 to comply with the federal Clean Water Act, and can treat up to 440 mgd, with an average of 133 mgd—she pulled out five jars showing the various levels of water purity as sewage traveled through the plant.

The jar of water containing completely untreated water had only a slight coating of residue on the bottom; I am not sure I would have drunk it, especially knowing the source, but I have seen worse-looking water on hiking trips. Each successive jar was slightly cleaner and by the final one, I doubt that anyone could have told you the water had been in the sewer system only 12 hours earlier, which is the average length of time it takes for water to pass through the treatment plant.

We left the conference room, donned yellow hard hats, and headed to the first treatment building, where bar screens remove larger items such as rags and sticks. Our leader's statement, "We once found a pair of dentures, which the owner wanted back," prompted understandable "That's sick" and "Gross" responses from my cohorts. More screens in another building remove smaller grit, which along with larger objects goes to a landfill. Primary treatment ends in a series of metal tanks, where mechanical skimmers remove floating material from the water. Heavier material sinks to the bottom.

Until 1995 this completed the treatment process, removing about 60 percent of organic solids. Secondary treatment began late that year, following five years of construction, which cost $573 million, more than a decade of debate, and more than 200 special permits. After primary treatment, pumps push wastewater up to aeration tanks, where oxygen and bacteria flood the liquid, creating an environment in which the bacteria can feed on dissolved and suspended organics. The wastewater then flows into 13 round tanks, the big pools of water visible from Discovery Park, which let bacteria settle out. By this point the water is clear enough to attract groups of gulls. A final phase chlorinates and dechlorinates the water, which flows 95 percent organics-free out into Puget Sound, 240 feet below the surface and three-quarters of a mile from shore.

This output part of the water cycle has not always worked so well in Seattle. The earliest known "sewer system" consisted of wood troughs or boxes, which emptied into Elliott Bay and Lake Union. Permanent pipes made of vitrified clay did not get laid until 1885. Five years later, in a report that still has ramifications, sanitation engineer Benezette Williams recommended combining sewage and storm runoff in one system. The simple reason was that a single, dual-purpose pipe cost less. Although Williams recognized that raw sewage should not enter the city's freshwater lakes, he thought it safe for untreated sanitary waste to flow into the Duwamish River, Elliott Bay, and off West Point.

The sewer system could not keep up with the growing population and by 1945 more and more beaches around the city displayed "Polluted Water: Unsafe for Bathing" signs. At least 30 pipes disgorged untreated material into Lake Washington. Sewage dumped into Puget Sound came out of pipes just offshore. By 1958, sewage from 425,000 people, about 53 percent of the metropolitan population, discharged untreated into the Sound. An additional 80,000 people connected into systems that expelled treated sewage into Lake Washington.

Degradation of Seattle's waters led to a historic vote in 1958 that established regional wastewater treatment facilities and a collection system to carry sewage to the new facility. Eight years later, Metro, which King County absorbed in 1992, completed the primary treatment plant at West Point. The site was chosen because sewage already went there, the currents in Puget Sound could disperse treated wastewater, and the site, at the time an army base, was relatively isolated.

The establishment of West Point and the other wastewater treatment plants in the system has helped to reduce pollution in the waters of the greater metropolitan Seattle area. We can swim in the various lakes and in Puget Sound. Raw sewage washing onto shore is no longer our biggest concern at beaches (now we complain about goose poop). But there are problems; we still foul our streams and lakes with contaminants.

One source for these contaminants is the Combined Sewer Overflow (CSO) system, a remnant of the 1890 Williams report. One disadvantage of the Williams single-pipe system is overflow. When too much stormwater enters the pipes in large rain events, the pipes spill without treatment into Lake Washington, Lake Union, the Ship Canal, Green Lake, and Elliott Bay. On average about 1.5 billion gallons a year (bgy) flows out of CSOs, down from an estimated 30 bgy in 1960, when on average about 40 times a summer, rainstorms led to raw sewage overflowing the sewer system into Green Lake and Lake Washington, making both lakes unfit for swimming. Both the city and King County are actively working to eliminate CSOs, with a projected completion date of 2030.

The second source of contaminants comes from industry, agriculture, and our own yards, parks, and roads. Recent studies from the USGS report a brew of compounds in our nation's streams that would put a witch to shame, including pesticides, steroids, antibiotics, prescription drugs, plasticizers, and household chemicals such as N, N-diethyltoluamide (aka DEET), tri(2-chloroethyl)phosphate (fire retardant), tricloran (antimicrobial disinfectant), caffeine, and carbaryl (pesticide). One study found 36 pesticides, including 16 at or above levels set to protect aquatic life, in streams and rivers in the Pacific Northwest. Another identified 82 organic wastewater contaminants (OWCs) from waterways; a third collected 38 chemical compounds in treated wastewater and drinking-water supplies; and a fourth found concentrations of pathogenic bacteria, such as fecal coliform, *E. coli*, and enterococci, exceeding Washington state safety standards.

Although most of these compounds undergo rigorous preapproval testing, little is known about their fate after their intended use. We don't know what happens when these chemicals mix together or what new compounds result when they degrade. We have only begun to understand how trace amounts of antibiotics in water foster the development of bacteria resistant to these drugs. We don't know how some hydrophobic pesticides get concentrated in sediments. Nor has the EPA assessed the risk to aquatic organisms of many of the pesticides found in streams.

For example, in Thornton Creek a USGS survey found 21 pesticides, 12 of which lacked criteria for risk to aquatics. Of those, four were found at some of the highest levels in the creek. Three others, carbaryl, chloropyrifos, and diazinon, for which levels have been set, exceeded those levels. The USGS also found PCBs in Thornton, as well as DDT and its notorious breakdown product DDE, which may indicate disturbance of buried, contaminated soils.

Who knows what noxious potion will result when organic wastewater compounds mix with pesticides and bacteria such as enterococci and *E. coli*?

I don't think it makes sense to let Taylor drink that water or even to walk in it. Nor does it seem safe to let kids play in Thornton Creek or swim at beaches near its outlet. And Thornton is no worse or no better than any other urban stream in Seattle.

We may not know exactly what these compounds do to us, but we do know they are not good for our local salmon and other fish. Pesticides impair a salmon's sense of smell, reduce their stamina, interfere with their hormones, and depress their immune systems. Hormone compounds can transform male fish into female fish, make males become intersex (displaying female and male reproductive tissues), and slow sperm motility. Detergents, including biodegradable ones, can ruin the protective external mucus layers of fish, damage gills, kill fish eggs, and cause fish to absorb double the amount of chemicals they would normally absorb. Not necessarily the news you want to hear if you eat fish or other seafood.

As Pogo said, "We have met the enemy and it is us." We are the polluters. We wash our cars in our driveways and flood our waterways with oil, grease, and detergents. We spray our yards, roadsides, gardens, parks, and golf courses with insecticides, rodentcides, and herbicides, which seep into streams and sewage pipes. We flush prescription drugs down our toilets. We let our pets poop in yards and parks and don't pick it up. On a larger scale, shipyards, oil refineries, and pulp and paper mills release toxic heavy metals directly into water bodies.

Seattle and King County agencies are trying to reduce the use of pesticides. They have started to educate people about the problems and to offer them alternatives. An analysis of pesticide sales at large hardware stores, however, shows that people are still buying them. When I walk around my neighborhood I see little signs stating that pesticides and fertilizers have been applied. I try to avoid letting Taylor walk on these lawns or any lawn that lacks weeds. Even organic fertilizers can be bad because people often use too much, which washes into the streams and creates a surplus of phosphate that leads to algal blooms. When the algae die, bacteria boom, sucking up excess oxygen and leading to the death of salmon.

It doesn't help that pavement covers huge tracts of urban land. Miles of impervious surfaces lead to increased runoff, lower summer flows, higher peak flows, increased erosion, and a higher sediment load. Water no longer soaks into soils but instead washes off pavement carrying biological and chemical contaminants into streams, lakes, and Puget Sound. Flushing material into storm drains doesn't always help because many pipes end up ejecting untreated stormwater into Lake Washington and Puget Sound.

Obviously we are not going to rip up pavement and replace it with green space, but each one of us does influence the complete water cycle. We can consciously make a decision to reduce or eliminate our lawns. We can wash our cars at car washes instead of in our driveways. We can avoid using pesticides and fertilizers, reduce our use of them, or at least apply them correctly. We can properly dispose of pharmaceuticals. We can collect runoff from our roofs. We can use water-efficient washing machines and dishwashers, low-flow toilets, showerheads, and faucets; and we can regularly fix leaks. We can pick up our pets' poop. We can eliminate pavement or redirect runoff from pavement to yards.

We in Seattle should know the importance of conserving and protecting water. We get conniptions when Copper River salmon finally arrives. We spend hundreds of thousands of dollars for houses with views of Puget Sound and Lake Washington. We have the nation's largest ferry system and own more boats per capita than anywhere else. Our single biggest civic celebration, Seafair, centers on water. We have built our reputation around our liquid abundance and the water cycle that nourishes it. It is a legacy worth protecting.

More than any other bird he has successfully matched his wits against those of
man, and his frequent easy victories and
consequent boastings are responsible in large
measure for the unsavory reputation in
which he is held.

WILLIAM LEON DAWSON, *THE BIRDS OF*
WASHINGTON, 1909

It is a warm Wednesday in late March 2001 and I am driving around Highlands Vista, a recently built subdivision on the east side of Seattle. I do not normally do this. I try to avoid the suburbs, but on this early spring day I have ventured into this labyrinth of McMansion-filled streets in the name of science. Next to me sits John Withey, a graduate student at the University of Washington. We are looking for a place to trap and band crows, as part of John's thesis work. "This is good territory for crows because of big, worm-rich yards, few predators, and a weekly supply of trash bins. We just need to find a quiet street with some open space and few houses," he says. After circling for 20 minutes, we find a roadway at the edge of the suburb and park between two houses and across the street from a yet-to-be-built-on lot of Douglas-firs and western red cedars.

We get out and begin to set up a contraption called a net gun. It consists of a three-sided, five-inch deep, 24-by-18 inch metal pan, where the net sits, and a metal frame, which holds the pan off the ground and supports four tubes, each filled with a metal weight attached to a corner of the net. To shoot the net, John uses a single .308-caliber shell blank, which, when fired, propels the four slugs and the net out and over crows. After carefully folding the net into the pan and stretching out two weighted strands of rope, which will help spread the net out when shot, John pulls a machete out of his backpack and cuts ferns and grasses to hide the net gun.

"Crows recognize the net gun as a trap and won't land if they see it," he explains. "Even birds that have never seen it will be wary. On the UW campus, where I trap extensively, I have to set the net gun up in the dark, in shrubs, and hide the strings attached to the anchor weights." We then run an electric trigger cord along the street from the gun to my car.

To attract crows, John puts out the equivalent of a five-star meal for them—a used Burger King box with french fries, some Mrs. Cubbison's Cheese Puffs, and pieces of County Fair enriched white bread. By 8:45 A.M. we are ready to catch crows. Our first avian gourmand appears almost immediately, landing on a nearby light post where it caws once and then flies to a Douglas-fir. Despite the delectables under its perch, the crow does not drop to the street.

Two taste testers land a little after nine. They hop around the food and one picks at the Burger King box, while the other appears to be deciding between a cheese puff and the bread. It prods one then the other before ultimately plucking up Mrs. Cubbison's colorful product and strutting around with a Day-Glo cigar sticking out of its beak.

Crows continue to land by the food over the next two hours, periodically interrupted by us either adding more food or rearranging it. Several vehicles drive down the rain-splattered street and all avoid our "trash" in the middle of the road. No one stops to ask why we are sitting in a car watching garbage in the street. Before we set up the trap, John had called the police to let them know that he would be shooting the gun.

Just as we are thinking that we will not catch any birds, 15 to 20 materialize out of nowhere and land by the food. John shoots the net, which makes a surprisingly loud sound. A neighbor yells "What happened?" out her second-story window. John yells back, "We're catching crows," and we rush toward the pile of birds. Most appear to be dead, wrapped in the net. Only a few wriggle. John takes off his sweater, places it over the more active ones, and we begin the process of untangling the eight birds.

I am surprised by how calm the crows are as we methodically unwrap their wings, beaks, and claws from the thin green thread. Once free they become more agitated so we put each bird in a sock, headfirst. This calms them, although, they try to escape by pulling the socks off. John had not expected to catch so many birds, so like any good field biologist would do, he sacrifices his own socks and walks around barefoot on the wet pavement. Within ten minutes we have the eight crows untangled, socked, and laid out on a ratty, patchwork blanket in the back of the car. One crow has a brown hood, three are in dark blue, three wear white, and one is clad in gray.

Their legs stick straight up and their tails straight out. Their feet are in a variety of positions. Like all members of the passerine, or perching bird, group, which includes most of the small birds found in cities, crows have four separate toes. Each toe of the birds in my car looks like yellowish, gray-stacked beads and ends in a three-eighths-inch-long black nail. The toes feel like reptile skin. Three face forward and the fourth backward and all attach to the leg at the same level, an arrangement that provides excellent gripping power and dexterity. They have stout legs, good for walking and for what appears to be their favorite mode of ground travel, a two-footed, springing strut. They also have stout beaks, which they use to pry open food, shred garbage bags, and bite an unsuspecting writer's finger.

John and I take about 45 minutes to measure wing and beak lengths, weigh each bird, snip feathers for DNA studies, and attach three colored bands and one numbered aluminum Fish and Wildlife Service band, two on each leg. Holding the final crow erect by wrapping my hand around the tail and legs, I feel like I am grasping an oversized black Popsicle. Up close I can make out subtle shades of black and purple on its head feathers, which look like hair, they are so fine.

As I gaze into the eyes of the bird in hand, it stares right back, adding to one of my few urban natural history fears. Crows often intimidate me. Whenever I see a small gathering of them I look around to figure out why they have banded together. I can't help feeling that they know something I do not and that they have the advantage. I sense this intelligence in the bird I hold, as if the crow is memorizing my features in case I ever venture onto its turf again. I hope it will not spread the word about how John and I have handled it and its seven compatriots.

I first met John at a presentation about Seattle's urban crows, at Camp Long in West Seattle. He was wearing a straw hat adorned with a small scarecrow holding a "Help" sign and surrounded by three crows perched on thin wires. I was one of about 20 people in the room. I had gone to the talk because I had developed a relationship with crows. They are one of the few animals—

along with our dog Taylor, squirrels, house finches, robins, and a few other bird species—that I encounter every day. Unlike other birds, however, crows seem to participate actively instead of passively in their day-to-day activities; they play, create mischief, watch me when I walk by, gather in groups for lengthy conversations, and problem-solve. They are thinkers, and I like them for that.

I am not alone in my appreciation of our local crows. In William Leon Dawson's *The Birds of Washington*, written in 1909, he described how early sawmills kept free-roaming pigs, which took advantage of the mills' proximity to water and wandered down to the beach to dig up clams at low tide. Crows, in turn, took advantage of the pigs by landing on their backs. Dawson wrote, "The minute the industrious rooter turned up a clam, the Crow darted down, seized it in his beak and made off; resigning his station to some sable brother, and leaving the porker to reflect discontentedly upon the rapacity of the upper classes."

John began his talk by describing the habits and haunts of crows, including one of the big misconceptions about them. "I don't deny that crows take eggs and young of other birds, but they are not as bad as some people believe," he said. Instead, crows are like the class clown in school who gets in trouble for talking in class when others are just as noisy but less conspicuous. Other less-obvious predators include dogs and cats, sharp-shinned hawks, rats, mice, garter snakes, gray squirrels, chipmunks, and raccoons, most of whom operate at night.

This misplaced accusation led to one of the more sordid tales of Seattle's avian past. In 1919 the Seattle Board of Park Commissioners asked the Sportsmen Association to find experienced gunners to kill crows in city parks. One of those selected, William Elliott, wrote to the board that "we did good service [at Volunteer Park]. . . . During the summer months I would go to the Park before sunrise and shoot crows until 7 o'clock." His weapon of choice was a small caliber shotgun, which used a cartridge no bigger than one's little finger. He appears to have shot crows for eight years before stopping, but he wanted to start up again when he saw crows destroy a robin's nest. Another request was made to kill crows in 1933. Jacob Umlauf, head gardener for the park department, supported the idea, but I could find no further record of depredation.

John then moved into his main topic. "I am trying to figure out why so many crows now live in Seattle," he said. In a situation similar to their more detested distant cousins, Canada geese, crow numbers have boomed since the 1960s from less than a few hundred birds in the city to the point where a monthly survey conducted by John and eight groups of volunteers finds an average of 1,700 crows in two hours of searching. What is odd is that it appears that the breeding rate of Seattle's urban crows is a bit below average, certainly not enough to account for the bird's dramatic population increase.

John and his advisor theorize that the carving out of second-growth forests for new suburbs on the east side of Lake Washington drives the population boom in Seattle. Crows prefer the suburbs, with their many open spaces and abundant food supplies, over the forests, which lack food and provide few nesting sites. "We see Seattle as a sponge, soaking up the excess population of suburban birds," John said. "I call it the Young Urban Crow or YUCKIE hypothesis."

Although Seattle is popular with the younger set, this does not mean that these crows find a better home here than in the suburbs. For one thing, urban property is scarce because each family, which is centered around a monogamous pair, defends its own territory. John believes that Seattle's breeder population has filled up the available territories, which means that juveniles who move to Seattle and look for mating possibilities will not find a place to settle. Seattle crows are so desperate for space that at least a dozen pairs nest in a 60-block section downtown, including one on a utility box tucked up and under the Alaska Way Viaduct. (Breeding season is one of the times when people notice crows, because adults will scold and swoop down on anyone who passes beneath a nest with nestlings or fledglings.)

Food is the other limiting factor. Crows find a high volume of edible material in what James Gorman of the *New York Times* calls "the French fry ecosystem," but as most people know, this food does not exactly meet many USDA recommended daily-allowance standards—even for crows. Grubs, mealworms, roadkill, and adult insects offer far more nutrition. Studies show that suburban adults who stick to that diet produce more and larger young than their urban counterparts. While edible items are plentiful in Seattle, a nutritious meal is more likely in the suburbs.

Survivorship is also lower in the city. Predators eat young crows and crow eggs. Crows get struck by cars and trucks, run into unnatural hazards such as windows, land on electric poles, and get killed by eagles, red-tailed hawks, and great horned owls. Predation on crows occurs in the suburbs but not to the degree that it does in the urban core.

So if living in the city is not as good for them, why do so many crows abandon the suburbs to live in Seattle? We have to look no further than the young humans who come into the city from the suburbs; Seattle is where the action is whether you are a young crow or a teenager. Each wants to get away from parents, chill with friends, gossip, and maybe make a bit of trouble. Nutrition and reproduction are not high on the agenda yet.

The birds also leave, at least initially, because young crows cannot easily find breeding space, but if they wait long enough suburban development will eventually create new territory for crows to colonize. This is the central point of the YUCKIE hypothesis: as sprawl slashes into the forests surrounding Seattle, crows who had journeyed into the city during their youth now move out to the newly created, unclaimed, crow-friendly territory to breed and propel the upward climb of bird numbers.

Two weeks after hearing John's talk at Camp Long, I joined him at Foster Island, one of the testing grounds for the YUCKIE hypothesis. Once a month John counts the crows that roost in the alders, maples, and oaks at the north end of the arboretum. He chose this spot because upwards of ten thousand crows spend the night here from November through February. Being social birds, crows gather in roosts to converse and share information. In the summer breeding season, the number may drop as low as 300 because they stay and defend their nest territory instead of socializing.

We met at 7:00 A.M. at the boat dock below Husky Stadium to watch the daily spectacle of thousands of crows flying en masse away from the roost just across the Montlake Cut. We were alone except for the UW women's crew team silently and gracefully gliding by a pair of mallards. I heard a few crows in an advance wave, but mostly urban sounds of speeding cars, airplanes, and an occasional honk of a Canada goose dominated the airwaves.

"I am studying the roost because I want to know if the winter roost adequately reflects the year-round population of crows," John said. To test this, John and his volunteer groups drive different routes monthly and count every crow they see. They then compare their numbers with numbers obtained during the annual Christmas Bird Count, a nationwide event where birders go out and count every bird they can find. "By comparing the two totals, I can see whether the winter data is an accurate gauge or whether it only reflects winter numbers, which could include urban, suburban, and rural crows," he added. Counting crows and knowing the true number in Seattle is essential if biologists want to get a true understanding of why the crow population is changing.

We stopped talking when the trickle of birds leaving Foster Island became a current, growing from 25 to 60 to over 100 per group. Crows headed west down the cut, southwest toward Capitol Hill, and northwest over the stadium. With my binoculars I could also pick out additional crows flying due north over Union Bay. The sky looked like someone had taken a fountain pen and flung ink onto azure paper. Black lines of birds streaked across the airspace above us. Dawn had triggered the crows' natural instinct to go out, explore, and forage.

One big pool formed in the Lombardy poplars directly across the ship canal from us. The birds conversed, preened, and warmed up, getting ready for their daily job as one of the most visible scavengers in the city. This is not the only gathering point for crows in the early morning. Thousands more land in Husky Stadium parking lots. Several hundred venture to Green Lake. Others convene at the Montlake Fill and still more congregate for a final conversation at parking lots and fields around Seattle.

They then return to their previous day's haunts or if they learned of a better spot at the roost they may follow their cohorts to the new location. Perhaps a Taco Bell or 7-Eleven to rummage through a Dumpster or some kindly person's backyard, where a fresh supply of peanuts awaits. They may know of a busy street where cars serve up fresh road kills. Lazy homeowners, who let their garbage cans overflow, provide meals, too, as do finicky homeowners, who get in the act by keeping nice grassy lawns, a haven for fat, juicy earthworms and larvae. Crows eat just about anything and quickly learn where they can consistently find a good meal.

Thanks to our sloppy, consumptive lifestyle, food in the french-fry ecosystem is plentiful and served regularly. As we do with Canada geese, we provide a smorgasbord of food, without considering that our actions are one of the reasons these birds, which many people despise, thrive in Seattle. We should at least thank the crows for cleaning up so much of the junk on the ground.

John takes advantage of the birds' daytime habits of spreading around the city to furnish data for the YUCKIE hypothesis. He and his assistants have banded over 400 juvenile crows, including our eight crows, in both the suburbs and on the UW campus. They also radio-track an additional 30 crows, each of which wears a small backpack consisting of Teflon straps and a plastic-coated, battery-powered radio transmitter about the size of a pack of Life Savers. Since a crow's 20-year life span is much longer than the battery, John uses dental floss, which eventually breaks, to hold the straps together.

Three weeks after John and I catch our crows, he invites me to join him to search for radio-tagged birds. Our plan is to head over to the east side of Lake Washington, to turn on a receiver in areas where John suspects that tagged crows live, and to drive until we locate one. The receiver is connected to a directional finder, made from a single five-foot-long aluminum rod with three parallel three-foot-long rods attached about one foot apart at right angles to the longer pole. A rubber handle at the bottom makes it easier to hold. Each bird transmits on a specific frequency. The finder picks up signals up to two miles away in the city, with better reception in suburban and flatter areas.

After searching for 20 minutes we pick up our first signal at the northeast corner of Bridle Trails State Park, a 482-acre park, about three miles northeast of downtown Bellevue. The signal is a faint scratchy pulse. We drive east, stop at Ben Franklin School, get out the directional finder, return to the park, drive north into a denser development of stores, and make a U-turn as the pulses get louder. The signal volume increases as we move west, where it is so loud I hear the staccato pulses from inside the car. We stop and John gets out behind a Red Apple grocery.

Four juvenile crows sit together on a roof edge overlooking a Dumpster. Perfect crow habitat. A quiet street, good trees for perching, and a ready food source of human detritus. We no longer need the antenna to hear the beeps. After searching for another five minutes we find our bird sitting in a Douglas-fir next to a small set of apartments. John jots down the bird's banding colors—white over red on its left leg and orange over white on its right leg—and location.

He later tells me that this bird stayed around the Red Apple for about two months, moved south to Bellevue, and then disappeared, probably because its transmitter died. Of the other birds tagged near Bridle Trails, one died of unknown causes, one appears to have been killed by a BB-gun or sling-shot, and one wintered near Southcenter, 10 miles south, before setting up a home territory near Totem Lake, four miles north of the Red Apple.

From the Red Apple we drive north of Kirkland to attempt to find a crow near St. Edward State Park. We spend nearly an hour searching, walking down the middle of empty streets holding our antenna and periodically using binoc-ulars to search trees for a radio-tagged crow, whose beeps pip quietly in John's receiver. I feel like we are in some biologist's surreal fantasy movie about des-perado researchers wandering lonely suburbia in search of fantastic beasts. Any time now a group of rival researchers will leap out and John will have to defend his theory to the death. We never find the bird. No one even asks what we are doing.

John says that this is typical for him. Many hours of searching, little inter-action with people in the study area, more hours logging data, and short bits of time with crows in hand. On one occasion, though, one of John's volun-teer crow watchers had a little too much human interaction. During the 2000 field season, Kirkland police handcuffed the volunteer because someone appar-ently reported him as a Peeping Tom when he was scoping for a radio-tagged bird near an apartment complex. John has yet to be handcuffed but has had a humbling encounter. During one of his searches a woman asked him what he was doing and he patiently described his work with crows. She replied, "Oh, I thought you were doing something scientific."

When I ask John why he studies urban crows instead of a less common bird out in some exotic place, he responds that he likes working with them because people can relate to the birds and their environment. "Everybody has a crow story," he says. "People know the suburbs. They can understand the consequences of a changing environment. I think that there has been a cultural coevolution between people and crows. Where once we persecuted them, now most people have learned to live with crows and they with us. I still get people asking me why I study crows but I have met more with curiosity than challenge.

"My fieldwork has given me more faith in humanity and the basic goodness and cooperativeness of people. I also like how you can't generalize about crows, that they make people nervous, and that there is a little edge to our interactions with them. I like to end my talks with a Tony Angell quote from his book *Ravens, Crows, Magpies, and Jays.* 'These birds are more than descriptions by weight, measure, color, and distribution, for behind their amber eyes are answers to questions we may never learn to ask.' They keep my work fresh and interesting."

After crows have finished their day of scrounging, eating, and avoiding John's net gun, they head back to Foster Island, though they do not return immediately to the roost. Before descending upon the arboretum, crows will meet up, often in the same locales where they had their postdawn get-together. Biologists don't fully understand these preroosting aggregations (PRAs) but hypothesize that birds gather primarily to gain the protection of being in a larger group. More eyes help spot potential predators, such as bald eagles and red-tailed hawks, while a large group can better foil an attack. PRAs may also serve as a kind of crow bar with birds sharing information on food and younger birds learning from older birds.

One of my favorite parts of the winter day is the daily ritual of crows on their determined flights back toward the roost. Some days I see only a few pass by my office window, their black bodies silhouetted against the ashen sky. On other days I may encounter hundreds streaming straight down Ravenna Boulevard or across Capitol Hill. No matter how many birds I see and no matter where I am, I still try to take the time to observe them.

I don't expect to see anything new or exciting. I stop and stare because watching the crows' return to the roost connects me to the natural patterns that define place. Their flight reassures me that nature's rhythms are in order and gives me another piece of the puzzle of my home. I also feel a connection to place in other cities when I see crows flying at dusk to roosts. It is like seeing an old friend, comforting and familiar. I have the same feeling when I see the big dipper when traveling or a chunk of Salem Limestone in a building I have not seen before. These bonds to the natural world help establish my bearings and keep me headed in the right direction. By learning about the stories of my home, I expand my connections to the larger world.

For my final crow adventure I return to Foster Island, this time to walk the trails around the roost at dusk. I am in the center of a cosmic crow maelstrom. Birds arrive from the north, east, and west. Most come in groups. Many are playing, chasing each other, dive-bombing their roostmates, enjoying the last flight of the day. One even lands in the water about 20 feet from the shore at the north end of the peninsula and sort of butterfly-strokes to the breakwater, where it disappears into a darkened crevice. Wave upon flying wave arrive, the birds starting high above the water, then swooping low before a final climb into the leafless trees dotting the shoreline.

The birds' chattering and squawking sounds like one of those rain sticks one can buy at nature stores. For a short time the tremor of competing voices drowns out all city sounds. When a new group lands and jockeys for position, they sometimes force whole tree loads to whorl above in a frenzy of wing beats and scolding. The inky mass at Foster Island eventually calms down about 45 minutes after sunset.

This winter dispersal and return of crows is perhaps Seattle's grandest daily natural-history display. Nowhere else in the city can one see so many wild, large, living beings at one time, except at certain sporting events. Nowhere else can one so easily escape the paved roads, manicured lawns, bleating cars, and push, push, push of the city. Despite the chaos of crows, entering this maelstrom calms, humbles, and awes me.

I have few opportunities in Seattle to experience the fecundity of the wild, to revel in populations maximizing their potential to use, but not over-use, the land's resources. Gone are salmon runs so thick you could walk across them or forests so dense you could barely walk through them. The Foster Island roost of crows, while not completely a natural phenomenon, at least touches on the nature of wildness.

Although I am thrilled by the large roost at Foster Island, I recognize that it represents a downside of urbanization. When human settlement expands into once-wild areas, bird communities respond by becoming denser, as the crows have done in the greater Seattle area. In this equation, it is not so much suburban versus urban that matters but developed versus wild. Surplus food, fewer predators, and new nesting potential (e.g., chimneys, eaves, and ledges) generally lead to increased fecundity and may help winter survivability. At first glance this might seem to be a good thing—more birds than before—but when ornithologists take a closer look they discover that higher numbers do not mean greater diversity.

What they find is that three species—pigeons, starlings, and house sparrows—all nonnatives, dominate most urban habitats. No matter what the local environment—coastal chaparral, temperate forest, grassland, or eastern broadleaf forest—these three species will be found within the most developed sites. They are the McDonalds of the avian world, successful, aggressive, and bland.

This homogenization has come at the expense of native species. Native birds lose out because of competition from aggressive aliens, reduction in arthropod populations, and higher potential for disease and chemical contamination. Loss of broad expanses of forest and grassland, with their layers of understory, shrubs, trees, and snags, leads to fewer ground and cavity nesters, as well as to fewer birds dependent on interior forests for nesting. Nonnative vegetation favors nonnative birds, which often have more plastic food and nesting requirements. Fragmented habitat also leads to increased nest predation and parasitism by creating more edge habitat that is not protected and is more accessible.

A drop in a native population can be the beginning of the path to extinction. Ecologists call these small-scale losses "local extinctions," and while some may consider such events inconsequential in the larger picture of a species, others argue that we must pay attention to them. In his passionate exploration of urban wildlands, *The Thunder Tree*, writer Robert Michael Pyle lists three reasons for paying attention. The first is that local extinction often occurs at the edge of a species' range, one of the most important frontiers for natural selection and speciation. Second, extinction rarely happens in one fell swoop; the first and usually smallest steps go unnoticed until momentum reaches a crisis point.

The final and least measurable of all consequences of depletion is what Pyle calls the *extinction of experience*. "I believe that one of the greatest causes of the ecological crisis is the state of personal alienation from nature in which many people live," he writes. When we lose touch with nature we lose awareness, appreciation, and respect. We cannot find this intimacy on television, with our own pets, or at the Zoo. We, and especially children, need to be able to see, touch, smell, and hear the wildness around us. As Pyle writes, "What is the extinction of a condor to a child who has never known a wren?"

Homogenization also plays a part in Pyle's extinction of experience. Urban residents may not see animals because people tend to disregard or discount the mundane and prosaic, a phenomenon I call "ignorance of the common." I am less excited by and tend not to notice the species I encounter on my daily walks. I see starlings, gray squirrels, and pigeons, and rarely do I note anything more than that they are respectively, a dark bird, a chattering mammal, and a fat bird. I have fooled myself into believing that I know these species because I see them so regularly, but what do I know besides the names we have given them, that they live in my neighborhood (and many other neighborhoods), and that they dwell here year-round? I do not ask questions about these species, not even basic ones about nesting, breeding, eating, or surviving.

We are missing a splendid opportunity to address this lack of relationships. I understand that Seattleites may not want to connect to nature through starlings, house sparrows, and pigeons, but Seattle has a second tier of common birds—Canada geese, gulls (twelve species but grouped here as one), and crows—each of which is charismatic, well known, and relatively easy to approach. In addition, their populations are not going to drop anytime in the near future. These are our fellow citizens of Seattle. Perhaps we can begin to develop a relationship to wildness by first getting to know the birds we see everyday.

Just as important, crows make the city a more interesting place to live. They are part of the reason I can survive in an urban landscape, away from the wild places I love. Like the crows, I was drawn back to the city because I wanted to be in an area where it is easy to hang out with my friends, where food is plentiful, and where I have a variety of opportunities to find what makes me happy, including a connection to nature.

I knew that I was leaving a remarkable place when we moved away from Moab. But I also knew that I could find beauty and wildness in the Northwest. However, I didn't expect such wildness so close to my home. I am constantly amazed by the plants, animals, and geology of Seattle, and how even short doses of wildness—walking under a canopy of bigleaf maples, sitting next to a small creek, or hunting for fossils in a 30-story sky-scraper—fill me with wonder. In writing this book, I have come to realize that like the crows, like the eagles, and like Thornton Creek, I am resilient and adaptable. I have found my niche in this least-wild place.

The Eagles

Page 15. State ecologists define a territory as an area where a pair of eagles resides. There may be more than one nest in the territory. Seattle is defined as the area that borders Lake Washington. In 1999, there were only 12 territories.

Page 18. Meriwether Lewis wrote, "below this fall at a little distance a beatifull little Island well timbered is situated about the middle of the river. in this Island on a Cottonwood tree an Eagle has placed her nest; a more inaccessable spot I beleive she could not have found; for neither man nor beast dare pass those gulphs which seperate her little domain from the shores." Raynolds wrote on July 12, 1860: "A remarkable fact is that the eagle's nest, described in 1805, as quoted, still remains in the cottonwood, on the island in the stream, and as we came within sight a bald eagle of unusual size was perched in the tree by its side."

Page 21. Watson, James W. and D. John Pierce. 1998. *Ecology of bald eagles in western Washington with an emphasis on the effects of human activity: final report.* Washington Dept. of Fish and Wildlife, Wild Management Program, Wildlife Research Division.

Page 25. Within King County there were 42 territories and 69 nests in 2003.

The Fault

Page 30.   The 1949 quake occurred at 11:55 A.M. with an epicenter near Olympia. Eight people died. Damages were more severe than in the Nisqually quake. The 1965 quake hit at 8:29 A.M., with an epicenter 13 miles southeast of downtown Seattle. Three people died from falling debris and three more apparently from heart attacks. Damages were also more extensive than in 2001.

Page 31.   Atwater and colleagues in Japan subsequently found evidence that a tsunami from the 1700 quake destroyed a ship off the coast of Japan. Tsunami waves trapped the ship for 18 hours off the coast, until a storm arrived and destroyed the ship. Two men died and nearly 30 tons of rice were lost.

Page 34.   Geologists have had the beginnings of a picture of the Seattle fault since the 1960s, they just didn't realize it. In 1965, a short paper appeared in the *Journal of Geophysical Research*. Written by University of Puget Sound geophysicist Zdenko Frankenberger Danes and nine high school students who did much of the fieldwork for Danes, the paper described gravitational anomalies around Puget Sound. Danes accounted for these anomalies, which indicated significant variations in the subsurface geology, by proposing that several, active faults had ratcheted the rocks under Puget Sound out of their original positions. The most active and most significant structure was a "double fault striking approximately at azimuth 105 degrees through Hood Point, Bremerton, southern Seattle, and Renton." Few realized the significance of this paper until the 1980s.

Page 35.   Shown on early maps as the largest island (200 acres) in a group of five, Kellogg was originally shaped like a massive slug, long and narrow with two tentacle-like expanses extended north. It appears to have been named for two signers of the original plat of 1870, S. Kellogg, county auditor, and David Kellogg, notary. In 1891, the name Edwards Island, replaced Kellogg, with the original name not appearing again until the 1930s.

Page 35.   Information on Kellogg Island and cultural resources of this area comes from *Continued Archaeological Testing at the Duwamish No. 1 site (45KI23)*, Office of Public Archaeology, Reconnaissance Reports No. 11, March 1977, by Jerry V. Jermann, Thomas H. Lorenz, and Robert S. Thomas and from *The Duwamish no. 1 site: A lower Puget Sound Shell Midden*, Office of Public Archaeology, Research Report No. 1, 1981, by Sarah H. Campbell.

Page 36.   Captain George Vancouver first noted this anomalous point of land during his round-the-world voyage of discovery. In 1792, he and his crew were some of the first Europeans to see Puget Sound. Vancouver wrote, "we arrived off a projecting point of land, not formed by a low sandy spit, but rising abruptly in a low cliff about ten or twelve feet from the water side."

Page 36.   According to Edwin F. Thor McKnight's 1923 thesis for his bachelor of science degree in geology, the submerged forests "were for the most part concealed from view" but became a "considerable menace to navigation" after 1916, when creation of the Lake Washington Ship Canal lowered the lake level by nine feet. McKnight wrote that two or three boats were sunk by trees. To combat this hazard, the U.S. Coast and Geodetic Survey and U.S. Army Corps of Engineers removed 186 trees, all Douglas-firs, using dynamite and a steel drag line. In 1957, diver Leiter Hockett descended down to the trees near St. Edwards in 90-foot-deep water, an eighth mile from shore. Hockett "found himself engulfed in a densely forested bottom" with many still upright trees in a 40-by-40-foot area. And finally, in 1991–92, tree salvager John Tortorelli illegally harvested about $165,000 worth of trees and sunken logs. Officials only discovered Tortorelli's actions after a Metro sewer line between Renton and Mercer Island started spilling effluvium. Tortorelli was arrested in 1994 and found guilty of theft, trafficking in stolen property, and criminal profiteering. He was sentenced to eight concurrent terms ranging from 12 to 43 months and ordered to pay restitution.

The Plants

Page 43.   The Locks opened officially on July 4, 1917. Thomas Mercer proposed the name Lake Union on July 4, 1854. On the day that Doc Maynard, Arthur Denny, and Carson Boren platted what became downtown Seattle, Maynard had had a bit to drink, leading to his slightly askew rendering of the land. The fire started in a basement on First Avenue just south of Madison Street. Henry Yesler arrived late in 1852 and by the next year had established the city's first industry: logging.

Page 43.   This quote comes from Stewart Holbrook's *Holy Old Mackinaw*. Written in 1938, it is an enjoyable, if not always true, account of the "natural history of the American lumberjack."

Page 47.   According to a history of Seattle schools, Oak Lake formed from overflow from Haller Lake (about one mile north) and was located at about N 107th Street and Midvale Avenue N. I could find no information on when the lake disappeared or when the oaks were removed.

Page 47.   The best information on prairie fires is in *Indians, Fire, and the Land in the Pacific Northwest*, edited by Robert Boyd, and Richard White's *Land Use, Environment, and Social Change: The Shaping of Island County, Washington*.

Page 48.   John Harvey was an Englishman who jumped ship in San Francisco to join the Gold Rush and met E. A. Clark, who had left Pennsylvania in 1850. They staked their claims in Seattle on April 10, 1852. Both were 24. Harvey later worked for Henry Yesler logging lots on Beacon Hill. He invested some $2,000 in improvements to his claim. He became one of the pioneers of Snohomish in 1860 and his descendants now operate Harvey Airfield on his property there. Clark was Seattle's first photographer. His famous first photo of the city shows Sarah Yesler in front of her home and includes an elevated plume from Seattle's first water system. He took the photograph (one of only two of his that survived) in 1859 and within a year was dead. Paul Talbert, who has researched the history of Seward Park, gave me this information.

Page 49. Taylor, Ronald and Theodore Boss. 1975. "Biosystematics of Quercus garryana in Relation to its Distribution in the State of Washington." *Northwest Science.* 49: 2 49–56.

Page 51. The loss of the great trees of Ravenna is one of the abiding mysteries of Seattle. By the 1890s the trees had become one of Seattle's biggest attractions. Visitors included naturalist Enos Mill, Teddy Roosevelt, and famed pianist Jan Paderewski. Clear-cutting of most of the city's other forests led to a push to preserve Ravenna as a city park and in 1910 the city acquired the land through condemnation for $135,663. Within a few years, however, the parks department had cut down the Roosevelt tree, supposedly because it was rotten. By the early 1920s all the big trees were gone. Some blamed the trees' demise on auto pollution, some on a big storm in 1925, and others on chimney smoke from the growing neighborhood. An article in the *Seattle Post-Intelligencer* (December 17, 1972), which contains the most complete record of the mystery, leans toward then superintendent of parks J. W. Thompson as the culprit. Writer William Arnold describes Thompson as a "hard talking, hard drinking engineer, who wouldn't care much what happened to the trees." The mystery will probably never be solved because all records had long been destroyed by the time Arnold penned his piece.

Page 53. Having native trees as the most common trees is unusual for a large city.

Page 56. *Me-Kwa-Mooks* is usually translated as "shaped like a bear's head." Coll Thrush, an expert on the history of Native Americans in the Seattle area, disagrees with this translation. He says, "I'm not fluent, but there's nothing in Me-Kwa-Mooks that even remotely resembles anything about bears or heads. There are lots of place-names involving the suffix denoting head (-qid), so this one would have that too, I'd imagine, if that's what the name meant."

Page 56. Arthur Lee Jacobson gave me the list of 58 native plants in the herbarium. It includes plants collected between 1889 and 1910. I based my analysis of plant extirpation in Seattle on Jacobson's book, *Wild Plants of Seattle*, a mind-bogglingly thorough field guide to every plant in the city. Together with Jacobson's *Trees of Seattle*, they are books that every local plant enthusiast should own.

Page 57. The quote is from May Theilgaard Watts's *Reading the Landscape: An Adventure in Ecology*, a first-rate book on how to interpret landscape. Watts writes in the first person about her adventures, which include visits to forests, bogs, and old school yards. Her style is engaging and informative. The book opened my eyes to an entire new way of looking at landscape. A more modern take on Watts is Tom Wessel's fine *Reading the Forested Landscape: A Natural History of New England*. Although written for eastern forests, it offers good lessons for any landscape.

Page 58. The best source of data on Seattle and Washington bogs is George B. Rigg's *Peat Resources of Washington*, Bulletin 44, Division of Mines and Geology, State of Washington. The report culminated Rigg's nearly 50 years of studying sphagnum bogs. I have also been told by a geologist who has studied the subsurface soils that there was a bog just north of the Opera House at the Seattle Center and one near Rainier Vista (northwest of the intersection of Martin Luther King Way and Columbian Way), which was formed by a landslide. Modern bogs are disappearing, too, especially in areas of rapid development outside of Seattle. Laws do protect modern bogs but they suffer from external landscape changes, such as increased impervious surfaces, which increases runoff and alters the narrow chemistry of bog waters. One study found a 69 percent loss in acreage of bogs in King County between 1958 and 2002.

The Creek

Page 62. It is unclear exactly where Thornton Creek begins. I have seen maps that place the headwaters at a dirty brown pond at the south end of Evergreen–Washelli Cemetery, NE 105th and Meridian Avenue N. From there the water enters a drainage pipe and flows underground until NSCC. Others show small ponds along Meridian as the headwaters. I chose NSCC because it is the first spot that looks like a beginning on the land.

Page 65. There are two papers that I believe describe this bog but the location descriptions are not exact. The earlier one, "The Effect of Some Puget Sound Bog Waters on the Root Hairs of Tradescantia," written by George Rigg in 1913 (*Botanical Gazette* 55, 314–326), refers to a Green Lake bog, located a little over 1,760 meters north of the lake. Rigg wrote that the bog was "just north of the city limits," at the time 85th Street, which locates the bog at roughly Northgate. By the time Rigg described the bog, it had been divided into small garden tracts. Plants in the remaining acres of bog included a small orchid and sundew. Three years later, Göte Turesson wrote "Lysichiton camtschatcense (L) Schott, and its Behavior in Sphagnum Bogs" (*American Journal of Botany* 3, 189–209), which includes a photo showing trees and low vegetation at the bog described by Rigg.

Page 65. Since writing this chapter, plans for the south lot have changed dramatically. King County now owns 3.9 acres at the west end of the lot, which it has converted into parking spaces for a transit center. The city of Seattle has plans to buy 2.7 acres at the east end, which it will probably use for some kind of stormwater detention. Another developer is slated to buy 5.9 acres and build retail and commercial space, 300 or more mixed income residential units, and a public plaza. A 22-member stakeholder group is evaluating plans. Daylighting of Thornton is still a possibility.

Page 68. The odd names of parks on this watershed—Park 6, Park 2, and Park 1—result from the Forward Thrust park proposal in the 1960s. At one point, 16 park properties were planned along the two forks of Thornton. Only three made it.

Page 69. One of 11 children, Edith was born May 10, 1868, in California. She bought her land with gold coin and faithfully paid her taxes every five years. She quit teaching sometime between 1903 and 1910 and moved to Whatcom County to live with her father, a doctor and pharmacist. She became deputy treasurer in 1917 and treasurer in 1921. The accident that killed her occurred three miles north of Ferndale. Alfred Lorenz, the man who ran her off the road, said at his trial, "I was not so drunk that I didn't know what I was doing."

Page 74.   The north fork begins at Ronald Bog at NE 175th Street and Meridian Avenue N and flows through Twin Ponds, Jackson Golf Course, Park 1, and several smaller ravines and wooded areas before reaching the confluence.

Page 74.   Al Blinheim's grandparents, August and Wilhelmina Fischer, originally owned this land and cleared it of trees for farming and grazing. By the 1920s, real estate agents were promoting what they called Fischer's Low-Land Meadows. One brochure described how new homeowners could "turn the mellow loam, plant the seed, and live the year thru on harvest." In addition, amenities such as city lights and Cedar River water came without being "TAXED TO THE BONE," since the property sat outside city limits.

The Stone

Page 84.   The best source of information about building stone in the state is Dave Knoblach's "Washington's Stone Industry—A History" (*Washington Geology*. Vol. 21, No. 4, pp. 3–17). Perhaps the best-known stone structure is the capitol building in Olympia. Built between 1922 and 1928, the dome is one of two self-supporting stone domes in the United States.

Page 85.   Weathering by salt and ice is a fate met by many sandstones in urban environments. Probably the best-known sufferers are the ubiquitous brownstones of New York and Boston, which were popular from the mid-1800s to early 1900s. These eastern rocks are essentially the same as our local variety, starting life as sediments washing out of a now-eroded mountain chain, 200 million years ago when dinosaurs frolicked across a tropical New England.

Page 86.   The Smith Tower opened on July 4, 1914, after four years of construction. Lyman Cornelius Smith was a former shotgun manufacturer turned typewriter maker (Smith Corona) when he decided to build his tower in Seattle. He died before completion of the building. The only taller buildings were in New York City. Smith Tower remained the tallest building west of the Mississippi River until construction of the Humble building in Houston, Texas, in 1963.

Page 87.   The earliest Salem quarries opened in 1827. With the arrival of rail in the 1850s, Salem became more popular around the country, peaking in production in 1912 with 10.5 million cubic feet (Wilkeson's peak was 1.7 million cubic feet). The Salem became popular because the stone cuts cleanly and evenly in all directions and because of its central location; builders used Salem to rebuild Chicago after its Great Fire. Because of its popularity many articles and books have been written about Salem Limestone. Two of the best are *In Limestone Country* (Beacon Press) by Scott Russell Sanders, which describes the natural and cultural history, and *The Salem Limestone in the Indiana Building-Stone District* (John Patton and Donald Carr, Indiana Department of Natural Resources, Geological Survey Occasional Paper 38), a technical paper by two geologists who worked with the stone for many years.

Page 89.   *Rapakivi* is a Finnish word meaning "weathered rock" or "crumbly stone," from *kivi* = rock or stone and *rapautua* = weather (verb). The term originated because the Finnish rapakivis tend to disintegrate more easily than other granitic rocks of the region, not necessarily a good endorsement for a building stone. Granite comes from the Italian *garnito*, meaning "grained."

Page 89.   Geologists have argued for decades about how this texture formed, with no one producing decisive, unequivocal evidence. They do agree, however, that the large feldspar crystals indicate slow cooling underground. As a group, feldspars are one of the most common minerals of the Earth's crust. They occur in all three rock types—igneous, metamorphic, and sedimentary—and they range in color from white to sky blue.

Page 89.   Rapakivis are not the oldest rocks used in Seattle's buildings. The Morton Gneiss, from Morton, Minnesota, is 3.5 billion years old The Morgon, also sold under the trade name of Rainbow Granite, is the oldest commonly used building stone in the country. In Seattle it was used on the Seattle Exchange Building, built in 1929 at Second Avenue and Marion Street.

Page 90.   The word *travertine* comes from the Italian *travertino*, a corruption of *tiburtino* or the stone of Tibur (now known as Tivoli). In the fifteenth and sixteenth centuries, builders pilfered travertine from the Colosseum and used it in the Piazza di San Marco in Venice and Pallazzo Farnese in Rome.

Page 92.   A fossil-rich layer of German limestone deposited at this time makes up the floors of the entry and elevator floors at the Grand Hyatt Hotel in downtown Seattle. The slices of gray rock contain some of Seattle's largest building stone fossils, four-inch-wide ammonites, which look like a top view of a cinnamon roll. Ammonites were relatives of squids and octopuses. They went extinct at the same time as the dinosaurs, 65 million years ago.

The Geese

Page 96.   Information on Operation Mother Goose comes from *Small Game Reports*, produced annually by what used to be known as the Washington Department of Game and now as the Department of Fish and Wildlife. I also interviewed three of the principals, Ellis Bowhay, Curt Hedstrom, and Bud Angerman in 2000.

Page 98.   Manuwal's report, *Nuisance Waterfowl at Public Waterfront Parks in the Seattle Metropolitan Area* (Wildlife Science Group, University of Washington, 1990), is not an easy report to locate. I finally obtained a complete copy of it in late 2003, almost three years after I finished most of the work on this chapter.

Page 99.   Quoted in *Seattle Post-Intelligencer*, November 21, 1990.

Page 99.   Quoted in the *Seattle Times*, July 31, 1991.

Page 99.   Numbers come from *Seattle Times*, July 31, 1991, and July 8, 1992, and from the *Seattle Post-Intelligencer*, August 9, 1993, which is also where the aerial census data came from.

Page 100. U.S. Department of Agriculture, *Final Environmental Assessment and Finding of No Significant Impact and Decision for Management of Conflicts Associated with Non-Migratory (resident) Canada Geese in the Puget Sound Area*, November 1, 1991. Price is listed as primary writer of this EA.

Page 103. Three studies document goose defecation rates, which account for the variability in my numbers. Each looked at Canada geese but in different environments. B. A. Manny, W. C. Johnson, and R.G. Wetzel studied geese in Michigan to determine how they affected nutrient loads in water bodies. "Nutrient additions by waterfowl to lakes and reservoirs: predicting their effects on productivity and water quality," 1994. *Hydrobiologia* 279–280, 121–132. J. Bethard and G. Gauthier's study appeared in 1986 in the *Journal of Applied Ecology* 23, 77–90, "Assessment of fecal output in geese." The final report was another EA on geese, this time in Anchorage, Alaska.

The Bugs

Page 111. Crawford, Rodney L. "An Annotated Checklist of the Spiders of Washington," Burke Museum *Contributions in Anthropology and Natural History*, No. 5.

Page 111. Ross, Kenneth and Robert L. Smith. 1979. "Aspects of the Courtship Behavior of the Black Widow Spider, Latrodectus hesperus, with Evidence for the Existence of a Contact Sex Pheromone," *Journal of Arachnology* 7, 69–77. Ross and Smith's study found that of 25 courtship encounters, only one male "was eaten immediately after mating. However, several were later found dead in their mates' webs."

Page 111. Born in Walla Walla in 1909, Exline received her M.S. (1932) and Ph.D. (1936) from the UW. She researched spiders in Peru and Ecuador, taught at the UW, and was taxonomist and consultant for a National Science Foundation project on spider biology.

Page 113. Additional information about dragonflies can be found in Dennis Paulson's *Dragonflies of Washington* (Seattle Audubon Society, 1999).

Page 113. Frank Carpenter, one of the world's premier insect paleontologists, found this species in the Carlton Limestone Member of the Wellington Formation, near Elmo, Kansas. On several expeditions from 1925 to 1935, he collected 8,000-plus specimens at the site, representing over 17 Orders, 52 Families, 93 Genera, and 150 Species.

Page 114. Another story relates that the seven spots on a ladybug symbolize the seven sorrows of the Virgin Mary.

Page 114. Oregon State University entomologist Jeffrey Miller found the first *Harmonia axyridis* in a potted geranium on July 18 at a friend's house in Kirkland. He said he noticed it because it did not look like any species he had seen before.

Page 115. Lutz and Owen wrote about their yard explorations in two books. Lutz, Frank E. 1941. *A Lot of Insects* (New York: G. P. Putnam's Sons). Owen, Jennifer. 1991. *The Ecology Of A Garden: The First Fifteen Years* (Cambridge University Press). Crawford's numbers come from a study in *Northwest Science*, Vol. 35, No. 1, 1979, "Autumn Populations of Spiders and Other Arthropods in an Urban Landfill."

Page 116. Theodore Savory wrote, ". . . the harvestmen are surely the comedians among the Arachnida: animals with rotund bodies ornamented with little spikes, with two eyes perched atop, back to back, like two faces of a clock-tower, with ungainly legs insecurely attached, with feeble jaws, and an undying thirst . . ." in his book, *Arachnida*.

Page 116. Early English names for harvestmen were shepherd spiders and father longlegs. Craneflies are also called daddy longlegs and there are daddy longlegs spiders in the family Pholcidae. The most common pholcid spiders found in U.S. homes are both European immigrants, *Pholcus phalangioides* and *Holocnemus pluchei*.

Page 116. This dearth of knowledge is based on mites' small size, their incredible diversity, and their lack of apparent charisma. As one mite researcher wrote me, "How many kids fondly remember going mite-watching with their grandpa?" Mites are ubiquitous (detritivores, fungivores, micropredators of tiny animals, plant parasites, animal parasites, nest commensals of vertebrates and insects. Just about anything a small organism can do, they do). To determine how many mites there were in the Pacific Northwest, I was told, "Add up the total number of species of plants, mammals, and birds found in your region. Multiply by two. That will give a conservative estimate for mite richness on these species. Don't forget to add humans! We have two host-specific mites of our own. For freshwater mites, I would guess between 200 and 400 species in Washington state. For marine mites, throw in another 20 species. Soil mites are anyone's guess, but probably 500 to 1000 species."

Page 117. "Milliped" has been the preferred term in America since 1911. Millipede is British.

Page 117. Some creationists use this as a sign that a creator had a hand in this scenario. After all, how could something so novel come to be without a "planner." One wonders what tricks said planner was playing when she created intestinal parasites, spiders that can only mate once because their reproductive organs break off inside the female, or wasps that lay their eggs in still living but paralyzed tarantulas—the newborn wasps feed on the tarantula.

Page 118. In Ian Fleming's *Dr. No*, the villain tried to kill James Bond with a centipede, described by Fleming as "five inches of gray-brown, shiny death." In the movie version, the centipede became a tarantula, neither species of which would have done much damage to a big, strong guy like Bond.

Page 118. Collinge, Walter E. 1935. "Woodlice, their Folk-lore and Local Names," *The North Western Naturalist* 10, 19–21. Collinge also wrote that some people believed that seeing a sowbug out during the day meant a sign of rain and that swallowing sowbugs helped cows "to promote the restoration of their cud."

Page 119. Byrne, David N. et al. 1984. "Public Attitudes Toward Urban Arthropods," *Bulletin of the Entomological Society of America* 30, 40–44.

Page 120. Information on entomophobia comes from Hardy, Tad. 1988. "Entomophobia: The Case for Miss Muffet," *Bulletin of the Entomological Society of America* 34, 65–69.

The Weather

Page 127. The original source for these documents is David Laskin's enjoyable and fascinating *Rains All the Time: A Connoisseur's History of Weather in the Pacific Northwest* (Sasquatch Books). It is another book that all northwesterners should own. Another fun source of weather information and trivia is Walter Rue's *Weather of the Pacific Coast* (The Writing Works, Inc.).

Page 128. Weather records have been kept in Seattle since 1891. Records were taken at the federal building in downtown until 1972. Since 1945, SeaTac Airport has been the official weather station. Statistically our driest days of the year are July 30 and August 4, both of which had measurable rainfall only 7 out of 105 years. The three days with the highest average temperature, 77 degrees, in 52 years at the airport are July 30 and 31 and August 1. At the federal building, the high days are July 21 to 28, with the same average. November 19 is the wettest day, with rain recorded on 79 out of 105 years.

Page 130. Albright's information was never published in a scientific journal but was reported in a September 8, 1988, *Seattle Times* article by Hill Williams (no relation).

Page 133. Mass, Clifford. 1981. "Topographically Forced Convergence in Western Washington State." *Monthly Weather Review* 109, 1335–1347.

Page 134. Mass, Clifford et al. 1986. "The Onshore Surge of Marine Air into the Pacific Northwest: A Coastal Region of Complex Terrain." *Monthly Weather Review* 114, 2602–2627.

Page 135. In the summer of 2003, a headline appeared in the *Seattle Times* asking "Will the 70-degree days ever end?" They did.

Page 136. Church, P. E. 1974. "Some Precipitation Characteristics of Seattle." *Weatherwise*, December 27, 1974, 244–251.

Page 138. This story comes from Charles Prosch's *Reminiscences of Washington Territory*, which has a delightful little chapter on our not-so-bad weather.

The Hills

Page 143. Galster, Richard et. al. 1994. "Engineering Geology of Seattle and Vicinity." In *Geologic Field Trips in the Pacific Northwest,* Vol. 2, Donald Swanson and Ralph Haugerud, eds.

Page 144. The Thomson quote comes from a letter he wrote in 1897, quoted in Stephen Evans's "Draining Seattle—WPA Landslide Stabilization Projects, 1935–1941." *Washington Geology,* Vol. 22, No. 4, 3–10, 1994.

Page 145. When owners of some of these houses sued the city, King County superior court judge Kathleen Learned ruled against them stating: "It is no small thing to reengineer the basic geology of the region, which is what the Plaintiff's position would lead to."

Page 146. Magnolia is named for the madronas that grow on the hill. This conundrum exists because a 22-year-old navy lieutenant, George Davidson, who visited the area in 1856 while leading a U.S. Coast and Geodetic Survey trip, thought the trees blooming on the edge of the hill were magnolias. We have been stuck with the name ever since.

Page 146. Booth, Derek B., and Barry Goldstein. 1994. "Patterns and Processes of Landscape Development by the Puget Lobe Ice Sheet," *Washington Division of Geology and Earth Resources Bulletin* 80: 207–218.

Page 147. Originally known as Eden Hill and then Galer Hill, for Jacob Galer, who built a house on the hill in 1884. Changed to Queen Anne in the late 1880s because of the houses being built in that architectural style.

Page 151. Beacon Hill received its name in 1889 from Union Army veteran M. Harwood Young, a representative of the New England and Northwest Investment Company. He wanted to honor another regraded hill from his hometown of Boston.

Page 153. A great deal of speculation exists as to the origin of the name Capitol Hill. According to *The Hill With a Future: Seattle's Capitol Hill 1900–1946* (Jacqueline B. Williams, CPK Ink, 2001), the name Capitol Hill did not appear until 1901 when developer James A. Moore started to promote the 160 acres he had purchased on July 10, 1900.

Williams states that Moore named the land "either for an area in Denver or because he planned to build the state's capitol building on his property." She concludes that either is possible and neither definitive.

The Invaders

Page 156. Leopold Trouvelot, of Medford, Massachusetts, imported several European gypsy moth eggs in 1868, hoping to breed them with North American varieties. His goal was to produce a better silkworm. During his experiments several caterpillars escaped and within 25 years, state and federal governments were trying to eradicate the moths. On March 6, 1890, Eugene Schieffelin released 80 starlings in Central Park because he believed that every bird mentioned by Shakespeare ought to be in America. A half century later they made it to Seattle, with ten starlings showing up at Fort Lawton in December, 1945.

Page 156. Pimental, et al. 2000. "Environmental and economic costs associated with non-indigenous species in the United States." *BioScience* 50 (1), 53–65.

Page 157. Martha Flahaut, a curator of zoology at the Washington State Museum (now the Burke) in the 1930s and 1940s, reported on the introduction of these squirrels in 1941 in *The Murrelet* (Vol. 22, 63–64.) She wrote that the squirrels had multiplied rapidly and spread out to a radius of at least three miles from Woodland.

Page 157. Storer collected the slug in the yard of William F. Thompson, director of the International Fisheries Commission, 3621 43rd Avenue. The slug now floats in a jar of ethanol at the California Academy of Sciences. No one knows when or how it arrived in Thompson's yard. By 1943, Allyn Smith of the Academy was able to collect 19 specimens at 1223 8th Avenue NW. The owner reported that he had first noticed the slug in 1940 because of "its depredations on bearded iris and succulents."

Page 157. Reichard, Sarah. 1994. *Assessing the Potential of invasiveness in woody plants introduced in North America.* (Thesis: University of Washington, Seattle).

Page 160. The USDA introduced tamarisk into the United States from the Middle

East in the early 1800s for erosion control. Nurseries in California began to sell the plant in 1861. One geographer estimated that tamarisk moved up the Colorado River system at a rate of 12 miles per year.

Page 161. Mobley, L. 1954. "Scotch Broom, A Menace to Forest, Range and Agricultural Land." *Proceedings 6th Annual California Weed Conference*, 39–42.

Page 162. The catalog is in the collection of the Oregon Historical Society, but most of it is reprinted in "David Newsom: The Western Observer" by David Newsom. Ivy was listed on planting lists for Kinnear Park 1890–1892 and in the parks nursery at Volunteer Park in 1891. The nursery had 1,000 cuttings growing at the time.

Page 165. Pollan's article appeared in the *New York Times Magazine*, May 15, 1994. He is not alone in comparing Nazis with the anti-invasives people; he is just one of the more prominent and less sensational writers to do so.

Page 165. Reichard, Sarah H. and Peter White. 2001. "Horticulture as a Pathway of Invasive Introductions in the United States," *BioScience*, Vol. 51, No. 2, 103–113.

Page 166. Rosenweig, Michael. 2001. "The four questions: What does the introduction of exotic species do to diversity?" *Evolutionary Ecology Research* 3: 361–367.

Page 166. Kirchner, J. W. and A. Weil. 2000. "Delayed biological recovery from extinctions throughout the fossil record." *Nature* 404: 177–180.

Page 166. Gould, Stephen Jay. "An Evolutionary Perspective on Strengths, Fallacies, and Confusions in the Concept of Native Plants," *Nature and Ideology: Nature and Garden Design in the Twentieth Century*, Dumbarton Oaks Colloquium on the History of Landscape Architecture, No. 18, 11–19, edited by Joachim Wolschke-Bulmahn.

The Water

Page 169. Two of the earliest white explorers of this route were Civil War Gen. George McClellan (1853), then only a captain, and Capt. Abiel W. Tinkham (1854), both searching for routes over the mountains and both remembered in peak names in or near the Watershed.

Page 170. At the time of the fire, most of the city's water came from a privately owned pumping station on Lake Washington. Located at present-day Colman Park, the station provided two million gallons per day. During the fire, when a messenger sent word to "Give her all she'll take" to the pump crews, they responded, "We've already given her all she'll take." The original vote on the $1 million bond was supposed to have occurred in November 1888, but city officials made a filing error and had to postpone the election until July 8. The two books covering the history of Seattle's water system are *The Seattle Municipal Water Plant* written in 1914 by John Lamb and Mary McWilliams's *Seattle Water Department History: 1854–1954*, published in 1955. Both books are basically descriptive, with little or no analysis or insight.

Page 170. The city acquired its first piece of land, Sec. 19 T22N, R27E, site of Landsburg intake, by condemnation on July 27, 1898. The last acquisition, which took place in 1996, involved trading 14,420 acres of land, which included 70 city-owned parcels in 10 counties. The city bought the land over a 30-year period with the specific plans of trading it for 17,000 acres of USFS land.

Page 170. The other four cities are New York, San Francisco, Boston, and Portland.

Page 172. The dam, known as a timber crib dam, was made by building a rectangular frame of cedar logs (the crib), filling it with gravel and boulders and covering the entire structure with planks. It raised the water level to 1,543 feet. An addition added six more feet before a washout in 1911 prompted rebuilding of the wood structure to its final level of 1,546 feet. Concerns about seismic safety compelled engineers to replace the timber crib dam in 1988 with a concrete structure, known as the Overflow Dike. Cedar was renamed Chester Morse Lake in 1955 in honor of the former superintendent of water, who homesteaded at the lake in the 1890s.

Page 174. During the last Ice Age, when small alpine glaciers crept down the upper Cedar, a tongue of the massive Puget lobe, the southernmost extension of the continent-covering Cordilleran ice sheet, pushed up into the Cedar and the two forks of the Snoqualmie, creating ice dams that impounded long narrow lakes. As the ice barrier grew in height, more and more sediment or moraine was deposited at the mouth of the valley, which pushed the lake progressively upvalley. After the glacier withdrew for a final time, the two forks of the Snoqualmie eroded down through the glacial debris and drained the former lakes. The Cedar, in contrast, happened to flow at the time on bedrock and could not cut down through the more resistant rock.

Page 174. Mackin, J. H. 1941. *A Geologic Interpretation of the Failure of the Cedar Reservoir, Washington.* University of Washington, Engineering Experiment Station Series Bulletin No. 107, Seattle. Another good source is Bliton, William. 1989. *Cedar River Project.* Washington Division of Geology and Earth Resources Bulletin 78.

Page 178. The fish ladder opened in September 2003. By early November, 79 chinook and 17 coho had returned to the watershed. Biologists documented 15 redds in the Cedar.

Page 181. The history of the sewer system comes from a report prepared in 1958 by the Brown and Caldwell consulting firm. The title is *Metropolitan Seattle Sewerage and Drainage Survey.*

Page 182. Ebbert, James, et al. 2000. *Water Quality in the Puget Sound Basin, Washington and British Columbia, 1996–1998.* U.S. Geological Survey Circular 1216. Barnes, Kimberlee et al. 2002. *Water-Quality Data for Pharmaceuticals, Hormones, and Other Organic Wastewater Contaminants in U.S. Streams, 1999–2000.* U.S. Geological Survey Open-File Report 02-94.

The Crows

Page 190. Crow killing in Seattle paled in comparison to crow killing in the Midwest. The preferred Midwest method was to decorate a known roost tree during the day with hundreds of foot-long steel tubes, each containing a stick of dynamite and several pounds of iron pellets. They would then be detonated electrically at night, after the birds had returned. State game officials killed 26,000 birds in Oklahoma in one roost in 1937 and another 18,000 the following year, while the Illinois State Department of Conservation killed 328,000 crows in roosts near Rockford, Illinois. *Life* magazine reported on the Illinois crow killings in the March 25, 1940, issue. The story included pictures of a man and boy clubbing wounded crows to death and kids sitting on a sled loaded with dead crows. The article made no apology for the killings and began "Least popular U.S. bird is the crow."

Page 192. Starting in 1973, Seattle City Light kept a tally of crows killed by transformers, the large canlike devices at the top of utility poles. They called it the crow-bituary. The birds died when they touched their beaks to the bare wires that carry electricity into transformers and received jolts of 13,000 to 26,000 volts. The number rose from 116 in 1973 to a peak of 591 in 1988, when City Light began to replace the 50,000 transformers and to install crow guards. They no longer keep the crow-bituary. No one knows why crows liked the transformers but some speculated it might be to get rid of fleas. Others blamed crows' curiosity; they appear to have been attracted to the 60-cycle hum of the electric current. Late spring and early summer had the most deaths.

Page 192 The name alludes to its status before construction of the Lake Washington Ship Canal in 1916 dropped the lake level nine feet and transformed the island into a peninsula.

Page 192. Other roosts near Seattle include one south of Snohomish on the Old Snohomish–Monroe road; one in Brier; one south of I-90 on the east shore of Lake Washington (Newport Marina or Mercer

Slough area); and one east of southcenter mall in the Renton Wetlands area. No one has completed a thorough survey of crows in these areas but during the fall and winter all except Brier have several thousand crows.

David B. Williams is the author of *A Naturalist's Guide to Canyon Country.* He has written for local and national newspapers and magazines. He grew up in Seattle, lived in southern Utah for nine years, and returned in 1998. He lives with his wife, Marjorie, and dog, Taylor.

Printed in the United States
126356LV00002B/142-261/P